T0326434

Rethinking the Theory of Money, Credit, and Macroeconomics

Rethinking the Theory of Money, Credit, and Macroeconomics

A New Statement for the Twenty-First Century

John Smithin

LEXINGTON BOOKS

Lanham • Boulder • New York • London

Published by Lexington Books
An imprint of The Rowman & Littlefield Publishing Group, Inc.
4501 Forbes Boulevard, Suite 200, Lanham, Maryland 20706
www.rowman.com

6 Tinworth Street, London SE11 5AL, United Kingdom

British Library Cataloguing in Publication Information Available

Library of Congress Cataloging-in-Publication Data

Names: Smithin, John N., author.
Title: Rethinking the theory of money, credit, and macroeconomics : a new statement for
   the twenty-first century / John Smithin.
Description: Lanham : Lexington Books, an imprint of The Rowman & Littlefield Publishing
   Group, Inc., [2018] | Includes bibliographical references and index.
Identifiers: LCCN 2018033338 (print) | LCCN 2018035921 (ebook) | ISBN 9781498542821 (Electronic) |
   ISBN 9781498542814 (cloth : alk. paper)
Subjects: LCSH: Money. | Credit. | Macroeconomics.
Classification: LCC HG221 (ebook) | LCC HG221 .S6437 2018 (print) |
   DDC 339.5/3—dc23
LC record available at https://lccn.loc.gov/2018033338

Printed in the United States of America

IN MEMORIAM

Hana Smithin

(neé Heřmanksa, bývala Ciprisova)

June 17, 1934, Brno-Tuřany, Moravia

December 16, 2017, Aurora, Ontario

Řekni, mi Řekni, kde je moje milá?

Contents

List of Figures

List of Tables

Preface

A few years ago I chanced to meet with Lord Robert Skidelsky the noted British historian, public intellectual, political commentator, and biographer of Keynes, at an academic conference. He told me that he was working on a book tentatively to be entitled *Unsettled Questions in Macroeconomic Policy*. I thought that this was a great title, as has been the case with many of Skidelsky's books over the years. I wished, not for the first time, that I had had the ability to come up with something similar. The reference is obviously to John Stuart Mill's *Unsettled Questions in Political Economy* of 1844 (Robbins 1967, viii–xiii). Mill presumably thought that he had himself settled those questions only four years later in the *Principles of Political Economy* of 1848. If so, however, he was deceiving himself. In the form presented by Mill all of the outstanding questions have remained "unsettled" for the past 175 years. Moreover, any and all attempts to challenge economic orthodoxy, such as the valiant effort by Keynes in the mid-twentieth century, have been rebuffed by an uncomprehending economics profession. I was very interested to hear about Professor Sidelsky's revival of the idea of "unsettled questions." This is because as he has been working on his project I have been working on a book, this book, that I think finally does settle the issues in dispute after all this time.

At the time of writing Skidelsky's book has not yet appeared, but in a working paper released in 2015, on the subject of austerity policies in the United Kingdom (UK), he elaborated on what he thought some of the unsettled questions still are— paying particular attention to the second of Mill's old collection of essays, entitled "Of the Influence of Consumption on Production." This was Mill's half-hearted and unconvincing defense of "Say's Law" of markets, that "supply creates its own demand" (Skidelsky 2015, 2). This is the truly asinine idea that there can never be a "general glut" of commodities (Mill's words) and that, therefore, there can never be depressions, recessions, negative growth, mass unemployment, and so on. Never mind that all of these things have actually have happened repeatedly, on occasions too numerous to mention, over the past 325 years since the early days of capitalism. This certainly includes Mill's own time of writing *circa* 1829–30. Theories about nonexistent systems of barter exchange notwithstanding, it seems to me that even the most rudimentary attempt at developing a realist social ontology of the economic system in which we actually live would soon reveal that "effective demand" has to be in the form of money. I most certainly hope that this point has been made sufficiently clear in the present book, in chapters 3, 4, and 5, for example.

In the context of economic policy in the contemporary UK, Skidelsky (2015, 2) identifies fiscal theory as one the "main unsettled questions of today." But, again, it really should not be. There have always been factions of economists who have insisted that frugality, or austerity, in the government budget is a precondition of economic growth. On the other hand, there are also factions who have urged the opposite. In reality, however (and perhaps needless to say), neither is accurate. What is true is that if there is ever to be economic growth obviously there must be sufficient effective demand to pay for the various goods and services that are being produced. As has just been pointed out, this means that there must be enough *money*. In turn, "money" in the contemporary world is nothing other than a subset of the liabilities of certain financial institutions, including banks and the so-called near-banks. Therefore, if there is ever to be enough money in existence to pay for all the output that is produced, it must have been the case that someone, somewhere, in the economy (more realistically some sector of the economy in the aggregate), was willing to go into debt to a sufficient extent to enable profits to be earned by others. This could be the government, of course, but it does not *have* to be the government. It could equally well be the private sector or the foreign sector. Keynes, it seems, understood this point perfectly well. In the situation in the 1930s, when there was insufficient borrowing in his view by the private sector, the remedy was a policy of "loan expenditure" by the government. This was defined as "a convenient expression for the net borrowing of the public authorities on all accounts whether on capital account or to meet a budgetary deficit" (Keynes 1936, 128–29). On the other hand, in an earlier era when the government option was not available, Keynes (1936, 355) was clear that "in a society where there is no question of direct investment . . . [by . . . public authority] . . . the . . . objects, with which it is reasonable . . . to be preoccupied, are the domestic rate of interest and the balance of foreign trade." As Skidelsky (2015, 7) points out, one thing that Keynes certainly did *not* envisage was "a budget balanced at a much higher level of both taxes and spending than [earlier generations] would have accepted." Yet, somehow, these "tax-and-spend" policies, typically favored by those of a basically socialist orientation seeking to enlarge the role of the public sector per se, did come to be associated specifically with "Keynesian economics." This was already true in the immediate postwar period and continues down to the present day. In the present book I hope that these and all of the other fiscal *connundra* are indeed successfully cleared up in chapters 2, 7, and 10.

In my own view another one of the most important currently unsettled questions, not specifically treated by Skidelsky, and yet vital for understanding contemporary political economy, is the relationship between fiscal policy and monetary policy. This turns out to be important above all for the stability of the economy. This is because in most jurisdictions the key monetary policy instrument is what I call the nominal *policy rate* of interest. In the United States, for example, the nominal policy rate of interest is called the "federal funds rate." It is alternatively called the "overnight rate" in Canada, the "overnight call rate" in Japan, and the "main refinancing rate" in the Euro-zone. The historical banking literature also made frequent reference to such things as the "discount rate" or "bank rate," meaning by such expressions the rate of interest at which the central bank would lend directly to the commercial banks.

Currently, in many jurisdictions the nominal policy rate set is set at intervals of about six-and-a-half weeks or so, and is actually changed quite infrequently, often no more than once or twice a year. But the problem with this, as will be shown in chapter 2 below, is that a nominal interest "peg," of any kind, and at any level, including a peg for the nominal policy rate, is conducive to economic instability. Moreover, whether the nominal policy rate is set high or low the instability can go in *either* direction. Depending on what is happening elsewhere in the economy, or the rest of the world, there could either be an "inflationary boom" or a "great depression," and having decided to simply fix the nominal policy rate, the central bank would be powerless to stop either of them. The solution, as I have argued on many occasions in past, and now again in detail in chapter 2 of this book, is for the central bank to pursue a real interest rate rule. Ideally, the *real* policy rate of interest should be set at a "low but still positive level" (Smithin 1994, 2003a, 2009a, 2013a) or perhaps even at zero, as is suggested in chapter 11 below.

Returning to the problems of J.S. Mill in the mid-nineteenth century, Lionel Robbins (1967, iv), the noted historian of economic thought and former Chair of the Department of Economics at the London School of Economics (LSE) was apparently of the opinion that the first of the 1844 essays, "Of the Laws of Interchange between Nations," was one of Mill's most important contributions. This essay dealt with the role of demand (again), but now in the context of the determination of the so-called "terms of trade" between nations. Given our previous discussion of Say's Law, however, the various conclusions that might be reached on this subject are also going to depend on what this "demand" is supposed to consist of, commodities or money. Chapters 9 and 10 of this book, therefore, return to the issue for the present day. The most important conclusion to be drawn is simply that as demand must always be expressed in terms of money, then the *real* exchange rate (the reciprocal of the terms of trade) is actually a *monetary* variable, in every sense of this term. It is therefore entirely susceptible to be influenced by the policy initiatives of the domestic government provided, at least, that they do not abdicate this responsibility by trying to permanently fix the nominal exchange rate.

Robbins (1967, xi) was rather less complimentary about the three remaining essays of Mill's total of five than of the first two, but nonetheless thought them interesting enough. Taking these contributions in reverse order, Mill's last essay was "On the Definition of Political Economy; and on the Method of Investigation Proper to It." I would have thought that logically this should have been placed as the first rather than the last essay of the series. In the present book I do just that. Here, the survey of methodological issues, "Methodological Problems in Monetary Macroeconomics," does come first. Mill's fourth and penultimate essay was "On Profits and Interest." It dealt, in particular, with the independent or separate determinants of the latter as compared to the former. In this book chapter 6 on "Interest, Profit, and Wages" similarly deals with the ontological distinctions between interest and profit, and their separate relationships to wages. This is bound to lead to some consideration of the necessarily monetary nature of interest, as opposed to the category of profit and, thereby, to such issues as the old debate about the "forced saving effect" (i.e., the effects of inflation on the rate of interest and on capital accumulation). In fact this was one of Mill's main concerns in 1844. In the present volume the forced saving effect is reinterpreted, for the twenty-first century, as a negative relationship between the inflation rate and the *real* rate of interest (in chapters, 2, 5, and 10). As there is also a credible argument to be made on ethical grounds that the optimal value of the real rate is actually zero (see chapter 11), this leads to a complete re-evaluation of the traditional ethics-based argument *against* the conscious pursuit of "growth and jobs friendly" economic policies (again see chapter 11). Finally, Mill's remaining essay "On the Words Productive and Unproductive" also seems, amazingly enough, to get right to the point of my current book. Robbins (1967, xi) makes it clear that the expression "productive" expenditure in Mill is supposed to refer only to spending on those items that in some sense add to the physical capital stock, whereas "unproductive" is meant to refer to pure consumption. From the point of view taken here, however, this seems to be another quite nonsensical distinction on the part of abstract theorists. It would simply never occur to anyone actually trying to make a living by selling the one thing or the other. This type of attitude has caused all sorts of problems throughout the development of the history of economic thought. It leads directly to as the "quagmire of capital theory" as I call it in chapter 1 which always seems to ensnare those economists so inclined into an endless, and ultimately fruitless, task of trying somehow to attribute causality to and precise mathematical relationships between concepts that are impossible either to define or quantify. A list of such imprecise and confusing concepts would include such things as even the very idea of "capital" itself, the meaning of "net" investment, how to calculate the supposed capital/output ratio, what is meant by the concept of "capacity utilization," and so on. A realist social ontology which is concerned primarily with social facts and institutions that are both ontologically subjective but also epistemologically objective must dispense with all such vague and misleading notions. This issue, in fact, comes up immediately in chapter 1, on methodological issues, and is then discussed in some detail in chapter 7 on "Alternative Approaches to the Theory of Economic Growth." In the end, all that we really need to know is that *both* so-called investment goods and consumption goods need to be "produced," and that the effective demand for both of them must be in the form of money.

As mentioned in chapter 1 below, I view this book as the culmination of a long series of works, authored and co-authored, and edited and co-edited, dating back to my PhD thesis, *The Incidence and Economic Effects of the Financing of Unemployment Insurance* (Smithin 1982). And it is not even a culmination, as it turns out. The empirical aspects have now been pushed much further forward in a PhD thesis completed thirty-six years later by Reed Collis at York University, Toronto, entitled *Three Essays on Monetary Macroeconomics*: *An Empirical Examination of the Soundness of the Alternative Monetary Model and Monetary Policy in Canada* (Collis 2018).

In each of my previous works I have acknowledged the contributions of very many people (including of course my co-authors and co-editors) who have helped me to come to understand monetary macroeconomics over the years. I would like all of those acknowledgments to stand. Friends and colleagues who have helped with issues specifically relating to the current book are typically mentioned in footnotes and references. These include Shakeb Abdul-Hakim, Torrey Byles, Jana Campbell (Ani Yeshi Llamo), David Fields, Mathias Grasselli, Geoff Harcourt, Geoff Ingham, Celine Mano, Samhruddi Thakkar, Prashant Singh, Brenda Spotton Visano, Martin Watts, Leo Zelmanovitz, and Frederick Zhou. I would also like to acknowledge all that I have learned about monetary economics from a series of PhD theses on that topic completed at York University over the past twenty-five years, including those by John Paschaksis (1993), Eric Kam (2000), Jong-Chul Kim (2011), Alberto D'Ansi Mendoza Espana (2012), Aqeela Tabassum (2012), and Reed Collis (2018). Together they make up a formidable "Toronto School" (perhaps we might call it) of monetary science.

During the writing of this book I suffered a devastating emotional and psychological blow. Hanička Smithinova, my true love, spouse, best friend, mentor, intellectual sparring partner, and most everything else, passed away peacefully, but after a long struggle with illness, in Aurora, Ontario, on December 16, 2017. The only way I could even begin to cope with this loss, and eventually complete this book, is by dedicating the whole project to her memory.

Chapter 1

Methodological Problems in Monetary Macroeconomics

INTRODUCTION

The late Robert Heilbroner (1919–2005) was an economics professor and a well-known "public intellectual" in the United States. He was the author of the classic bestseller *The Worldly Philosophers* (Heilbroner 1999), a work which went through seven editions between 1953 and 1999. By a very large margin this is the most widely read book on the history of economic thought ever published. Heilbroner had this to say about another, even more famous, book by John Maynard Keynes *The General Theory of Employment Interest and Money* (Keynes 1936):[1]

> I can think of no single book that has so changed the conception held by economists as to the working of the capitalist system.

That had indeed been Keynes's ambition, as is very clear from a letter to George Bernard Shaw (Keynes 1934–35, 40) written on New Year's Day 1935:

> To understand my state of mind . . . you have to know that I believe myself to be writing a book on economic theory which will largely revolutionise—not, I suppose, at once but in the course of the next ten years—the way the world thinks about economic problems. When my new theory has been duly assimilated and mixed with politics and feelings and passions, I can't predict what the final upshot will be in its effects on action and affairs. But there will be a great change, and, in particular, *the Ricardian foundations of Marxism will be knocked away.* . . . I can't expect you, or anyone else, to believe this at the present stage. But for myself I don't merely hope what I say—in my own mind I'm quite sure. (Emphasis added)

In the end Keynes did not succeed, certainly not permanently, in this "Essay in Persuasion."[2] Otherwise, the world would hardly be in the mess it is in today. Nonetheless, the author's objectives are plainly stated. Why then, did the vital message not get through, and why are Keynes's often brilliant insights now almost completely lost? One reason which contemporary Keynesian and Post Keynesian economists seem quite reluctant to accept, is that there were indeed flaws in Keynes's work which, all along, have blocked others from achieving a full understanding. Another is that, in the meantime, after a hiatus in the mid-twentieth century in which it seemed that Keynes had won the intellectual argument, the academic discipline of so-called macroeconomics (and to some extent the entire field of economics itself) has gone totally off the rails. In 1969, a volume of academic essays appeared with the optimistic title *Is the Business Cycle Obsolete?* (Bronfenbrenner 1969). Subsequently, however, the economics profession apparently collectively decided that if the business cycle no longer existed it would be necessary to re-invent it. That seems to have been their objective ever since, with (a cynic might say) arguably a considerable degree of success.

In a recent book entitled *A History of Macroeconomics* De Vroey (2016) identifies two main eras in the historical development of mainstream macroeconomics in the universities. (The author does not discuss any of the heterodox schools of economic theory, either on the right or on the left of the political spectrum.) The first is the period in which a (supposedly) "Keynesian" macroeconomics held sway, dating from the late 1930s down to the mid-1970s.[3] The title of the Brofenbrenner volume seems to indicate that this approach did have at least some success for the first thirty years or so. The second phase was then the "era of DSGE macroeconomics" (De Vroey 2016 xiv) originally initiated by Lucas, from the mid-1970s down to the present. The acronym DSGE stands for the "dynamic stochastic general equilibrium (model)," an appellation which in itself gives a strong hint about the preoccupations of the leading participants. Thirty years into the development of this program nobody was writing books with titles like that of Brofenbrenner. Instead, economic policy-makers and commentators had had to deal with such episodes as the global financial crisis (GFC) of 2008, the subsequent "Great Recession," multiple crises in the Euro-zone, chronic payments imbalances, and a great many other manifestations of the myriad problems of globalism. To be fair, it is not clear that body of theory that was called "Keynesian" in the post–World War II period did actually contribute very much to the economic prosperity of that time. It certainly had very little connection with the ideas of John Maynard Keynes, or to the doctrines that he thought would bring about change. Another book published toward the end of the pseudo-Keynesian era (just before the optimistic Brofenbrenner volume) was entitled *Keynesian Economics and the Economics of Keynes* (Leijonhufvud 1968) which succinctly makes the point.

According to De Vroey (2016, 376) the DSGE modeling strategy is a "progressive" research program, presumably in the sense in which the philosopher of science Lakatos (1978) has used this term. However, the actual narrative of De Vroey's book does not really bear this out. To the contrary it is made clear that the main interest of researchers following this line of inquiry is, and seems always to have been, the internal consistency of the theory itself (De Vroey 2016, 379). There is no attempt to provide a realistic social ontology, or to find solutions to actual economic problems. To take just one example of this attitude, John King reports that an authoritative graduate level textbook by Wickens (2008), published by an Ivy League university press, frankly avoided any discussion at all of what is surely the "defining characteristic of the capitalist mode of production" (King 2012, 3), namely wage-labor, and had no index entry for "unemployment."[4] It seems also telling that De Vroey's history, though published in the year 2016 ends in 2008, after which date the focus presumably would have had to shift to the several "empirical problems" faced by the DGSE program, rather than the purely "conceptual problems" (Smithin 1990a, 1990b) that were of primary interest to the participants. This terminology of empirical and conceptual problems comes from the work of another philosopher of science (Laudan 1977) the author of *Progress and its Problems*. Here is a book which now, in hindsight, seems highly relevant to the fates of both of the mainstream programs discussed by De Vroey. The main idea of Laudan's work was that the success or otherwise of the competing research programs depends on them being able to solve *both* empirical and conceptual problems not just one or the other. It is also argued that a program which is failing in one of these areas will not actually be replaced by another more promising approach unless the new program seems likely to be able to succeed on both fronts. This explains why some research programs linger on for decades in the graduate schools long past their apparent "sell by" date.

Professor Paul Krugman's trenchant statement about the practical relevance of the DSGE program (made in the immediate aftermath of the GFC of the early twentieth century) is by now very well known. According to Krugman, as previously quoted by Smithin (2013a, 33):

> Most macroeconomics of the past thirty years was spectacularly useless at best and positively harmful at worst.

Regardless of one's evaluation of Krugman's own views on macroeconomic theory and policy (which are widely known as he is also a public intellectual), I would say that the only possible quibble with this is that it tends to understatement. At around the same time as Krugman's declaration, work by such writers as Skidelsky (2009) in *Keynes: The Master Returns* and Davidson (2009) who wrote on *The Keynes Solution* seemed very briefly to herald a Keynesian renaissance. However, as might indeed have been predicted by those familiar with the state of the academic debate described in De Vroey's book, this "Keynes moment" as some have called it, quickly passed in both academia and in policy-making circles. Therefore, the upshot of the discussion so far, taking all of the above references together, is simply to reinforce the point that there is an urgent need for a *new* statement and a *new* beginning. This is the purpose of the current book, to reset the agenda for the twenty-first century.

It is significant that Heilbroner, quoted above as approving of Keynes was also, according to his own biographers and commentators, a life-long supporter of socialism, albeit one with a very hard-headed attitude to the strengths and weaknesses of that particular social system. For this reason, the highlighted portion of the quote from Keynes's letter to Shaw (himself a prominent socialist) is particularly interesting. What did Keynes actually mean by "knocking away the Ricardian foundations of Marxism"? In fact, neither modern Post Keynesians, a group that we might perhaps take to represent the left of the academic spectrum, nor the so-called "Austrian" economists on the right, think that there is any serious opposition between Keynes and Marx. For the Austrians, whose primary interest was and is, the advocacy of free markets and the demonstration of the power of market forces, all of "state socialism" (including Marxian communism), "interventionism," and "inflationism" were simply variants on the theme of "etatism" (Mises 1978, 13–26). Keynesianism is dismissed as merely the twentieth-century incarnation of age-old inflationism (Hayek 1994, Mises 1978, Sennholz 1978). On the Post Keynesian side, Lavoie (2014, 44–45) in a work entitled *Post Keynesian Economics: New Foundations,* advocates a hybrid approach that is sometimes labeled "Classical-Keynesian" or "Post-Classical" and which can accommodate both Ricardo and Marx, as well as more recent heterodox economists such as Kalecki, Kaldor, Joan Robinson, Sraffa, and others. Similarly, King (2012, 4) explicitly calls for a "Keynes-Marx synthesis."

It therefore seems that Keynes's claims about the shakiness of both the Ricardian foundations and the Marxian superstructure must be investigated at deeper level than that of macroeconomic theory per se. In fact, they relate directly to questions of social ontology, and more particularly the ontology of money. From this point of view, and using the terminology of writers such as Ingham (1996, 2000, 2004a, 2004b, 2018), Lawson (1997, 2003, 2016), and Searle (1995, 1998, 2005, 2010), Keynes's (1933a, 1993b) notion of a monetary theory of production implies a view of money as a "social relation," a "social institution," or a "social fact." These are relationships between people arising from collective intentionality which, although not dependent on, or reducible to, the purely material properties of the physical world, are nonetheless capable of having definite causal effects in that world. Philosophically speaking the ontology of the social world must be a version of emergentism.

One possible interpretation of Keynes's statement about Marx and Ricardo is therefore that he recognized (at least implicitly) that his own revolutionary approach did indeed have very different philosophical, ontological, and methodological underpinnings from those of his predecessors.[5] The same sort of insights about the different visions of how the macro-economy functions as a social system might then also readily be extended forward to Keynes's opponents among his own contemporaries and immediate successors, and ultimately to the discussion of the serious methodological problems that seem to abound everywhere in current macroeconomic analysis.

MONETARY ANALYSIS VERSUS REAL ANALYSIS

Keynes himself would almost certainly have claimed that the difference between himself and the "Classics" (Keynes 1936, 3, fn.), including in the latter both Marx and also the neoclassical economists of the late nineteenth century, was in the treatment of money. Joseph Schumpeter would have agreed and in his posthumously published *History of Economic Analysis* (Schumpeter 1954, 276) he made a sharp distinction between "real analysis" and "monetary analysis." The title of Chapter 6 of Schumpeter's book, about pre-classical and classical theories of money, is actually "*Value and Money*" (emphasis added). Moreover, the subtitle of the first section of the chapter is specifically "Real Analysis and Monetary Analysis."

Schumpeter describes *real analysis* as conducted solely in terms of quantities of inputs and outputs, often physical quantities, but presumably also including various types of volume indices of these quantities. As the name implies, it proceeds by taking for granted that all economic knowledge can be acquired simply by studying relationships among and between the goods and services themselves, as well as the attitudes of human beings toward these commodities. Money is thought of as secondary, and the economy operates as essentially a barter economy. Indeed everyone who has studied any economics at all at the college or university level is familiar with the various slogans and catch-phrases expressing this point of view, such as "money is neutral," or "money is a veil." To the contrary, in *monetary analysis* (Schumpeter 1954, 277–78), money and monetary variables are of primary importance and are:

> introduced on the very ground floor of the analytical structure.

Monetary analysis abandons the idea that all the essential features of economic life can be represented as barter. It takes into account a separate and "relatively autonomous" monetary sphere (Ingham 2004a, 61). It goes without saying that, for Schumpeter, Keynes's system itself is the primary example of monetary analysis.

Keynes (1933b, 408–11) had similarly made a clear distinction between a "real-exchange economy" and a "monetary economy." For Keynes:

> a monetary economy. . . [is that in] . . . which. . . money plays a part of its own and affects motives and decisions and is . . . one of the operative factors. . . . The course of events cannot be predicted, either in the long period or in the short, without a knowledge of the behaviour of money between the first state and the last.

He continues (far too optimistically) "everyone would . . . agree that it is in a monetary economy in my sense . . . that we actually live." The problem is that not everyone has agreed with this, far from it. Not Ricardo, for instance, and certainly not the contemporary adherents to the DSGE program, one of whose proudest accomplishments was to produce a theory of "real business cycles" (De Vroey 2016, 261–81, Scarth 2014, 7–101).

As for Marx it is true that a number of writers, such as Bellafiore (1989, 2004) Graziani (1997), Moseley (2016), and others, have drawn attention to the fact that "money [in some sense] *pervades* the Marxist conception of the economic process" (Graziani 1997, 26, emphasis added, my interpolation). For example, Moseley (2016, 28) writes that "the general analytical framework of Marx's theory of surplus value is the circuit of money capital, $M - C \ldots P \ldots C' - M'$,[6] where $M' = M + \Delta M$." Moseley is, in fact, of the opinion that Marx's method is an example of monetary analysis in Schumpeter's precise sense. However, a major difficulty with this is that Marx is not mentioned specifically as an exemplar of monetary analysis by Schumpeter. As already suggested, writing in the mid-twentieth century the seemingly most obvious choice (to Schumpeter) was that of Keynes. For example, Schumpeter states that "once and for all . . . as a matter of fact . . . [the importance of money] . . . is recognized by modern economists" and also that "monetary analysis has established itself" (Schumpeter 1954, 278). There is a further assertion that "monetary analysis has once more conquered in our own time" (Schumpeter 1954, 276). These references are clearly about Keynes's impact on the economics profession of the mid-twentieth century, not to Marx eighty or ninety years earlier. Furthermore, from this point of view, all of the later mainstream macroeconomics research programs, including neoclassical Keynesianism, soi-disant monetarism, and both wings of the DSGE camp, can be interpreted together as a reactionary counter-revolution against monetary analysis—a highly "successful" one at that. Macroeconomic analysis has been evolving backward for around six decades, and very rapidly indeed as of late.

How then to adjudicate the different opinions about Marx and money implicit in the above discussion? The main issue is clearly the nature of the actual "money stuff" (Ingham 2004a, 6) of which the M, M', or ΔM consists.[7] Once again, it has everything to do with the ontology of money. There also exists another distinction, very closely related to that between real and monetary analysis, namely that between a commodity theory of money and a credit theory of money (Ingham 2004a, 6, Wray 2004, 238). Moreover, based largely on the first three chapters of the *Treatise on Money,* Keynes (1930, 3–43) is usually regarded as having put forward a version of credit theory. As for Marx, it has seemed inescapable to most commentators that in common with both his classical predecessors and later neoclassical opponents, the underlying conception was that of a commodity theory of money. For example, the economic sociologist Ingham (2004a, 61) writes as follows:

> Like Adam Smith, Marx held that "[g]old confronts other commodities only because it previously confronted them as a commodity. . . ." Forms of credit are derivative: bank notes and bills of exchange are money in so far as they directly *represent* both precious metals and/or commodities in exchange (original emphasis). . . . Marx's *analytical* position is similar to that of classical economics (original emphasis). [. . . it . . . implies that money can be analytically "bracketed"] . . . Emphasis . . . on the labour theory of value prevented Marx from recognizing the . . . relative autonomy of the production of abstract value . . . [*via*] . . . credit-money. . . . At times Marx appeared to . . . gras[p] that capitalist credit-money can be created autonomously outside the sphere of the production and circulation of commodities; but then he thinks that it plays an essentially *dysfunctional* role (original emphasis). Bank credit "could expand beyond its necessary proportions" and become ". . . the most effective . . . [vehicle] . . . of crises and swindle." . . . Marx held the conventional . . . view that credit instruments . . . were, or rather should be, no more than functional substitutes for hard cash.

If M is supposed to be a "money commodity" which is a characteristic Marxian phrase, it becomes very difficult to see how the argument could ever reach beyond the boundaries of Schumpeterian real analysis. On the other hand if the M and M' were supposed to be quantities of a means of (final) payment, denominated in an abstract unit of account, and which also represents a binding social commitment (Ingham 2004a, 2004b, 2018, Searle 2010, Smithin 2013a, 2013b, Wray 2012), then the characteristic problems of a genuine monetary analysis would be present. Neither the physical properties of the money stuff, however, nor any other concept of intrinsic value would be relevant. What I mean by characteristic monetary problems would include that of being able to theoretically reconcile, or make commensurate, the different magnitudes $(C' - C)$ and $(M' - M)$ in the circuit. Also, the all-important issue of whether, or not, there is actually enough money in existence at any point in time to purchase the full value of the output (Smithin 2016b). To put this point into something more like the standard economic jargon (and regardless of the specifics of the real theory of value connecting C and C') the question is whether the M and M' are supposed to be real magnitudes, in one sense or another, or nominal magnitudes, that is, simply quantities of dollars, pounds, or yen as such. For a truly monetary analysis it is the latter assumption that would have to be made. It would also have to be made clear exactly *how* the nominal magnitudes in the accounting framework are relevant to, or necessary for, the functioning of the real production system.

In what sense then did Keynes think that he was knocking away the Ricardian foundations of Marxism? It seems clear from many of Keynes's remarks about Ricardo, not least in the *General Theory* itself that, to Keynes, that archetypal classical economist was (in anachronistically Schumpeterian terms) definitely an exponent of real rather than monetary analysis. Clear examples are to be found in Keynes's (1936, 190–92) critique of the concept of the natural rate of interest in Ricardo, in the Appendix to Chapter 14 on "The Classical Theory of Interest," and later at the end of Chapter 17 on "The Essential Properties of Interest and Money." In the latter place, he speaks of conventional economists, unaware of these properties, as being "safely ensconced in a Ricardian world" (Keynes 1936, 224). Similar sentiments are expressed in the famous footnote to Chapter 1 (Keynes 1936, 3, fn.) previously cited, in which Keynes not only names Ricardo as the founder of the "classical" economics to which he (Keynes) was adamantly opposed, but also extends the definition forward in time to include the neoclassical economists of the late nineteenth century.

As to Keynes's specific views on Marx, interestingly enough there are only three brief references to this larger-than-life figure in the *General Theory*,[8] in two of which Marx is indeed bracketed specifically with Ricardo. In the third (Keynes 1936, 155) Marx is unfavorably compared to Gesell (who assuredly *is*, in Keynes's view, an exponent of monetary analysis). Gesell is said to have championed "an anti-Marxian socialism [*sic*] . . . based . . . on an unfettering of competition instead of its abolition."[9] Keynes goes so far as to say that "I believe the future will learn more from the spirit of Gesell that that of Marx."

Looking at matters in this way does not detract from Moseley's and other contributions in drawing attention to the fact that discussion of the monetary circuit *begins* with Marx. Indeed, Keynes (1933a, 1933b) himself, in some published and unpublished writings before the *General Theory*, had already recognized Marx's ideas as potentially relevant to his own project (Tarshis 1989, 36–37). According to Keynes (1933b, 81):

> The distinction between a co-operative economy and an entrepreneur economy bears some relation to a pregnant observation by Marx,—though the subsequent use to which he put it was highly illogical. He pointed out that the nature of production in the actual world is not, as economists seem often to suppose, a case of $C - M - C'$, *i.e.* of exchanging commodity (or effort) to obtain another commodity or (effort).That may be the standpoint of a private consumer. But it is not the attitude of business, which is a case of $M - C -M'$, *i.e.* of parting with money for commodity (or effort) in order to obtain more money.

Unfortunately, this allusion to the Marxian monetary circuit via the monetary theory of production did not survive into the published version of the *General Theory* in 1936. Nor did Keynes seem at all confident about the concept in debates about interest rate theory (in the *Economic Journal,* and elsewhere), the following year. This was one of the main reasons why writers of the Franco-Italian circuit school in the late twentieth century, such as Graziani, Parguez, Schmitt, and others found it necessary to develop the theory of the monetary circuit in far more detail, arguing that to advance the idea of a monetary theory of production it is necessary to go well beyond Keynes's tentative discussion (Graziani 2003, Parguez and Seccareccia 2000, Rochon 1999, Schmitt 1988). Therefore, even if recognizing that Marx was in essence a commodity theorist, and Keynes an embryonic credit theorist, it is certainly the case that to fully develop the implications of a credit or claim theory of money, something like Marx's notion of the monetary circuit is indispensable.

In the final analysis it is not really credible to argue that *either* of Keynes or Marx succeeded in developing a fully fledged credit theory of money or, in the case of Marx, that he (Marx) was ever really interested in in doing so. Nonetheless, they both contributed ideas that have been, and still are, the necessary conditions for the continuing development of a viable credit theory. To be able to go further and make that theory a reality these ideas still do have to be connected up with those of money as a social relation, the endogeneity of money, the importance of bank credit creation, and so on. Such concepts are the key inputs for an adequate explanation of how profit is actually generated (as opposed to *valued*) in the economic system that Weber called the "method of enterprise" and Marx called "capitalism" (see chapter 4 below). But we would have never arrived at this position were it not for the pioneering contributions of both Keynes and Marx. Having made this point, it still seems fair to say that Keynes, were he still alive today, might legitimately claim to have traveled much further down this road than did Marx.

METHODOLOGICAL PROBLEMS IN
MAINSTREAM MACROECONOMICS

We now return to the all-important question of why is that contemporary mainstream macroeconomics is in such a state that serious writers, including many of those quoted above, have gone so far as to suggest that it should be done away with altogether. With the above discussion as a starting point it is possible to identify a number of methodological problems that beset the subject as currently practiced, and also to suggest ways in which these problems might be resolved. I will argue that the same solutions would benefit equally teaching and research, and ultimately public policy itself. There are four major methodological problems which need to be identified and addressed before any remedies may be suggested. These are listed below.

Drawing on the idea of real versus monetary analysis, discussed in detail above, the first of these problems is simply (1) *the basic premise of neoclassical microeconomic theory that beneath the "veil of money" economic activity is fundamentally a question of barter exchange*. This is the same issue already explored in the previous discussion about the different implications of a commodity theory of money versus a credit theory. In an important paper written nearly thirty years ago this problem was dubbed "the barter illusion" by Dillard (1988). The focus is inevitably on Keynes's real exchange economy, and money and credit take a back seat. It is clear from the recent histories by De Vroey and Scarth, cited earlier, that very little has changed in the interim.

A second and closely related problem can be posed as (2) *the virtual identification of the term "economy theory" with the use of differential and stochastic calculus to solve the optimization problems of the representative agent, or agents.* These mathematical exercises are conceived of as precisely a "theory of choice" about how the atomistic agent interacts with the material world, essentially without the intervention of money. This second problem might therefore be called the *Microfoundations Delusion* from the title of the book by King (2012) cited above. The end game of the search for the "microfoundations of macroeconomics" turns out to be nothing other than the DSGE model itself, with all of its obvious weaknesses and essential inapplicability as a vehicle for the pursuit of social science.[10] A few years ago, in the jacket copy for King's book, I explicitly linked these two notions, of barter exchange and microfoundations, as follows:

> The "illusion" has been with us for a very long time whereas the "delusion" is of relatively more recent vintage. Together they have blocked mainstream macroeconomics from achieving a basic understanding of monetary and macroeconomic phenomena at a time when this is most urgently needed.

Differential calculus is actually the mathematics of infinitesimal change, so perhaps we can identify the underlying source of the delusion (if not its full brain-stultifying application in contemporary graduate schools) as going all the way back to Alfred Marshall's motto *"natura non facit saltum"*—nature does not make leaps—from the front-piece of the *Principles of Economics* (Marshall 1890). But, Marshall's motto was deeply unsuitable for the social sciences on all counts. In the first place, in reality nature does make leaps, all the time. Secondly, and most importantly for present purposes, we are not actually dealing primarily with *natura*, that is with the so-called "brute facts" of natural world (Searle 1995, 1998), but with the social world. This has a different ontology, in which "revolutions," including those in the literal political sense of the term, are simply par for the course (Smithin 2009a, 47–49).

This reference, once again, to social ontology brings up the third serious methodological problem, namely (3) *the reliance on statistical probability theory as the main empirical method in economics*, under the label of econometrics. The problem here is that strictly speaking the theorems of statistical probability theory do not apply in the social world. This was a point that Keynes had already made quite clearly as early as the *Treatise on Probability* (Keynes 1921). Later on, when Keynes (1937) was finally asked to sum up the contribution of his *General Theory* in a famous article in the *Quarterly Journal of Economics*, great stress was laid on the presence of fundamental uncertainty in the socio-economic environment, as opposed to probabilistic risk. There is already a very large literature on this topic by Post Keynesian and other heterodox economists.[11] On the more general topic (of the different ontologies of the social world and natural world) the reader can consult, for example, Ingham (2000, 2004a, 2018), Lawson (1993, 2003), Searle (1995) on *The Construction of Social Reality*, the same author on *Making the Social World* (Searle 2010), Smithin (2013b) on "The Requirements of a Philosophy of Money and Finance," and Zelmanovitz (2016) on *The Ontology and Function of Money.*

The fourth, final, (and perhaps decisive) problem is (4) *the failure (and in truth the incoherence) of any and all attempts that have been made at deriving capital theory.* This applies, in particular, to the efforts of the mainstream school and also to those of the Austrian school. However, there is really no satisfactory treatment by any economic school. On the confusions of capital theory, we can do no better than consult Geoff Harcourt's (1969) summary of the issues in a classic article in the *Journal of Economic Literature* which has never really been answered. According to Harcourt's mentor Joan Robinson, writing earlier in the 1950s and as quoted by Cohen and Harcourt (2003, 201):

> The production function has been a powerful instrument of mis-education. The student of economic theory is taught to write $Q = f(L, K)$ where L is a quantity of labour, K a quantity of capital and Q a rate of output of commodities. He is instructed to assume all workers alike, and to measure L in man-hours of labour; he is told something about the index-number problem in choosing a unit of output; and then he is hurried on to the next question, in the hope that he will forget to ask in what units K is measured. Before he ever does ask, he has become a professor, and so sloppy habits of thought are handed on from one generation to the next.

The sloppy habits of thought have persisted, and continued to vitiate any type of economic theory derived on the basis of capital-theoretic arguments. The conceptual confusions about capital are in fact very closely related to the same sorts of confusion about money that have just been discussed. The credit theorist Mitchell Innes (1914, 355) had already made this very point over one hundred years ago, in a passage that is the more impressive for having been written at a time when the international gold standard was still in force. According to Innes, in the real world "every banker and every commercial man knows that there is only one kind of *capital*, and that is *money*" (emphasis added).

IS ANYTHING WORTH SALVAGING FROM THE WRECKAGE?

We need to pause at this point to ask just what is left of the program of the mainstream school. I suppose that a truly honest intellectual answer would have to be "not very much." But this can be a tough sell, in particular to people who have already invested a lot of time and energy in learning the various techniques (including myself) but also, more importantly, to the current cohort of PhD students and young Assistant Professors on whom the future will depend. I think that the wording in the discussion above has made enough caveats to cover any potential objections. The criticism was of econometrics as the *main* empirical method, the *virtual* identification of economic theory with differential calculus, and so on. It is not suggested that these techniques will disappear entirely, or that it was a waste of time learning them (Smithin 2013a, xii–xiv). For example, I will go on below to suggest a greater use of numerical methods (i.e., computer simulation methods) as one option for the pursuit of fruitful research projects. If so, then one possible source of trial or starting values for the parameters would clearly be exercises in time series econometrics. The emphasis here, however, should be very much on the words "trial" and "exercises." If so, the procedure would not violate any strictures against the use of statistical probability theory as the "main" empirical method. Rather the time series econometrics would be an information-gathering exercise only, as part of the first stage of an "abductive" (or "retroductive") mode of investigation (Lawson 1997, 24–26). Any attempt at an *explanation* (note emphasis) of a specific sequence of events would belong to the second stage which could legitimately include (non-stochastic) computer simulation methods. Nonetheless, these preliminary econometric exercises would still allow young researchers to deploy more-or-less the full range of their technical skills so painfully acquired in graduate school. Similarly, in a detailed process analysis it is always possible to mathematically work out the hypothetical "long-run multipliers," at the end of the process, by calculus. Once again, however, what is really important is the investigation of the actual process itself.

Having made these concessions it is then reasonable then to point to the opposite, and really more serious danger, that of making so many caveats as to return to an untenable status quo. The point of making the concessions is to be able to attract interest in, and allegiance to, the project on the part of the current cohort of graduate students, and this can be achieved by retaining at least some of the results and techniques that continue to play such a large role in contemporary graduate training. However, if the results are ultimately to be of any value it is equally important not to comprise methodological first principles.

WHAT IS THE CORRECT METHODOLOGY FOR MONETARY MACROECONOMICS?

As a counterpoint to the seemingly insuperable problems facing the contemporary economics profession in its less than half-hearted attempt to study monetary phenomena, we can also list four possible alternative methodological principles that might help us to do better. There is not a strict one-to-one correspondence between the four problems identified above and the set of solutions. Therefore, each of the solutions will be labeled with Roman numerals (i) to (iv) rather than repeating the list (1) to (4) of the previous discussion.

The first correct principle is (i) *to use explicitly macroeconomic methods.* Simply put, the nature of money both *necessitates* and *justifies* a macroeconomic approach. Such a statement then immediately raises the question of what a "macroeconomic" approach actually is. For some time now there has been a pronounced tendency, on the part of mainstream economists and also (particularly) self-described Austrian economists, to actively disparage macroeconomics—on the grounds that these methods involve only the mechanical manipulation of aggregates and averages without behavioral content. But, if the objective really is to study a monetary system, and indeed any sort of social system, this attitude is wildly off the mark. It is deeply unscientific. In reality, only the social institution of *money itself* can bestow sufficient organic unity on the economic system to make any kind of rational decision-making feasible, much less a scholarly analysis of that decision-making. The alternative strategy, of reduction and atomism as applied to a money-less economy, is rather the equivalent of "nonsense as game" (Fletcher 2000, as quoted by Smithin 2002, 441).[12]

And the whole point of a "game" in the context of scientific research, according to Fletcher, is that:

> by operating according to known rules and limiting the range of possible outcomes the game is more certain than life . . . and confers upon the player [*i.e.*, the researcher] a characteristic sense of freedom and security.

It has to do mainly with bolstering the psychological well-being and self-esteem of the analyst rather than having anything to do with actual research in the sense of finding things out. Anyone acquainted with the contemporary mainstream economic literature will surely recognize the parallels (intended) to be drawn with such research programs as neo-Walrasian general equilibrium theory, the microfoundations approach, the DGSE model, and the whole can of worms opened up by the very idea of "game theory" itself. The actual significance of macroeconomic analysis, despite the repeated assertions to the contrary, is that it is the only way to make a genuinely behavioral analysis, including money, at all possible. It is definitely *not* just a question of appealing to mathematical aggregation and averages. To his credit Schumpeter, writing in the mid-twentieth century, was very well aware of this aspect of the problem. In fact, the title of another subsection of Chapter 6 of the *History of Economic Analysis* (1954) was the "Relation of Monetary Analysis to Aggregative or Macroanalysis." Schumpeter argues that it is a distinct *advantage* that macroeconomic analysis "attempts to reduce the variables of the economic system to a small number of monetary aggregates, such as total income, total investment, total consumption, and the like" (Schumpeter 1954, 278). This is the only way to render the system comprehensible. Significantly, Schumpeter also states that monetary analysis is "almost always" [*sic*][13] combined with macroanalysis precisely because "monetary aggregates are homogenous, whereas most nonmonetary aggregates are but *meaningless heaps of hopelessly disparate things*" (emphasis added).

The second important principle is that we should (ii) *take seriously the notions of endogenous money and bank credit creation* and their importance for the successful operation of the economic system. This should follow logically as soon as the difference between real and monetary analysis has been recognized. Although there are currently various competing claims being made about scholarly priority on this particular issue (see, for example, Smithin 2016a, 64–65) my own view is that this is one of the "main collective contributions" of the various heterodox schools of monetary economics, such as Post Keynesian theory, in both its horizontalist and structuralist versions, circuit theory, modern money theory (universally known by its acronym MMT), and others.

Third, and as already indicated by the reference to Schumpeter, we should (iii) restrict attention to relatively small models of both closed and open economies. The former are useful primarily for theory, and the latter for practical policy analysis. Relatively small models are required to ensure that the logic of each approach is fully comprehensible, both to those who are constructing the models and, just as importantly, to those who are using them. In the standard economic jargon, there should be no "black boxes."

The fourth and final correct principle is then (iv) *to "make use of only two fundamental units of quantity, namely, quantities of [real] money-value and quantities of employment"* which is a quote from the *General Theory* itself (Keynes 1936, 41). The point is to avoid the quagmire of capital theory and Keynes, for one, was quite clear that this was his intention. The interpolation is necessary because Keynes in 1936 actually talked only about "money values" rather than "*real* money values." This left several hostages to fortune in the shape of later accusations about "money illusion" and so forth—supposedly the opposite pole to barter illusion. The change in wording simply acknowledges the various modern debates about the concepts used in compiling both the national income and expenditure accounts and aggregate price indices, including the important issue of stock-flow consistency. One of the most important question that needs to be answered is whether, or not, it is possible to construct a relevant and useful macroeconomic theory without recourse to the dead-end of capital-theoretic reasoning, and yet one that at the same time is well able to cope with important long-run questions such as growth, development, and technical change, as well as short-run stabilization policy. The argument of this book is that such a project is wholly viable (it is certainly necessary) and that Keynes did much to point the way in this direction, even if ultimately he was not able to deliver such a theory in full detail.

IS THERE A BETTER WAY?

A few years ago, in Smithin (2009a, 56), I explicitly argued that one way forward is simply to take a step back, and return to practice of monetary macroeconomics in the style of such writers as Keynes himself, the later Hicks, and the Post Keynesians. But, having said this does it mean that there is nothing that the methods and technology of the twenty-first century can add? Of course not. This, clearly, is where developments in modern computer technology come in.

In the mid-1980s, my colleagues Omar Hamouda, Bernard Wolf, and myself organized a conference in Toronto at which one of the speakers, one of whose co-authors was a Nobel Prize winner, put forward the attractive notion of a modern-day Keynes, "surrounded by a high-tech 'circus' with . . . personal computers . . . current problems being attacked by . . . intuition . . . aided by current technology" (Bodkin, Klein, and Marwah 1988, 9–10).[14] The fact of the matter is, however, that in the 1980s the relevant technology was not yet available. I had already made an attempt in this direction myself, in my doctoral thesis (Smithin 1982) on *The Incidence and Economic Effects of the Financing of Unemployment Insurance (TIEEFUI)*,[15] and the computers of those days could hardly be called "high-tech." Now, in the twenty-first century the situation is quite different as is illustrated, for example, by the pioneering work of Godley and Lavoie (2007) on *Monetary Economics* which used these methods to good effect. These days there need be no hesitation in suggesting that non-stochastic numerical methods in discrete time can provide (a) a theoretical method that can handle fundamental uncertainty, (b) a comprehensive process analysis capable of dealing with historical time, (c) a robust empirical method based on the principle of abduction rather than induction (Lawson 1997, 2003), and (d) nonetheless the ability to retain at least some of the results and techniques of time series econometrics which (as already stressed) continue to play a large role in the training of contemporary graduate students.

The reference to *non-stochastic* simulation methods, albeit with periodic shocks to the system (including those caused by changes in market psychology in all its manifestations), is intended to take seriously the presence of fundamental uncertainty rather than probabilistic risk, as discussed above. A *discrete time* specification is appropriate for two main reasons. The first is that in the business, accounting, and social worlds generally, time is organized into discrete units, years, quarters, months, weeks, and so on (Blaise 2000, Landes 1983).[16] The second is the frequently made observation that the characteristic time series of business and economic data are well approximated by low-order difference (as opposed to differential) equations. One writer who has made progress with the use of non-stochastic numerical methods is Keen (e.g., 1995, 2009), who nonetheless argues strongly in favor of a continuous time specification. However, this seems to be because Keen is primarily interested in nonlinear or "chaotic" dynamics, much of the mathematics of which has been worked out in the context of physical systems in the natural sciences (Devaney 2011, 5), such as physics, biology, meteorology (*cf.* the iconic Lorenz system), and so on, and all such applications have used continuous time specifications. Therefore the remarks, made above, about the different ontologies of the natural and social worlds (and the inapplicability of differential and stochastic *calculus* to the latter) would seem also to apply to the choice between differential equations and difference equations in dynamic theory. Contrary to Alfred Marshall (1890), whose motto was quoted above, nature does "make leaps" (e.g., because of a sensitivity to initial conditions), but these take place in a very different manner to the ways in which the "*salta*" occur in the social context.

I would argue that there is no contradiction in both appealing to the presence of fundamental uncertainty in the social world and yet retaining the use of time series econometrics, in the first phase only, of an abductive empirical investigation. As already discussed, the econometric methods are required for two reasons (a) to provide plausible starting values for the parameters in simulation exercises, and also (b) for the researcher to be able to derive time series for the spontaneous changes that will necessarily occur in all of the policy variables and in real costs and productivity, as well as in the proxies for the evolution of different measures of market psychology. We would not be involved in hypothesis testing per se at this stage. The actual empirical investigation occurs only at the second stage of the abductive or retroductive process. The concept of "reflexivity," due to George Soros, the well-known financier and self-described philanthropist (Soros 2009), is also highly relevant to the development of the new empirical method. Soros's idea of reflexivity suggests that in situations involving conscious (or "thinking") participants, the views that these fallible agents form about the current state of affairs can in turn influence and change the situation itself. The experience of an economic recession, for example, may in itself incline market participants to a pessimistic view of the future and cause further disruption. It turns out that the new method is well able to isolate time series that can act as proxies for how these psychological states change over time (and then cause further shocks to the system) and hence in themselves have a definite causal impact on the real economy.

The argument therefore comes down essentially to the claim that the suggested numerical methods are able to satisfy all of the methodological desiderata put forward in the previous section. In fact, preliminary work by Collis (2016, 2018), Smithin

(2013d), and Smithin and Zhou (2014) has already shown how these methods might be put into operation in various types of both research and teaching contexts. The resulting methodology can be claimed to be genuinely interdisciplinary—involving social philosophy (social ontology), economic sociology, monetary macroeconomics, and political economy, in addition to making full use of the purely technical methods.

RELATION OF THE CURRENT VOLUME
TO PREVIOUS RESEARCH

In retrospect the body of work in the sequence to be found in Smithin (1994, 1996, 2003, 2009a, 2013a), that is, between my *Controversies of Monetary Economics* (*CME*) of 1994 (Smithin 1994) and the present work, continues themes that I first addressed more than thirty-five years ago in my PhD thesis (Smithin 1982). This took an entirely monetary or macroeconomic approach to public finance, and already included the concepts of endogenous money and bank credit creation. Much later, between my *Money Enterprise and Income Distribution* (*MEI*) of 2009 (Smithin 2009), and *Essays in the Fundamental Theory of Monetary Economics and Macroeconomics* (*EFTMEM*) in 2013 (Smithin 2013a), there was a further progression. In *EFTMEM* what, in *MEI*, I had previously called the "demand for inflation" (DI) schedule slopes upward instead of downward, in what I now take to be a thoroughly "Keynesian" manner.[17] The key to the change was a more detailed discussion of the transmission mechanism of monetary policy, together with the realization that in principle there is a *negative* relationship between the inflation rate and the real rate of interest on loans from the commercial banks. This is actually the historical "forced saving" effect. In *MEI*, in contrast, there was a positive relationship between interest rates and inflation, and hence a negative relationship between interest rates and growth. This was based on the artificially imposed *contra*-inflation preferences of central banks, implemented via restrictive monetary policy. I now see this not as genuinely an exercise in pure economic theory,[18] but rather as a prime illustration of one of the many ways in which the central bank itself can be a destabilizing factor—as has occurred multiple times in practice,

The current book intends to draw all of the above themes together into a new and definitive statement for the present era.

CONCLUSION

In the end, Keynes in 1936 did not permanently change the way the world thinks about economic problems. Neither did he knock away the Ricardian foundations of Marxism nor, for that matter, the ultimately similar "real" analytical foundations of the neoclassical economics of the late nineteenth century. The latter, in spite of the efforts of Keynes and others, meta-sized uncontrollably in the latter part of the twentieth century, and lives on to the present day to confound the best efforts of those charged with giving policy advice. Keynes's stated objectives therefore still remain as tasks for the current generation of young scholars in the twenty-first century. The project is doomed to failure, however, if these scholars continue to have to learn precisely the wrong set of principles and attitudes in the hothouse atmosphere of the graduate schools of contemporary academia.

Money is a social relation or social institution. It is neither a simple commodity nor merely a *numeraire*. It has deontic power, and important causal effects on the material world. In particular, credit creation and money creation are continuously necessary for firms to realize the profits, and workers to receive the wages, on which the method of enterprise (capitalism) itself depends. Orthodox economics errs by ignoring this, treating economic activity mainly as a question of barter exchange. There is a failure to understand that both inflation-adjusted real interest rates and (in international economic relations) real exchange rates are important *monetary* variables. The reader should not, however, be misled by this statement into thinking it relies on so-called money illusion (the bugbear of the neoclassical economist), nor on any supposed differences in the theoretical bona fides of macroeconomics and microeconomics. Though determined primarily in the money and financial markets, real interest rates and real exchange rates are certainly real enough in the common-sense meaning of the term, and are also important relative prices in the standard economic sense. These ideas are significant, not only for an understanding of how the system actually works, but also what advice should be given about monetary, financial, fiscal, and trade policy.

NOTES

1. This quote appeared on the front cover of a paperback edition of Keynes's book (originally published by Harcourt Brace in 1964) in a printing of 1991.

2. *Essays in Persuasion* was the title of volume of essays published by Keynes in the early 1930s, in the depths of the Great Depression (Keynes 1931).

3. Another recent work that should be consulted on this history is that by Bill Scarth on *Macroeconomics: The Development of Modern Methods for Policy Analysis* (Scarth 2014).

4. Later, according to King (2015, 4), "this astonishing omission was apparently rectified in the second edition." However, no substantive changes were made to the text.

5. Keynes (1936, 383) did famously assert, in contrast to classical Marxism, that "the power of vested interests is vastly exaggerated compared with the gradual encroachment of ideas."

6. This is the formulation found in Vol. II of *Das Kapital* (Marx 1885, 109).

7. The very title of Ingham's book was, in fact, *The Nature of Money*.

8. For further discussion of Keynes's attitude to Marx see, for example, Cottrell (1994, 6–10) in an interesting article.

9. A caveat is that here, as elsewhere (for example, in the notion of the "socialization of investment" from Chapter 24 of the *General Theory*), Keynes confusingly seems to use the term socialism in a somewhat different sense than that usually employed in discussions of comparative economic systems.

10. At best these constructs can only be made to "mimic" results that have previously been derived by other means, by changing the specifications of the objective functions and constraints to deliver a predetermined or desired result. See, for example, the paper on this topic by Kam, Smithin, and Tabassum (2016).

11. These are issues that Paul Davidson (1974, 1991, 2009, 29–43, 2011), for example, has been stressing for many years. In 1988, Hamouda and Smithin (1988a, 1988b) summarized much of the literature up to that point, fifty years or so after Keynes's own statement.

12. These ideas are explored by Fletcher (2000, 2007) in his biographical research on the Cambridge economist Dennis Robertson who ended up as one of the main opponents of Keynes in the 1930s. The idea of "nonsense as game" comes from literary criticism of the works of Lewis Caroll (the pseudonym of the Reverend Charles Dobson, the author of *Alice in Wonderland*). Robertson, in fact, was well known for using quotes from *Alice* as epigraphs for the chapters of his works on monetary theory. It is easy to see "Wonderland" as a metaphor for the imaginary world created by mainstream economists *via* purely abstract theorizing. See also Smithin (2002, 2009b).

13. In my view the first word here is redundant.

14. The "circus" was the name given to the small group of Keynes's closest followers in Cambridge in the early 1930s.

15. Ironically, in the Orwellian world in which we now live, the "unemployment insurance" (UI) of old has morphed into "employment insurance" (EI) even though (or perhaps because) the ratio of employment to the working-age population is much lower.

16. Even in finance there is a trading day in the stock market (e.g., from 9:30 a.m. to 4:00 p.m. for the TSX in Toronto).

17. In the current work this will be called the effective demand (ED) schedule.

18. The broader implication of this remark for the validity of the monetary theory found in most textbooks today seems to me to be quite obvious.

Chapter 2

The Basic Principles of Macroeconomics in an Alternative Monetary Model

INTRODUCTION

The purpose of this chapter, at an early stage in the development of the argument, is to set out the basic principles of monetary macroeconomics in an alternative monetary model (AMM) of economic growth, the business cycle, inflation, and income distribution. These principles differ considerably from those advanced in the standard macroeconomic textbooks. However, the latter have been demonstrably unsuccessful in the promotion of usable macroeconomic policy advice for the past several years, actually decades. A different approach is needed.

The AMM has had a number of antecedents over the years. Earlier attempts at working out an alternative model may be found, for example, in Atesoglu and Smithin (2006a, 2006b, 2007) and Smithin (1994, 1997, 2003, 2005, 2009a, 2013a). The latest version contains each of what I have described as the "desirable" (they really are the *essential*) features of such a model (Smithin 2013a, 219). These are (1) that credit creation and money creation are an integral part of the way in which the economy actually works, not just a superfluous addition to a barter exchange economy, (2) the money supply is always treated as endogenous, (3) there is a "*monetary* theory of the *real* rate of interest" (Burstein 1995, 5, emphasis added), (4) the monetary policy instrument of the central bank is a nominal interest rate, generically called the "policy rate" of the central bank, and (5) monetary policy is non-neutral in both the short-run and the long-run. Both monetary policy, that is changes in the *real* inflation-adjusted policy rate of interest, and fiscal policy, changes in government spending as a percentage of GDP and/or changes in the average tax rate, are seen to affect not only the ups and downs of the business cycle, but also the ongoing growth rate of the economy. No other approach to monetary economics combines all of these features.

I think that there is sufficient analytical material in what follows to identify, and fully explain, the various factors causing economic growth or stagnation, episodes of boom and bust, inflation and deflation, periodic financial crises, and so on, and how these might be mitigated or avoided. However, before going into the details, it will be necessary first to address an argument that is frequently made, particularly in difficult economic times, that the monetary production or "capitalist" economy is somehow inherently or irremediably unstable. One of the first tasks to be undertaken in this chapter is therefore an investigation of the conditions that might make this degree of instability an actual reality. The *stability* issue will, in fact, be seen to revolve around questions of monetary policy first and foremost, rather than (say) fiscal policy or even financial regulation as such.[1] The sine qua non for good macroeconomic performance is therefore at least some understanding on the part of policy-makers of such things as endogenous money, the role of credit creation by the banks, the relationship between the central bank and the commercial banks, and so forth. Unfortunately, such an understanding has never been much in evidence either historically or at the present time.

Once the point about stability is established the remaining results can then be worked out in the context of a theoretical closed-economy model, the AMM itself. A closed-economy framework is chosen simply for the purpose of clarity and completeness in dealing with the basic theoretical issues. However, clearly, later in the book the narrative will indeed have to be extended to deal with the important practical issues of the exchange rate regime, the balance of payments, and international finance. Even before moving on to the discussion of stability, therefore, the next section of this chapter will give a brief preview of these key questions of international political economy.

EXCHANGE RATE REGIMES AND
INTERNATIONAL ECONOMIC RELATIONS

Although the theoretical results derived below are worked out within the framework of the closed-economy version of the AMM (and are exhaustive in that context) it will also be insisted that the discussion has a very much wider sphere of practical application. In principle, the results derived in this chapter will hold up in each of the following circumstances, (a) for a closed economy under autarky (i.e., an economy that does not trade with the rest of the world), (b) for the world (or possibly a regional) economy treated as whole, (c) very importantly, in an individual open economy with a floating exchange rate and, (d) in an individual open economy with a "fixed-but-adjustable" exchange rate.

To explain these statements and applying a broad brush, we can identify four possible configurations for international economic relations. These are (1) a floating exchange rate, (2) a "fixed-but-adjustable" exchange rate, (3) an irrevocably fixed exchange rate, or hard peg, and (4) a currency union.[2] In an economy with a floating exchange rate, and as previously shown by Smithin (2013a, 2016a), the results would be qualitatively the same as those in the equivalent closed-economy model. This is a case of full "monetary sovereignty" for the government of the domestic economy (Smithin 2016a, 66, Tymoigne and Wray 2015, 24–25). In this case the results presented here do provide a reliable guide for making macroeconomic policy choices. All that would then be needed for a fully complete analysis is to later add results for the real exchange rate and the foreign debt position. In an economy with a fixed-but-adjustable exchange rate, and again qualitatively speaking, the results also resemble those of the closed economy (Kam and Smithin 2008, 2011, Smithin 2013a, 2016a). This is again a regime which allows for some domestic control over both monetary and fiscal policy. In both these cases, the domestic authorities are thus able to conduct monetary and fiscal policy more-or-less as they see fit. An important implication of this finding is that the old idea (from the Mundell-Fleming model of the 1960s), to the effect that monetary policy can be assigned to floating exchange rates and fiscal policy to fixed exchange rates (Fleming 1963, Mundell 1963b), is completely misleading.

Turning now to the other possible configurations we should note that in spite of the solid-sounding name, a putative "hard peg" for the exchange rate (such as a metallic standard, a credible fixed exchange rate regime, or a currency board with no loopholes) is actually an unstable arrangement, and will eventually break down. There are very many historical examples.[3] There is no effective sovereignty in this case, and it is simply not a viable policy choice in the long-run. The idea of a currency union which, in its late twentieth and early twenty-first-century versions owes much to the concept of an "optimal currency area" (OCA), another dubious idea originally due to Mundell (1961), is to do away with exchange rates altogether. It is a total abandonment of sovereignty. Ironically, even though the intent is to eliminate exchange rate problems, when initially applied the currency union will have very much the same (in)stability characteristics as a hard peg (cf. the actual historical case of the Euro-zone). Unless the domestic authorities are willing to give up control over economic policy entirely there are only two possible long-run outcomes. These are either (a) break-up of the system (which is the equivalent of an exchange rate crisis in this context), or (b) eventual evolution into a true federal state with a developed system of fiscal federalism. In the latter case, the different countries turn into mere Provinces, in the specifically Canadian sense of this term.

There are detailed proofs of these propositions in chapter 10 below. For now these statements should simply be kept in mind when attempting to apply the theoretical results to various practical situations. For a jurisdiction with a floating exchange rate, or with a fixed-but-adjustable exchange rate, the results do provide usable guidelines for the improved conduct of macroeconomic and monetary policy. However, jurisdictions stuck with either of the other types of arrangement are essentially in a self-imposed straightjacket. The only sensible policy advice that could have been given would have been for the decision-makers to think more clearly about basic economic theory, before subjecting their citizens to these problems.

"STABILIZING AN UNSTABLE ECONOMY"?

As explained in an earlier article (Smithin 2016a, 72–74) the above section heading is a reference to the title of a widely read book by Hyman Minsky (1986) the author of the "financial fragility hypothesis." The suggestion is that a capitalist economy is inherently prone to sequences of boom and bust, or in Minsky's words, of "inflations and debt deflations which have the potential to spin out of control" (Minsky 1992, 1), because of the nature of financial and banking system. Minsky (1992, 8–9) does concede the possibility of a stable configuration. In fact, the "first theorem of the financial instability hypothesis is that the economy [does] ha[ve] financing regimes in which it is stable." However:

> The second theorem . . . is that over periods of prolonged prosperity, the economy transits
> from financial relations that make for a static system to financial relations that make for
> an unstable system.

The implication is therefore that there is a sort of inevitability to the process, and that this must be remedied by some sort of financial regulation. The contemporary self-identified "Austrian" economist Pascal Salin, however, apparently disagrees with this assessment. Writing of the global financial crisis (GFC) of the early twenty-first century, Salin (2014) asserts that:

> Two main errors have been made about the recent crisis (and, probably, about any other
> crisis). First, the most widely accepted interpretation of the crisis consists in stressing
> that it was a consequence of the fundamentally unstable nature of the market mechanisms
> and, moreover, of the immoral behavior of bankers who were mostly concerned by . . .
> their profits so that they took too many risks. For those who hold such a view, it is obvi-
> ous that curing the crisis implies state interventionism which would be the only way to
> reintroduce stability in the economic system (through more regulations and so-called
> "recovery policies"). Unhappily, this approach is misleading and it can be shown that,
> quite on the contrary, the crisis has been a consequence of state interventionism. . . . The
> second most frequent error consisted in opposing only two main theories about business
> cycles . . . forgetting [a third] . . . the only one which . . . makes it possible to understand
> modern business cycles . . . so-called "Austrian theory" initially developed by Ludwig
> von Mises and Friedrich Hayek.

From my point of view this is an interesting passage because (it has always seemed to me) the Hayek-Mises theory of the cycle does not actually present a dramatically different view of how the boom and bust cycle unfolds than does the financial fragility hypothesis (see, for example, Smithin 2013a, 238–47, Toporowksi 2008).[4] The main difference for the Austrians, as Salin explains, is really only the idea that the inflationary boom (which then inexorably leads to crisis and a deflationary reaction) is set off by an inappropriately expansionary monetary or fiscal policy on the part of the governmental authorities rather than being caused purely by the greed of the private sector.[5] Nonetheless, both groups do seem to agree that excessive credit and money creation is somehow at the root of the problem, and that this can be cured by "turning off the tap," or so to speak.

However, in suggesting various methods to choke off the prior boom, neither camp seems to fully take into account the point made in chapter 1, that some substantial amount of credit and money creation is still going to be required even for the normal functioning of the system, and particularly for the realization of money profits. Going "cold turkey" (switching the analogy to a medical addiction) is not really an option. Schumpeter, as quoted by Solow (2007, 9), once wrote disparagingly of Salin's "recovery policies" as "capitalism in an oxygen tent." However, the patient will die if the air supply is cut off altogether. Keynes (1936, 322) on the other hand did seem to see the fundamental difficulty, writing that:

> The right remedy for the trade cycle is not to be found in abolishing booms and thus keep-
> ing us permanently in a state of semi-slump; but in abolishing slumps and thus keeping
> us in a state of semi-boom.

In terms of the big picture this seems to me to be the essential difference between the Keynesian approach to economic difficulties and the other suggested remedies at both ends of the political spectrum. These alternatives would tend to keep the economy permanently in a slow growth, high unemployment mode which is not going to be politically sustainable regardless of who is administering it. I suppose that common-sense tell us that we are all ultimately be looking for some sort of happy medium in terms of the flow of credit, but the difficult question is how this is actually to be achieved.

There are some obvious analogies between the current state of political economy after the GFC of the early twenty-first century and the comparable watershed three-quarters of a century earlier that deeply affected Keynes and others. That was also a period in which, in the absence of an effective response to crisis by orthodoxy, various heterodox approaches proliferated, both outside and inside the academy. In the 1930s the outsiders were dismissed by Robertson (1940, 29), and others, as "monetary cranks," but treated more kindly by Keynes (1936, 370–71) who called them "brave . . . heretics." The failures of orthodoxy in the early twenty-first century have naturally provoked a similar set of responses from outside academia (see, for example, Ingham, Coutts, and Konzelmann 2016).

Perhaps a more neutral term for the outsiders, then and now, would be something like "monetary reformers" and, to be fair, in a passage I have recently quoted elsewhere (Smithin 2016a, 66), nine decades ago Robertson did acknowledge that:

> It is easy to scoff at these productions: it is not so easy to see exactly where they go wrong. It is natural that practical bankers . . . conscious that the projects of monetary cranks are dangerous to society, should cling in self-defence to . . . tradition and accepted practice. But it is not open to . . . detached student(s) of economics to take refuge from dangerous innovation in blind conservatism. [They] . . . must assess with an equal eye the projects of the reformers and the claims of the established order . . . and . . . to this end must [themselves] build up . . . a theory of money—a critical analysis of . . . processes by which, under a modern system of banking money is manufactured.

What is not quite clear from this quote, however, is that there actually have always been two varieties of monetary reformer. Robertson seems to have had in mind those who advocate more credit creation.[6] However, both in the 1930s and now, there were and are other reformers who think exactly the opposite and, as with some of the academics whose views have already been discussed, advocate such things as "100 percent reserve banking" or similar in an attempt to restrain the perceived excesses of the bankers (Dyson, Hodgson, and van Lerven 2016, Fontana and Sawyer 2016). These two points of view about monetary reform are really diametrically opposed. To sort them out it will certainly be necessary to finally and belatedly take Roberston's advice and build up a detailed monetary model from scratch.

One class of proposals to regulate credit creation dates back to a period long before there was any academic economics profession to comment on them. The reference is to the so-called real bills doctrine, the name of which derives from a famous passage in Adam Smith's *Wealth of Nations* (Smith 1776, 304) about what he (Smith) thought prudent banking practice might be. Similar ideas, albeit with land rather than real bills as security, can also be traced back to the French-based Scots financier John Law writing seventy years earlier (Mints 1945). That suggestion, however, obviously did not work at all. It led to banking practices that were anything but prudent, for example at the time of the infamous Mississippi Scheme. The real bills doctrine was also advanced by "anti-bullionists" during the controversies of the early nineteenth century and by the "banking school" later in the mid-nineteenth century (Humphrey 1982, 27–29). Into the twentieth century a form of the real bills doctrine was "enshrined," as Humphrey (1982, 29) puts it, in the US legislation setting up the Federal Reserve System in 1913, and remained very influential in the United States down to the 1950s (Meltzer 2003, Sargent 1979). In our own time, and in spite of this long history, very many of the supposedly new proposals of twenty-first-century reformers do indeed bear a distinct family resemblance to notions of this sort.

Generically, real bills-type proposals are criteria for regulating overall bank lending in the context of a system in which the bulk of the money supply consists of the nominal liabilities of financial institutions, issued as a by-product of their credit creating activities, and without reference to a metallic standard. The suggestion is that if banks restrict themselves to short-term commercial lending to finance the production and/or distribution of goods in process, this would provide a system in which the money supply would change endogenously, be optimally responsive to the needs of trade, and yet also deliver price stability. Laidler (1989, 66) however unambiguously calls the real bills doctrine "the real bills fallacy." It is fallacious because any number of promises to pay can be issued in connection with the forward delivery of a given quantity of goods (the same goods can be sold any number of times) and, also, because the money value of any collateral supposedly backing the bills necessarily must contain a price component as well as a value component. Real bills-type criteria therefore provide no check to either goods price inflation or asset price inflation. Any arbitrary money price increases of (say) the goods concerned are automatically validated by forthcoming increases in the nominal money supply.

A REAL INTEREST RATE RULE FOR MONETARY POLICY?

To now explore the various questions about the stability of the system in more detail, first consider the following simple model of the supply of and demand for endogenous money. The endogenous supply of money is expressed as multiple of the lagged nominal wage bill, and the "voluntary" demand for money (Hicks 1967a, 14) as a fraction of nominal GDP.

$$Ms = \phi W_{-1} N_{-1}, \quad \phi > 1 \tag{2.1}$$

$$Md = \psi PY. \qquad 0 < \psi < 1 \tag{2.2}$$

Here the symbol M stands for the broad money supply in period t which in the modern world consists primarily of commercial bank deposits of one kind or another, and $W_{-1}N_{-1}$ is the aggregate nominal wage bill (of the previous period). The idea that the money supply depends upon the aggregate wage bill comes originally from circuit theory—in which it has been shown that firms in the aggregate must always be borrowing at least the equivalent of total wage bill (Graziani 2003, 27). It is important to note, however, that for the industrial system to be *viable* (in the sense of being able to generate positive monetary profits) the coefficient ϕ must actually be greater than one (Moore 1988, Smithin 2013a, 2016b). This margin therefore represents all other types of borrowing (speculative or not) over and above that needed to finance the aggregate wage bill. Implicitly, there is a one-period production lag in the model whereby the expression $Y = AN_{-1}$ maps lagged labor input into current GDP. This is the simplest possible specification that captures the fundamental idea that production takes time.

The equilibrium condition in the money market is therefore that the voluntary demand for money (meaning the willingness of agents to hold commercial bank deposits created in the previous period through the current period) should be equal to the money supply in existence during that period:

$$Md = Ms \tag{2.3}$$

Given the production lag, there must also, clearly, be a temporary Hicksian involuntary demand for those same money balances to be held over the turn of the period. However, only the voluntary part of money demand has any economic significance.

From (2.1), (2.2), and (2.3) it can be seen that the value of the aggregate price level P must satisfy (in the sense of being consistent with):[7]

$$P = (\phi/\psi)\left(W_{-1}/A\right) \tag{2.4}$$

which expression includes the ratio of two terms, ϕ relating to the supply side of the money market, and ψ which relates to the demand-side. Next, we propose a specification for the behavior of this ratio as follows:

$$\phi/\psi = \left[(\phi_0/\psi_0)\right]e^{-\lambda(r-r-1)}. \quad 0 < \lambda < 1 \tag{2.5}$$

This contains a version of Keynes's (1936, 196) "speculative" demand for money. Unlike in Keynes's treatment, however, there is also a speculative *supply* of money arising, as mentioned, from bank loans for all other things than the wage bill such as (quite literally) financial speculation, but also consumer spending, capital spending, and so on. Each of these certainly has a significant forward-looking aspect.

It is important to realize that the two relevant monetary magnitudes are themselves real variables (i.e., dollar values divided by price indices). Therefore the "speculation" must be supposed to be about real asset prices and real interest rates. This is, again, unlike in Keynes who was interested mainly in nominal interest rates and nominal asset prices. Next, taking natural logarithms we obtain:

$$ln\phi - ln\psi = (ln\phi_0 - ln\psi_0) - \lambda(r - r_{-1}), \tag{2.6}$$

And now define the term p_0 as $p_0 = (ln\phi - ln\psi)$. Equation (2.6) can thus be rewritten as:

$$ln\phi - ln\psi = p_0 - \lambda(r - r_{-1}). \tag{2.7}$$

The new term p_0 might be thought of as representing the purely psychological element of liquidity preference rather than speculation about changes in interest rates as such. It may perhaps best be identified with the more general notions of "bullishness" versus "bearishness" in the financial markets, such as Keynes had discussed in the earlier *Treatise on Money* (Keynes 1930, 128–31), rather than the specifically speculative demand of the *General Theory* itself. (The latter is represented here by the parameter λ.) As was also the case with speculative demand, both sides of the money market are reflected in p_0.

Once again taking natural logarithms of equation (2.4) and substituting in from (2.7), we can finally derive the following expression for inflation:

$$p = p_0 - \lambda\left(r - r_{-1}\right) + w_{-1} - a \tag{2.8}$$

Next, we will assume that the policy of the central bank is simply to fix the *nominal* policy rate of interest at whatever level including the supposed lower bound of zero. The main point about such a policy stance is that the central bank would not consistently be following any sort of feedback rule conditional on previous macroeconomic outcomes. The former stance is actually the sort of policy that central banks do seem to have been pursuing in recent years, up to the time of writing. In the United States, for example, the Board of Governors of the Federal Reserve System meets eight times per year to set the federal funds rate. However, actual changes are very rare, perhaps once a year or not at all, and even then only by a maximum of twenty-five basis points. The problem with this procedure is that it turns out that this is precisely the sort of policy that renders the economy unstable. It will lead directly to the sorts of problems already identified by the several authors quoted above, namely the episodes of boom and bust, inflation and deflation, Great Depressions, Great Recessions, bursting bubbles, GFCs, and so on. Indeed, going further back in time, this policy of setting (or fixing) a nominal policy instrument, such as a bank rate or discount rate, has almost always been what central banks have tried to do throughout history ever since these institutions first came into existence in the late seventeenth century, except perhaps during the heyday of monetarism in the 1970s and 1980s. As this is an unstable policy, these circumstances may well be enough to explain much of the actual historical experience.[8]

In context of our theoretical model, the nominal policy rate will be labeled i_0.[9] When the central bank has decided on the level of i_0 at one of its meetings, this setting will then be passed through to interest rates in general via the expression:

$$i = m_0 + m_1 i_0, \quad m_0 > 0, \quad 0 < m_1 < 1 \tag{2.9}$$

which is the monetary policy transmissions mechanism. Also, recall that the definition of the real interest rate (rather than the nominal rate) is;

$$r = i - p_{+1}. \tag{2.10}$$

The implication of (2.9) and (2.10) taken together is that, in principle, there must exist a negative relationship between the real rate of interest and the expected inflation rate of the form $r = m_0 + m_1 r_0 - (1-m_1)p_{+1}$.[10] This relation is, in fact, the old "forced savings effect" which played such a prominent role in the history of economic thought. Next, using these three equations (2.8), (2.9), and (2.10), it will now be shown that even if a real economic equilibrium is assumed to exist in this economy, a nominal interest rate peg will lead to inflationary instability. In the case where a real growth equilibrium exists, the natural logarithm of the real wage rate will also converge to its equilibrium value, implying that $w = w_{-1} = w_{-2}$, and so on. Thus, from (2.8) through (2.10), the following expression for inflation will emerge:

$$p = p_0 + w - a + \lambda\left(p_{+1} - p\right). \tag{2.11}$$

Lagging one period and rearranging then yields the following difference equation in inflation:

$$p = [(1+\lambda)/\lambda]p_{-1} + (1/\lambda)\left(p_0 + w - a\right). \tag{2.12}$$

It can immediately be seen that (2.12) is unstable. As $0 < \lambda < 1$, then $[(1+\lambda)/\lambda] > 1$. Therefore, under the assumed circumstances, there will definitely be inflationary instability (Smithin 1994, 2007, 2009a, 2013a). In fact, the instability can actually go in either direction depending on the nature of the initial shock to the system. In the real world, in fact, the situation will actually be still worse. This is because, as previously demonstrated by Smithin (2013a, 240–41) and contrary to our initial assumption above, it is *not* actually possible to achieve a real economic equilibrium in the presence of inflationary instability. If there is deflation, for example, there may well also be a growth recession.

How then to avoid these results? We can alternatively suppose that the central bank pursues a *real interest rate rule* for the real policy rate—along the lines I have suggested on several previous occasions (Smithin 2003, 2007, 2009a, 2013a, 2016a). Although such a policy will not be able to achieve any given numerical target for the inflation rate it will stabilize that rate, such that it is not accelerating or decelerating. The specific rule which would work in the present case is:

$$r_0(t) = r'_0 + \left[\left(1 - m_1\right)/m_1\right]p_{+1}, \tag{2.13}$$

where r'_0 is the real (inflation-adjusted) target for the overnight rate chosen by the central bank, and (t) is a time index. This is (still) an example of what is sometimes called a "park it" strategy for the policy rate of interest rate (Palley 2015, 17, Rochon and Setterfield 2007, 2012). What is being parked, however, is the target for the real policy rate r'_0 itself, rather any nominal interest rate. The rule set out in (2.13) will ensure that $r = r_{-1}$ in (2.8) and, therefore, given that in this case the equation for w also separately converges,[11] the inflation rate will eventually settle down to an equilibrium value (whether this be high, low, or even negative), given by:

$$p = p_0 + w - a. \tag{2.14}$$

This is a comprehensive theory of inflation for an economy with endogenous money. Cost push and productivity changes are relevant, but so also are the parameters of the explicit money supply and demand functions.

The analysis so far has set out the conditions in which outright instability will indeed be a problem, and has suggested that a *stable monetary policy*, in the sense of a real interest rate rule, is the way to avoid this. The next step is to embed this result into the complete AMM in the version previously described in Smithin (2013a, 221–22).

THE ALTERNATIVE MONETARY MODEL

The AMM consists of the following five equations, equations (2.15) through (2.19). The first of these (2.15) is a "Keynes-type" theory of growth (Smithin 2014, 456–58) which suggests that economic growth depends primarily on demand growth and profitability. The second (2.16) shows a three-way functional distribution of income between profit, interest, and wages. Equation (2.17) simply repeats the expression for inflation from (2.14) above, while (2.18) is a wage function explaining how real wages are determined. The argument of the wage function is (basically) that the bargaining power of labor increases in a growing economy. Finally, equation (2.19) shows that that there is an inverse relationship between the real rate of interest and expected inflation, derived by subtracting the expected inflation rate from both sides of equation (2.9). As mentioned previously, this last relationship is actually the historical "forced saving effect" which in the twentieth century came to be known as the "Mundell-Tobin effect" (Kam 2000, 2005, Smithin 2013a), after the ubiquitous Mundell (1963a) and Tobin (1965):

$$y = e_0 + e_1 k + (g - t), \qquad 0 < e_0 < 1, \quad (\text{economic growth}) \tag{2.15}$$

$$a = k + r_{-1} + w_{-1}, \qquad\qquad (\text{income distribution}) \tag{2.16}$$

$$p = p_0 + w_{-1} - a, \qquad\qquad (\text{inflation}) \tag{2.17}$$

$$w = t + h_0 + h_1 y. \qquad 0 < h_1 < 1 \quad (\text{real wages}) \tag{2.18}$$

$$r = m_0 + m_1 r'_0 - (1 - m_1) p_{+1}. \quad 0 < m_1 < 1 \quad (\text{real interest rates}) \tag{2.19}$$

The endogenous variables in the AMM are, y the growth rate of real GDP (where $y = [Y - Y_{-1}]/Y_{-1}$), k the (natural logarithm of) the average entrepreneurial markup, r the real rate of interest on loans of money, w the natural logarithm of the average real wage, and p the inflation rate (where $p = [P - P_{-1}]/P_{-1}$).

The exogenous variables are e_0, the net autonomous demand of the private sector as a percentage of GDP (which includes investment due to Keynes's "animal spirits"), g, government spending as a percentage of GDP, t, the average tax rate, r'_0, the target (determined by the central bank) for the inflation-adjusted real policy rate of interest, a, the logarithm of average aggregate labor productivity per employed worker, m_0 the markup in the banking or financial sector, p_0, an inverse measure of liquidity preference and, h_0, the intercept term in the wage function which represents the sociopolitical power of labor.

The symbols e_1, h_1, and m_1 are the given parameters of the model. The restrictions on the signs and magnitudes of these parameters are based on considerations of theoretical consistency and empirical plausibility.

In the discussion about the stability characteristics of the model we have already seen how two of these equations, namely (2.17) and (2.19), may be derived. There will be further discussion of the remaining components of the model in chapters 5, 6, and 7 to follow. For now the objective is to see how the five equations, equations (2.15) through (2.19), will work together in the context of a complete macroeconomic model.

THE BUSINESS CYCLE

By successive substitution in equations (2.15) through (2.19), it is possible to reduce the model to a single difference equation in economic growth, as follows:[12]

$$y = -e_1 h_1 m_1 y_{-1} + (e_0 + g) - (1 + e_1 m_1) t - e_1 m_1 (r'_0 - a - h_0) + e_1 (1 - m_1) p_0 - e_1 m_0$$

$$(2.20)$$

This is a first-order difference equation which is "convergent with oscillations," and is therefore a concise description of the business cycle in the world of the AMM.

There are three explicit *policy* variables in the above, changes in which will affect the ups and downs of the business cycle. These are, g, government spending as a percentage of GDP, t, the average tax rate, and r'_0, the target for the real policy rate of interest. Each of these is treated as an exogenous decision variable on the part of the fiscal and monetary authorities. It is true that in any actual economy there will be feedback on each of these from other elements in the system. For example, there may be a progressive tax system, automatic stabilizers, or a reactive monetary policy rule by the central bank. However, the rationale for treating the policy variables as exogenous is that they could all be made so if the authorities wished it. In short, in an empirical setting the current levels of each policy instrument are effectively what *has* been chosen by the society as a whole in the given circumstances.

As can be seen the initial effect of an increase in the government spending (as a percentage of GDP) is to set off a business cycle upswing, whereas an increase in the average tax rate has the opposite effect. Similarly, a reduction in the target for the real policy rate (an expansionary monetary policy) also has the effect of improving economic growth, whereas a higher target for the real policy rate (a contractionary monetary policy) will provoke a downturn.

In addition to these policy initiatives, there are a number of other Keynes-type influences on the cycle that need to be discussed. An increase in e_0, the net autonomous demand of the private sector (as a percentage of GDP) is another factor which sets off a boom. This may be the result of either an improvement in the "animal spirits" of the entrepreneurs or a spontaneous decline in the willingness of consumers to save rather than spend.[13] A decline in business confidence, or an increase in the overall propensity to save (this is Keynes's "paradox of thrift"), will both cause a downturn. In a similar vein we note that an increase in liquidity preference on either side of the money market (shown by a *fall* in the p_0 term), is also a change that sets off a business cycle downturn and vice versa. This is yet another issue on which Keynes's original insights seem to have been well founded. Overall the results of the model seem strongly to support a broadly Keynesian, rather than a classical or new classical, approach to macroeconomics (Fletcher 1987, 2000, 2007, Smithin, 2002, 2009c).

Another type of macroeconomic change that may occur is a spontaneous economy-wide technological innovation. This may be illustrated by an increase in the term a. Such a wave of innovation will cause a business cycle upturn, whereas a fall in productivity (a reduction in a) will lead to a downturn. Therefore, there does remain something of the logic the real business cycle (RBC) model in this framework, but along with the more demand-orientated factors (not to their exclusion). We might therefore say that the model is able to accommodate a Schumpeterian or Robertsonian approach to cycles (cf., again, Fletcher 2007, 67–70), as well as those of the traditional opponents of such writers.

A further possible cause of the business cycle would be a change in real costs. For example, a change in h_0, the intercept term in the wage equation, represents an increase in production costs that is brought about by wage bargaining but with no concomitant increase in productivity. This has the opposite effect to an improvement in technical efficiency, and will cause a downturn. A reduction in costs (whether achieved by astute wage bargaining by employers or otherwise) will cause an upswing.

Meanwhile the behavior of the inflation rate over the cycle is given by:

$$p = \left(t + p_0 - a + h_0 \right) + h_1 y_{-1}. \tag{2.21}$$

It can thus be seen how (depending of the source of the disturbance) that sometimes the ups and downs of the business cycle are accompanied by changes in the inflation rate in the same direction and sometimes not. Increases in e_0, g, t, and h_0, for example, will all tend to increase the inflation rate. However, in the first two cases this will be accompanied by an increase in economic growth, whereas for tax increases and real cost increases an increase in inflation is associated with lower economic growth.

THE STEADY-STATE

The steady-state of the system is represented by the following solutions for economic growth, inflation, the average profit markup, after-tax real wages and real interest rates:

$$y = \left[1/(1+e_1 h_1 m_1)\right](e_0 + g) - \left[(1+e_1 m_1)/(1+e_1 h_1 m_1)\right]t$$

$$- \left[e_1 m_1/(1+e_1 h_1 m_1)\right](r'_0 - a + h_0)$$

$$+ \left[e_1(1-m_1)/(1+e_1 h_1 m_1)\right]p_0 - \left[e_1/(1+e_1 h_1 m_1)\right]m_0 \tag{2.22}$$

$$p = \left[h_1/(1+e_1 h_1 m_1)\right](e_0 + g) + \left[(1-h_1)/(1+e_1 h_1 m_1)\right]t - \left[e_1 m_1/(1+e_1 h_1 m_1)\right]r'_0$$

$$- \left[1/(1+e_1 h_1 m_1)(a - h_0)\right] + \left[e_1 h_1/(1+e_1 h_1 m_1)\right](p_0 - m_0) \tag{2.23}$$

$$k = -\left[h_1 m_1/[1+e_1 h_1 m_1](e_0 + g)\right] - \left[m_1(1-h_1)/(1+e_1 h_1 m_1)\right]t$$

$$- \left[m_1/(1+e_1 h_1 m_1)\right](r'_0 + a - h_0) \tag{2.24}$$

$$+ \left[(1-m_1)/(1+e_1 h_1 m_1)\right]p_0 - \left[1/(1+e_1 h_1 m_1)\right]m_0$$

$$w - t = \left[h_1(1+e_1 h_1 m_1)\right](e_0 + g) - \left[h_1(1+e_1 m_1)/(1+e_1 h_1 m_1)\right]t$$

$$- \left[e_1 h_1 m_1/(1+e_1 h_1 m_1)\right](r'_0 - a) \tag{2.25}$$

$$+ \left[1/(1+e_1 h_1 m_1)\right]h_0 + \left[e_1 h_1(1-m_1)/(1+e_1 h_1 m_1)\right](p_0 - m_0)$$

$$r = -\left[h_1(1-m_1)/(1+e_1 h_1 m_1)\right](e_0 + g) - \left[h_1(1-h_1)/(1+e_1 h_1 m_1)\right]t$$

$$+ \left\{m_1\left[(1+e_1) + e_1 m_1(h_1 - 1)\right]/(1+e_1 h_1 m_1)\right\}r'_0 + \left[(1-m_1)e_1 m_1/(1+e_1 h_1 m_1)\right](a - h_0)$$

$$- \left[e_1 h_1/(1+e_1 h_1 m_1)\right]p_0 + \left\{\left[1+(m_1-1)e_1 h_1\right]/(1+e_1 h_1 m_1)\right\}m_0$$

$$\tag{2.26}$$

The striking thing about these results, as compared to orthodox models which assume the existence of so-called natural rates of growth, interest, and unemployment is that the forces which initially set off business cycles, in one direction or another, also impact the longer term growth path in the *same* direction. The finite horizon steady-state of the model is itself a moving equilibrium, and there is never any argument to be made that policy or other changes which "work" in the short-run will fail or be reversed in the long-run. Also, the model has the advantage of being able to explicitly identify the impact on the after-tax distribution of income. To some extent this answers the question of "*cui bono?*" (who benefits?) and hence may be able to explain at least some of the motivation for the strong political stances characteristically taken on issues of macroeconomic policy.

LONG-RUN MULTIPLIERS

Tables 2.1 to 2.3 work out the "long-run multipliers" for the AMM. First, Table 2.1 looks at the long-run impact of changes in the stances of fiscal and monetary policy.

Table 2.2 then deals with the impact of changes in market psychology and of business confidence. Also (in the third column) the impact of changes in the market power of banks and other financial institutions.

Finally, Table 2.3 reports the results for spontaneous changes in real costs and productivity.

The basic principles governing macroeconomic outcomes in the AMM may thus usefully be summarized by recording the signs of all the long-run multipliers together in Table 2.4. These are reported in the same order as in Tables 2.1 to 2.3.

For example, column 1 of Table 2.4 states that an increase in government expenditure as a percentage of GDP will increase the growth rate of real GDP. This comes at the cost of a somewhat higher inflation rate, but not of inflationary instability.[14] It will also increase the average after-tax real wage rate but actually reduce the average profit markup and the real rate of interest. These latter results about income distribution may thus give some clue as to which groups are likely to be in favor of, or might be opposed to, Keynesian economics broadly defined. The remaining results can be read off from the table in the same way.

THE POLITICAL ECONOMY OF FISCAL POLICY

The results recorded above, and those about fiscal policy in particular, bring us face to face with some of the most controversial questions of political economy. Notably, as both government spending *increases* and tax *cuts* have positive effects on growth it is clear that the analysis must in some way be relying on the Lernerian tradition of "functional finance" (Lerner 1943, Nell and Forstater 2003, Warner et al. 2000). This is the proposition that decisions in public finance should be judged by their actual results on the economy rather than meeting certain purely financial objectives (such as balancing the budget). But, if deficits are to be allowed, then this immediately raises a host of other questions. Where, ultimately, is the money to come from? Are there no limits at all to the various fiscal policy initiatives? How will the debt and deficit ratios themselves evolve? Is there an implication that the government must always run a deficit in order for the economy to be able to grow?

Table 2.1   Fiscal and Monetary Policy

	dg	dt	dr'_0
$dy\|$	$[1/(1+e_1 h_1 m_1)]$	$-[(1+e_1 m_1)/(1+e_1 h_1 m_1)]$	$-[e_1 m_1/(1+e_1 h_1 m_1)]$
$dp\|$	$[h_1/(1+e_1 h_1 m_1)]$	$[(1-h_1)/(1+e_1 h_1 m_1)]$	$-[e_1 m_1/(1+e_1 h_1 m_1)$
$dk\|$	$-[h_1 m_1(1-e_1 h_1 m_1)]$	$-[m_1(1-h_1)/(1+e_1 h_1 m_1)]$	$-[m_1/(1+e_1 h_1 m_1)]$
$d[w-t]\|$	$[h_1/(1+e_1 h_1 m_1)]$	$-[h_1(1+e_1 m_1)/(1+e_1 h_1 m_1)]$	$-[e_1 h_1 m_1/(1+e_1 h_1 m_1)]$
$dr\|$	$-[h_1(1-m_1)/(1+e_1 h_1 m_1)]$	$-[h_1(1-h_1)/(1+e_1 h_1 m_1)]$	$[(m_1(1-e_1)+ e_1 h_1(m_1-1)/(1+e_1 h_1 m_1)]$

Table 2.2 Business and Consumer Confidence and Market Sentiment

	$\overline{de_0}$	$\overline{dp_0}$	$\overline{dm_0}$
$dy\mid$	$[1/(1+e_l h_l m_l)]$	$[e_l(1-m_l)/(1+e_l h_l m_l)]$	$-[e_l/(1+e_l h_l m_l)]$
$dp\mid$	$[h_l/(1+e_l h_l m_l)]$	$[e_l h_l/(1+e_l h_l)]$	$-[e_l h_l/(1+e_l h_l m_l)]$
$dk\mid$	$-[h_l m_l/(1-e_l h_l m_l)]$	$[(1-m_l)/(1+e_l h_l m_l)]$	$-[1/(1+e_l h_l m_l)]$
$dr\mid$	$-[h_l(1-m_l)/(1+e_l h_l m_l)]$	$-[e_l h_l/(1+e_l h_l m_l)]$	$[m_l/(1+e_l h_l m_l)$
$d[w-t]\mid$	$[h_l/(1+e_l h_l m_l)]$	$[e_l h_l(1-m_l)/(1+e_l h_l m_l)]$	$-[e_l h_l(1-m_l)/(1+e_l h_l m_l)]$

The last question is easily answered in the negative simply by referring to Tables 2.1 through 2.3. The answers to the others have been much clarified in recent years by the research, in particular, of economists belonging to the so-called modern money theory (MMT) school. According to Tymoinge and Wray (2015a, 24–25) two prominent members of this school:

> A . . . main contribution . . . [of MMT] . . . has been to explain why monetarily sovereign governments have a flexible policy space unconstrained by hard financial limits. . . . We use the term "sovereign government" to indicate a government that issues its own currency. . . a monetarily sovereign government can *choose* among alternative exchange rate regimes—fixed, managed, and floating—which impact domestic policy space. (Emphasis added)

As has already been discussed above this last statement is actually not quite correct. That is, if by a fixed exchange rate we mean a hard peg. As we have seen, this is not actually a viable policy choice, and is not consistent with sovereignty. The most important part of this passage, however, is the broader claim that sovereign governments do not face binding financial constraints. To examine this idea in more detail, let D stand for the government budget deficit, $\$G$ stand for nominal government expenditure, $\$T$ for nominal tax collection, and R for the total of nominal interest payments on the national debt. Then, by definition:

$$D = \$G + R - \$T. \tag{2.27}$$

The usual argument that is made about this expression is that the deficit can be financed in one of two ways. Either the ministry of finance (MOF), or Treasury, can sell bonds B, to the general public, or, the central bank (CB) could actually buy bonds directly from the MOF (another branch of the same government) in exchange for its own liabilities, H. The former is called "bond financing" and the latter "money financing"

Table 2.3 Real Costs and Productivity

	$\overline{da}$	$\overline{dh_0}$
$dy\mid$	$[e_l m_l/(1+e_l h_l m_l)]$	$-[e_l m_l/(1+e_l h_l m_l)]$
$dp\mid$	$-[1/(1+e_l m_l h_l)]$	$[1/(1+e_l m_l h_l)]$
$dk\mid$	$[m_l/(1+e_l h_l m_l)]$	$-[m_l/(1+e_l h_l m_l)]$
$d[w-t]\mid$	$[e_l h_l m_l/(1+e_l h_l m_l)]$	$[1/(1+e_l h_l m_l)]$
$dr\mid$	$[(1-m_l)/(1+e_l h_l m_l)]$	$-[(1-m_l)/(1+e_l h_l m_l)]$

Table 2.4   Signs of the Long-Run Multipliers

$\frac{dy}{}$	$+$	$-$	$-$	$+$	$+$	$-$	$+$	$-$
$\frac{dp}{}$	$+$	$+$	$-$	$+$	$+$	$-$	$-$	$+$
$\frac{dk}{}$	$-$	$-$	$-$	$-$	$+$	$-$	$+$	$-$
$\frac{dr}{}$	$-$	$-$	$+$	$-$	$-$	$+$	$+$	$-$
$\frac{d[w-t]}{}$	$+$	$-$	$-$	$+$	$+$	$-$	$+$	$+$
	$\overline{dg}$	$\overline{dt}$	$\overline{r'_0}$	$\overline{de_0}$	$\overline{dp_0}$	$\overline{dm_0}$	$\overline{da}$	$\overline{dh_0}$

but these terms are highly misleading. Both involve bond sales and by definition all finance involves raising money. The symbol, H, by the way, dates back to the heyday of monetarism when the monetary base was called "high-powered money." This is by no means a good descriptive term, but it remains convenient to have a different symbol for CB liabilities than that used for the overall broad money supply, M. The supposed choices about how to finance the deficit can thus be characterized as

$$D = \Delta\$B_P + \Delta H, \qquad (2.28)$$

where $\Delta\$B_p$ represents the dollar value of bond sales to the public.

The argument of the MMT school and others, however, is not simply that a sovereign government could possibly set $\Delta\$B_p = 0$, and thus let the deficit be 100 percent financed by the issue of base money. The opposite choice could equally well be made. The point about the absence of binding financial constraints goes much deeper. The flaw in the standard argument is rather the restriction of the concept of money financing to the idea of financing via the monetary base. The implication of this is that, in order to make any more general statement about the overall supply of money, the analyst will be forced back to another dubious monetarist notion from the 1960s, namely that of the "money multiplier" (Friedman 1960, Goodhart 1989). This idea is completely invalid in the endogenous money environment (Kam and Smithin 2012, Lavoie 2010).[15] Recently, for example in Smithin (2016a, 68), I have sometimes suggested that a more meaningful expression might therefore be $\$G + R - \$T = \Delta M$, where M stands for the overall money supply rather than the base. However, I now think (see, for example, Smithin 2016c) that a much better notation would be:

$$\$G + R - \$T = \Delta M_F \qquad (2.29)$$

The new term ΔM_F can then be taken to mean that part of the change in the overall money supply which is specifically the result of fiscal policy. The total change in the money supply would then be $\Delta M = \Delta M_F + \Delta M_O$ where ΔM_O (positive or negative) is that part of the total change from all other causes. This notation makes clear the basic point that "finance" is always available to the sovereign government *via* an endogenous increase in the broad money supply, not just the monetary base, without necessarily putting upward pressure on interest rates.

It is clear where the money comes from, but what of evolution of the debt and deficit ratios themselves? To start thinking about this question, first note that in real terms the government budget deficit can alternatively be represented as:

$$\Delta B = G - T + rB, \tag{2.30}$$

where ΔB is the real change in debt (the real deficit itself), G is the level of real government spending, T is total real tax collection, and the expression rB represents real interest payments on the national debt. Dividing through by the level of real GDP, this expression becomes:

$$\Delta(B/Y) = g - t + r(B/Y) \tag{2.31}$$

Therefore, it is clear that an increase in $g - t$ (the primary deficit as a percentage of GDP) will indeed increase the debt/GDP ratio. However, this says nothing about whether any given figure for this ratio is a good or bad thing, or how it evolves. Another well-known algebraic formula for evolution of the debt/GDP ratio, however, is:

$$\Delta(B/Y) = (B/Y)[\Delta B/B - \Delta Y/Y] \tag{2.32}$$

where $\Delta Y/Y$ (= y) *is* the rate of economic growth. Combining (31) and (32) then gives:

$$\Delta(B/Y) = g - t + (r - y)(B/Y) \tag{2.33}$$

In the end, the dynamic behavior of the debt/GDP ratio thus depends on the expression $(r - y)$, the real interest rate less the GDP growth rate. Only if the real interest rate is higher than the growth rate will the debt/GDP ratio go on increasing. This is, of course, the unstable case constantly emphasized in the financial press. But how likely is it actually to occur? If, on the other hand, the real interest rate is less than the growth rate, the B/Y ratio settles down to some constant value and does not continuously increase. The frequently voiced concerns that the debt/GDP ratio might get "out of control," therefore, may well be disingenuous. For one thing both the interest rate and the growth rate itself are themselves affected by government policy. For example the real rate of interest may be increasing merely because the state CB itself is pursuing a "tight money" policy. This will always tend to increase the debt burden, both because of the higher interest rate itself, and also because same policy reduces the growth rate. Note, however, that this situation would be self-imposed to a large extent. It would always be possible to change the policy. One would like to think that MOF and CB officials would have the wit not to let this sort of situation occur but, needless to say, there are no guarantees about this in the actual world of affairs.

If it is accepted that running a budget deficit is possible, and may even be desirable, what then are the limits on the individual g and t ratios?

For spending, it should be stressed that the relevant order of magnitude is the current ratio of government expenditure on goods and service to GDP in the national accounts not the relative size of the total government sector. Therefore, in a mixed economy, there is never any real danger that government spending will "swallow up" the whole output of goods and services in the economy. Although there is no such thing as a natural rate of unemployment in the world of the AMM, and also no meaningful distinction to be made between so-called voluntary versus involuntary unemployment,[16] there must nonetheless be some sort of commonsense notion of full employment that is reached when the *measured* unemployment rate falls to some low level. To find out what this is we can postulate a relationship between growth and unemployment along the lines of "Okun's Law," a construct which at one time used to be a staple of the intermediate level textbooks.

Okun's law was based on empirical findings by Okun (1962) about how much growth in the economy was typically needed to reduce unemployment. For example, to get measured unemployment down by (say) 1.0 percent points the growth rate might have to increase by as much as 2.5 or 3.0 percent points. If u stands for the unemployment rate, u_1 for the Okun coefficient, and y for the rate of growth, this sort of relationship might well be illustrated in linear form by something along the lines of:

$$u = u_0 - u_1 y + u_2 u_{-1}, \quad 0 < u_1 < 1, \qquad 0 < u_2 < 1 \tag{2.34}$$

In this specific case, the equilibrium relationship between the unemployment rate and the rate of growth will therefore turn out to be:

$$u = u_0 / (1 - u_2) - u_1 / (1 - u_2) y, \tag{2.35}$$

This means that the maximum growth rate, in the sense of the growth rate that if maintained will eventually reduce the measured unemployment rate to zero, is given by:

$$y_{max} = u_0 / u_1 \tag{2.36}$$

Therefore, even if it were true that an increase in growth can only brought about by increased government spending (which it is not) the pragmatically defined level of full employment is reached long before government spending as a percentage of GDP reaches anything like 100 percent.

As for the issue of tax cuts, one obvious question that arises is that if cutting taxes is always a "good thing," and it is always possible to run a deficit, why not simply reduce taxes to zero? To see why not, we can again take a cue from the arguments of the modern neo-chartalist or MMT school (e.g., Bell 2001, Goodhart 1998, Mosler 1997–98, Wray 1998, 2012, Tymoigne and Wray 2015). The mantra of this group has been that "taxes drive money," meaning by this the assertion that it is the ability of the state to exercise sovereignty via tax collection that is actually the foundation for the very social institution of money itself. On this view the taxes do not really "pay for" the government spending, nor does budget have to balance. Nonetheless, the existence of tax obligations, and their efficient collection and enforcement, is crucial for asserting the claims and legitimacy of state-issued base money and hence, at a basic level, for the maintenance of the necessary financial and legal superstructure itself. It is true that in principle any tax cut from existing levels does tend to boost the economy. Nonetheless, both the power to tax and actual tax collection need to be retained as a fundamental part of the institutional structure of commercial society. That being said the taxes do not need to be very high, and certainly not punitive.

THE FALLACY OF A POSITIVE BALANCED
BUDGET MULTIPLIER

This is a subject that the supposed American Keynesian (Colander and Landreth 1996) and textbook author, Paul Samuelson, once called "a subject for advanced treatises" (Samuleson 1948, 245) even though it was a fundamental part of his political economy. It was a justification for what later came to be called a "tax-and-spend" policy. Samuelson (1948, 245, fn.) gave it the name of the "balanced budget multiplier."

According to Samuelson, an increase in government spending covered by an equal increase in taxes will still cause an increase in the overall level of aggregate demand. In short, the balanced budget multiplier is positive. Tax-and-spend policies were therefore thought to be wholly viable. Samuelson himself even went so far as to argue that to avoid inflation "taxes would probably have to be increased by *more than enough to balance the budget*" (Samuelson 1948, 245, original emphasis). From the perspective of subsequent political developments this was arguably the worst possible starting point for the advocacy of Keynesian policies. In effect, from the start Keynesian economics was also identified with (broadly speaking) leftist policies favorable to income redistribution. However, Keynes himself had specifically argued in the *General Theory* for a fiscal policy only of "loan expenditure" defined as "a convenient expression for the net borrowing of the public authorities on all accounts whether on capital account or to meet a budgetary deficit" (Keynes 1936, 128–29, fn.1). There was no mention of offsetting the stimulus with increased taxation.[17] Admittedly, at one stage Keynes (1936, 372–74) did suggest that his "paradox of saving" might reduce the force of one the main *political* justifications that had routinely been put forward in pre-Keynesian times in defense of an unequal distribution of income. This was the argument that the rich are likely to save proportional more than the poor and, therefore, if saving is a good thing an unequal distribution of income would be good for society. The paradox of saving would clearly undercut this argument. However, the original proposition itself was by no means unassailable and, whether true or false, has no bearing either on the specific policy proposals that Keynes put forward in chapter 10 of the *General Theory*, or on the actual macroeconomic effects of a tax-and-spend policy in the real world.

And, in fact, Samuelson's supposedly "Keynesian" policy would actually have led to lower growth with higher inflation, to stagflation. This can easily be seen in the context of the AMM as the balanced budget multiplier is unambiguously negative:

$$dy/dg\,|_{dg=dt} = -\left[e_1 m_1 / \left(1 + e_1 h_1 m_1\right)\right], \quad < 0 \tag{2.37}$$

The implication is that the depressing effect of the higher taxes on demand growth outweighs any positive impact of the government spending financed by those taxes. The inflationary effect of both changes meanwhile is in the same direction.

$$dp/dg\,|_{dg=dt} = \left[1 / \left(1 + e_1 h_1 m_1\right)\right], \quad > 0 \tag{2.38}$$

A balanced budget increase in government spending as a percentage of GDP (i.e., new spending wholly financed by increased taxation), also increases inflation.

GRAPHICAL ANALYSIS OF THE AMM

These points about the effects of fiscal policy and of macroeconomic policy in general may perhaps be more easily summarized using a simple graphical approach. The complete AMM is therefore depicted graphically in Figure 2.1. The effective demand (ED) schedule[18] has a negative intercept and a positive slope. All the short-run supply (SRS) schedules are flat, and the equilibrium SRS schedule is a horizontal line through the equilibrium point. The long-run supply (LRS) schedule is positively sloped but less steep than the ED. The intersection of the three schedules represents macroeconomic equilibrium and determines the steady-state growth and inflation rates.

Figure 2.2 then reprises the effect of an increase in government spending (as a percentage of GDP) not offset by any tax increases. In Figure 2.2, the ED schedule shifts down and to the right, but in the short-run the inflation rate does not change, as it takes time for the wage-push mechanism to begin to operate. There is an economic boom, but no immediate inflation. After a while, however, the very boom itself leads to an increase in cost pressures. The SRS begins to shift up, and the inflation rate rises. The boom nevertheless continues and the economy finally settles to a long-run equilibrium at point "D" in the diagram with admittedly a higher inflation rate, but also a permanently higher growth rate. The short-run behavior of the model is therefore reasonably consistent with that which has always been suggested in the standard textbooks. There is a big difference in the final analysis, however, in that a boom caused by fiscal stimulus (while it does cause higher inflation) is never entirely dissipated or eliminated. Thus the AMM restores basically Keynesian insights about the effects of government spending for the long-run as well as in the short-run.

Figure 2.3 then looks at the effects of the other type of fiscal policy, in this case a tax cut without any corresponding reduction in government spending. A reduction in the average tax rate shifts both SRS and LRS schedules downward and simultaneously the ED schedule also shifts down and to the right. The tax cut will certainly increase growth in the first instance without any immediate impact on inflation. After a while, however, inflationary pressure is reduced as the SRS shifts down. In the final equilibrium the

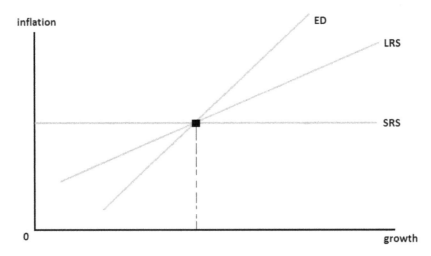

Figure 2.1 The AMM in Inflation/Growth Space. *Source*: Author.

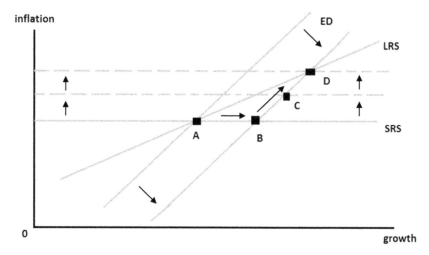

Figure 2.2 The Effects of an Increase in Government Spending. *Source*: Author.

inflation rate falls and, although the growth rate does slacken somewhat from the peak of the boom, it still ends up higher than it was at the beginning of the process.

Figure 2.4 then puts both the spending and tax sides of fiscal policy together, to look at the case of the balanced budget multiplier. In this experiment an increase in government spending is more than fully offset by tax increases. Contrary to the predictions of the pseudo-Keynesian textbooks of the 1950s and 1960s, effective demand falls and there is initially a sharp recession. Then there is something of a recovery, but the final growth path still ends up lower than it was at the beginning, with inflation actually higher. "Tax-and-spend" policies do not work. They lead only to stagflation. Note also that the existence of the recovery phase may well be quite misleading in terms of the debate about political economy. Politicians will no doubt claim that their policies are "working at last" after the initial recession.[19] However, the economy always ends up in worse shape than it was to start with.

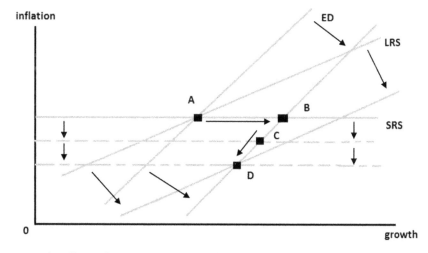

Figure 2.3 The Effects of a Tax Cut. *Source*: Author.

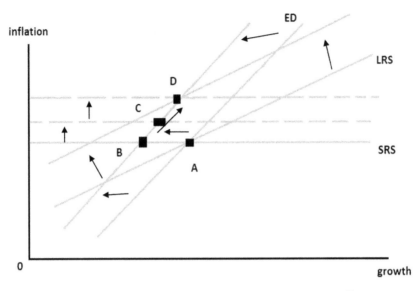

Figure 2.4   The Effects of a "Balanced Budget" Increase in Government Spending. *Source*: Author.

CONCLUSION

In this chapter we have already touched on all of the most important results that are the consequences of the adoption of a new, and very different, approach to money, credit, and macroeconomics. Each of the next eight chapters, 3–10, will go into more detail about the various individual components of the model. The final chapter, chapter 11, looks forward toward the development of a "philosophy of money and finance."

NOTES

1. This is not to say that questions of the overall "financial architecture," and of the macro-level regulatory, legal and supervisory arrangements, are unimportant for overall economic performance. In the context of North America, for example, one has only to think of the contrast between the financial arrangements of Canada and the United States in terms of "safety and security." There have only been two actual bank failures in the past hundred years in Canada (including the period of the Great Depression and that of the twenty-first-century global financial crisis, or GFC) compared to uncountably many in the United States. The statement in the text refers specifically to the question of macro stability. Similar remarks apply to fiscal policy, and a detailed discussion of the impact that the various fiscal policy changes can have on the economy (for better or worse) is to be found later in this chapter.

2. The "Keynes's Plan" of 1943 for an international clearing union (ICU) was never put into practice, and was superseded by the Bretton Woods agreement the following year. From the point of view adopted in this book, a common fault of both schemes was that far too much emphasis was placed on the issue of the stability of *nominal* exchange rates. In such an environment, success would only be possible if the nominal exchange rate is "fixed-but-adjustable" as described below.

3. For example, the failure of the restored gold standard in the early 1930s, the ERM crisis of 1992, the collapse of the currency board in Argentina in 2001, and so on.

4. Toporowski makes the point that Minsky's original PhD thesis was itself influenced by Hayek's writings, as Minsky acknowledged.

5. Private sector incentives, however, clearly must play a key role in the response to any policy initiatives.

6. As, for example, in the case of the Social Credit movement in the 1920s and 1930s (Dow 2016), which still has adherents today (Heydoorn 2014, 2016). The leading figure of Social Credit was Major C.H. Douglas who was actually one of Keynes's brave heretics, although he received a demotion in military rank from Keynes. According to Keynes (1936, 371) Douglas deserved to be "a private, perhaps, but not a major in the brave army of heretics."

7. It would not be correct to say that (4) *determines* the price level as this expression will also usually be embedded in some kind of simultaneous-equations macro model.

8. Monetarist policies, of course, also cause instability but in a different way.

9. I use this notation because in contemporary Canada the policy rate of interest is called the "overnight rate." It is comparable to the federal funds rate in the United States.

10. Here $\mathbf{r_0}$ is the real policy rate, the nominal policy rate minus expected inflation.

11. See equations (2.18) and (2.20).

12. In the next few equations endogenous and exogenous variables will be distinguished from parameters by being printed in bold type.

13. See chapter 6 below for the details of how this mechanism would actually work.

14. That is, the inflation rate will not be "ever-accelerating" as was frequently claimed in the tendentious, but nonetheless highly influential, anti-Keynesian analysis of the "expectations-augmented Phillips curve" in the 1970s and 1980s. This is because the central bank is pursuing the stabilizing real interest rate rule that was described above.

15. There is an algebraic relationship between M and H of the form $M = [(1+cd)/(cd +rr)]H$ where cd is the cash-deposit ratio and rr is the reserve ratio. This leads to the argument that if H changes by some given dollar amount M must also change, in the ratio $(1+cd)/(cd + rr)$. However, the argument fails badly in practice as each of $H, M, cd,$ and rr are endogenous variables.

16. In the *General Theory,* Keynes (1936, 6–13), presumably because of his background in Marshallian microeconomics, and I think mistakenly, laid great stress on this distinction. This was surely a tactical error at the time, given that the ultimate objective was to deal with real-world economic problems. The same sorts of confusions persist in the economic literature to this day. In the late twentieth century, for example, there was a frankly absurd controversy among mainstream economists as to whether or not unemployment was in fact a "choice" (De Vroey 2016, 220–22). This sort of thing does nothing at all to enhance the reputations of academic economists with the general public.

17. At other points in his career, but in different contexts, Keynes was certainly prepared to advocate higher taxes in specific circumstances. For example, in the World War II pamphlet *How to Pay for the War?* Keynes (1940) advocated higher taxes to restrain inflation. The results here, however, seem to show that Keynes was wrong about this.

18. It should be pointed out that the concept of effective demand used here is somewhat different than that employed by Keynes in the *General Theory.* In Keynes, according to Victoria Chick (1983, 65), "*effective* demand, in contrast to aggregate demand, is not a schedule . . . it is the *point* on the schedule . . . which is 'made effective' by firm's production decisions" (original emphasis). This is correct as far as Keynes's treatment is concerned. However, in the AMM what makes effective demand "effective" is that there has been just enough credit and money creation to sustain that rate of demand growth at every point along the ED schedule. This may not correspond to the firms' willingness to supply that amount of output at any given point. This is why there will be disequilibrium adjustments and explains how the model will eventually converge to a unique equilibrium.

19. The reader will no doubt be able to think of numerous real-world examples of this type of argument.

Chapter 3

The Role of Money and Banking in Capitalism

INTRODUCTION

From a common-sense point of view economic activity in a capitalist-type system is all about money (Smithin 2000, 1, 2010, 49, 2013a, 1). We continually speak and write about "making money," "losing money," "spending money," "saving money," and so forth.

The ongoing changes in computer and information technology over the last few decades have made no difference, at all, to the truth of this statement. The advent of personal computers, smart cards, the internet, and so on has certainly not led to the disappearance of money, in spite of the periodic "op-ed" articles in the popular and financial press stating either that this has happened, is about to happen, or will happen within the next generation. This type of argument eventually loses its force when essentially the same predictions are repeated decade after decade and never come true.[1]

Indeed, it is fairly obvious (except perhaps to writers of op-ed articles) that what has been going on is merely a change of form rather than substance. It is certainly possible to imagine a "cash-less society" in the sense of a payments technology which makes no use of bits of paper and small metal disks. However, such a cash-less society would hardly be "money-less," far from it. Indeed, how could it be? The purpose of "e-business" or "e-commerce" is also to make money exactly as before. In fact, under capitalism new technology would not be introduced at all if it could not be made "to pay" in the traditional sense.

A realist approach to social science must therefore insist that money retains the same importance in social life today that it has always had, if not more so. It is actually quite striking how twenty-first century financial problems, of which there have been many, continue to be discussed in very much the same sort of terms as they always have been throughout the twentieth, nineteenth, and eighteenth centuries, regardless of the state of technology.

Nevertheless, it remains a curious fact that many of the social science and business disciplines studying economic activity have paid far less attention to this "most important institution in capitalist society" (money) than it seems to deserve (Ingham

2004a, 195). This neglect goes back to a time well before there were any computers. It is almost as if the various recent predictions about the disappearance of money due to technology are supposed to finally validate the traditional approach—an approach which has *always* ignored money. It is true that there are many existing theories in social science about "what money does." For example, there are economic theories about money and inflation, political theories about money and power, sociological theories about money's cultural significance, and so on. What is missing, however, is any detailed discussion of what a philosopher would call the ontology of money (Mendoza 2012, Searle 2005, 1, 2010, 5, Zelmanovitz 2016). This would mean thinking about what money actually is, how it comes into being, and what is its nature. In business disciplines like accounting and finance, for example, it is just taken for granted that sums of money are the proper subject for discussion, but without any further inquiry. No business professor would ever think to ask what the sums of money, meticulously accounted for on the bottom line, actually consist of. In economics, as we have already seen in chapter 1, the most influential approach in today's academic mainstream has usually taught that money itself is not fundamentally important, and that what is really going on when economic activity occurs is a barter exchange of goods and services. The controlling idea of neoclassical economics has been that beneath the "veil of money" economics should deal with the real exchange of goods and services, and the determination of so-called relative prices rather than money prices. The problem with this sort of attitude is that most real world economic issues *do* seem to involve money, booms and depressions, financial crises, inflation and deflation, unexpected fluctuations in interest rates and exchange rates, deficits in the balance of payments, and so on. A monetary economy is a different thing altogether than a barter economy. However this only seems to receive any attention, if at all, when a major crisis comes along.

TWO COMPETING THEORIES OF MONEY: COMMODITY THEORY VERSUS CREDIT THEORY

In Schumpeter's view (as quoted by Ingham 2004a, 6), there are:

> only two theories of money which deserve the name . . . the commodity theory and the claim [or credit][2] theory. By their very nature they are incompatible.

The competing theories can be traced all the way back to the Greek philosophers Plato and Aristotle. In the modern era (as has been the case in very many other fields of intellectual inquiry) these ideas were revived to provide essentially two competing explanations of capitalism. On the one hand, Aristotle was a well-known "metallist" (Schumpeter 1954, 63–64) and, while Plato left only a few clues about his views on money, Schumpeter (1954, 54) was able to extrapolate:

> it must be observed that his [Plato's] canons of monetary policy—his hostility to the use of gold and silver . . . or his idea of a domestic currency that would be useless abroad . . . do agree with the logical consequence of a theory according to which the value of money is . . . independent of the stuff it is made of.

The contrary idea of a commodity theory of money is self-explanatory. It is the belief that the value of money derives from its intrinsic worth as a commodity (as, for example, with the precious metals like gold and silver). Such things were believed to be money because market forces had eventually made one or other of them the most acceptable item in trade or exchange in a given society. The commodity theory has thus also been called the "catallactic" theory, an expression which literally comes from the Greek for "to exchange" (Mises 1934, 462, Schumpeter 1954, 63). It holds that money is primarily a medium-of-exchange evolved spontaneously from barter for the purpose of minimizing transaction costs (Menger 1892). And because the precious metals were supposed to have been used historically as exchange media the catallactic/commodity theory is alternatively called "metallist" theory, as already noted above in the discussion of Aristotle's views. The value of metallic money in these circumstances is believed to be based on the intrinsic content of the metal itself. Metallic money is therefore a prime example of something that is both money and a commodity at the same time.

It was really a major weakness of traditional economic thinking that the only attempt made to understand the trading process—beyond a simple act of barter—was this assumption (it is no more than that) that market forces will naturally select one, or a limited number, of actual physical objects to serve as the money of exchange. To the contrary there have been very many well-documented historical periods when money was obviously not a substantial physical object, for example, when it was a piece of paper (such as bank note) or simply a book entry (Smithin 2013a, 2–3). Nonetheless, it continued to be held that these representations were merely symbolic of some more intrinsically valuable commodity underlying the whole transaction.

The idea that the value of money could be guaranteed in this way, for example by adherence to a commodity standard such as a gold standard or other metallic standard, was always extremely dubious. Nonetheless, it became something of a dogma when the international gold standard was in force in the period 1873–1914. At this stage, so superficially persuasive were these ideas that the gold standard came to seem almost like the "natural order of things" instead of simply a tacit agreement by the various states to keep to the so-called rules of the game. And, moreover, in spite of the fact (as we have already seen in chapter 2) that it was actually an *unstable* system.[3] Given this background, the achievements of some of the early credit theorists are the more impressive for having been written during this time period (cf. Innes 1913, 15, 1914, 51–54).

Some vestiges of the old way of thinking remain even to this day, but in the modern world, when the physical form of money may well be nothing more than electronic impulses in a computer network, the idea that money necessarily consists of some specific commodity is (or at least should be) impossible to sustain. The flickering numbers on the computer screen do not represent any particular commodity. They are only a generalized unspecific claim to a partial share of the total of goods and services available. They are "credits," in fact, and the claims only have force because they are socially recognized as such. This partial unspecific claim is what usually called the "purchasing power" of a particular sum of money. However, the actual amount of purchasing power possessed by any one individual or institution, although it is something that all economic actors must have in order to be able to participate in the economy at all, is itself subject to continual fluctuation as money prices change.

What, then, is money? In a credit or claim theory of money (Ingham 2004a, Schumpeter 1954) money is not thought of primarily as a physical object, or as representative of some pre-existing value, but as entries in a ledger, a system of accounts, or a balance sheet. The purpose of these entries is to record the various social relations of indebtedness. Debts are incurred and paid off by various balance sheet and accounting operations (Parguez and Seccareccia 2000). It then becomes a key issue for the analyst to decide exactly what it is in any given system that "counts as" making payments, that is, discharging debt, in the given circumstances.

The idea of credit money (or equivalently debt money) is sometimes expressed by statements to the effect that "all money is credit" or "all money is debt" or similar. For example, Geoffrey Ingham in his influential book, the *Nature of Money*, refers throughout to the system of "capitalist credit money." Ingham (2004a, 198) also explicitly states that:

> All money is debt in so far as issuers promise to accept their own money for *any* debt payment by *any* bearer of the money. (Original emphasis)

This corresponds also to the definition of money given by Hicks in his last book, the posthumously published *Market Theory of Money*. According to Hicks (1989, 42):

> Money is paid for a discharge of debt when that debt has been expressed in terms of money.

Taken together, these two definitions already seem to cover the historical special case of precious metal coins (and for that matter token coins also) as well as debt money. To make pieces of metal "money," for example, the issuer or guarantor of the coins would always have agree to accept them back in payment of obligations to itself. It was this acceptability feature that was the key to the coins being money not the physical properties of the bits of metal themselves (Ingham 2004a, 198). On this account, it would still need to be elaborated exactly why it is that the issuers of money are in a position in which other actors have incurred binding obligations to them. If this can be done, however, then the formal validity of money is explained.

Credit theories are also sometimes called "chartalist" or "cartalist" theories, from an adjective derived by Knapp from the Latin *charta* (Goodhart 1998, Wray 1998). Chartalism emphasizes the means-of-payment and unit-of-account functions of money rather than the medium-of-exchange. Money is "a debt-relation or a promise to pay that exists between human beings" (Bell 2001, 497). Alternatively and as already stated, "money is a social relation" (Ingham 1996, 225). General acceptability by the public is the necessary condition of money. In particular, in the "state theory of money," money is that which is accepted in payment of taxes or other obligations to the state (Innes 1914, 161, Knapp 1924, 95, Lerner 1947, 313, Wray 1998, 4).[4] This is one prominent method whereby the money issuer can enforce the formal validity of money. In the most general statement the value of money is simply based on social arrangements and social relations of indebtedness of one kind or another.

In the so-called property theory of money (De Soto 2000, Heinsohn and Steiger 2000), we find that some elements of the theory are consistent with the notion of money as credit. However other aspects of it continually harken back to the old notion that money must somehow be backed by what are (thought to be) real assets. This weakens the theory irreparably. As with all such approaches it is actually impossible to answer the basic question of what is "real" in the given context without a very substantial investigation into social ontology. The fundamental idea of the property theory is to distinguish mere possessional rights from property rights as such. The former are "restricted to the physical use of resources" (Heinsohn and Steiger 2000, 68) whereas the latter "encompass the *non-physical* uses of encumbering the property for backing money and collateralizing credit" (Heinsohn and Steiger 2000, 70, original emphasis). The intuitive idea is that property rights enable the use of resources as collateral. The collateral supposedly enables entrepreneurs to borrow money and hence expand their "capital." De Soto (2000, 39–68) therefore argues that a formal or legal property system is the key to the development of capitalism. Money is defined in terms of debt but, allegedly, collaterals are that which make debt possible. Money is "an anonymized claim to property" (Heinsohn and Steiger 2000, 85) and, on this view, the institution of money is built upon the institution of property in what is a somewhat strained analogy to the logical relation between language and law. As a general principle the notion that property rights are important in capitalism is unobjectionable. However, there is an awkward "chicken and egg" question to be answered in this case. Government, law, and money are *all* social institutions which may indeed be fundamentally based on language, as in "speech acts" (Searle 1995, 1998, 2010). But logically to derive from this a more complex social institution such as property, via a process of iteration, each of the more basic building blocks must already be in place. In conveying real estate, for example, it is not possible to say that a house is "worth" two million or three million dollars unless we already have some idea or concept of what a dollar actually is.[5]

The property theory does recognize both that the money of account is a primary function of money and that money is a credit relation. However, there are two faulty arguments in the theory. First, without the prior establishment of a money of account one cannot express any kind of credit relation. As just mentioned, the very concept of property, at least the one interesting to economists, must always have some definite monetary value. This monetary quantification of property is the reason *why* it can be used as collateral. As in the example of the house, the underlying concept of "property" itself, unlike the more primitive concept of "possessiveness," already presupposes a money of account. Second, not all loan contracts are based on collateral (Schumpeter 1954). Heinsohn and Steiger (2000, 83) recognize this, but argue that even without specific collateral creditors provide loans on the basis of the imputed and unspecific collateral owned by debtors. At the operational level of the practice of bank lending this is incorrect. A loan is based *either* on the expected cash flows yielded by business activity *or* on pledged collateral. Property theorists erroneously reduce the former to the latter. According to Minsky (1986, 233):

in structuring a loan . . . based on prospective cash flows, the loan officers may insist on a margin of safety in the form of pledged collateral. But this would not be the primary consideration: cash-flow-oriented loans are made on the basis of the prospective value added of . . . business endeavours.

Once again, "credit-worthiness" itself is essentially a social relation. Loan decisions are made by evaluating the future ability and willingness of the debtor to fulfill the commitment. This evaluation is a subjective judgment based on information obtained, and the trustworthiness of the applicant (a social relation), under the guidance of the general criteria of the bank. In such a loan, asset collateral is only an additional safety margin, and is not the fundamental reason for a cash-oriented loan. In summary, and as Max Weber (1927, 236) put the point, "from the evolutionary standpoint money is the father of private property" (not the other way round).

Credit and Debt

If we accept a credit or debt theory of money then, given current institutional arrangements, we are effectively arguing that the characteristic form of money in contemporary capitalism is bank money. This much is clear. However, once we have started talking about social accounting and thereby using terms like "credit money," "debt money," and so forth there are some obvious pitfalls that needs to be pointed out right away and dealt with.

First, it is obvious that the mere possibility of acquiring goods on credit does not in itself constitute a credit theory of money. Credit, in this sense, is also available even in the strictest commodity money system. The important factor is how this credit is eventually to be paid back. If all debt must eventually be paid with commodity money then the debtor is really no further ahead. In a credit *money* system, however, the debt is paid off with something that is itself credit. This was clearly stated in the quote from Hicks above, and see also the discussion by Innes (1913, 15–16) about the "errors" of Adam Smith.

Secondly, it is also necessary to deal with the implications of the simple fact that, in any banking or financial system, credit and debt are just the mirror images of each other. For every debt there is a credit and vice versa. If, for example, a commercial bank extends a loan to an individual or to a firm then that would (correctly) be described as the granting of credit. The loan is an earning asset to the bank. On the other hand if somebody makes a deposit *in* a bank then from the bank's point of view that is a debt or liability. This means that in discussing the various balance sheet operations we need to be clear about which side of the balance sheet it is that contains the entries that are the actual *money*.

Table 3.1 therefore presents a stylized version of the balance sheet of a commercial bank with some arbitrarily chosen numbers. On the asset side appear bank loans and an entry for "other" assets. The bank can extend credit by making loans, or by acquiring other types of asset in the financial markets, such as bonds or equities. The list on the liabilities side contains redeemable deposits, non-redeemable deposits, and (again) "other" liabilities. This last item includes the invested capital of the bank owners. The language of "redeemable" versus "non-redeemable" deposits is the sort of terminology

Table 3.1   A Hypothetical Commercial Bank Balance Sheet

Assets		Liabilities	
Loans	120,000	Redeemable Deposits	100,000 ◄——— **Money**
Other	50,000	Non-Redeemable Deposits:	40,000
		Other	30,000
	------------		------------
	170,000		170,000

that bankers themselves tend to use. Unfortunately, however, these expressions are far from ideal in the credit money context as they still contain echoes of the old-fashioned commodity theory of money. Therefore, what I mean by redeemable deposits is simply that the funds are available to be spent immediately, if the deposit holders choose to do so, whereas the non-redeemable deposits are not. It is important to note that there is no clear relationship between the idea of redeemable versus non-redeemable deposits and the notion of chequing versus savings accounts familiar to most people. For example, in using a debit card to pay for goods and services the user is often given a choice to withdraw funds from *either* a chequing account or a savings account. Therefore, both are actually redeemable, in the sense used above, in the given context.

It should be evident from Table 3.1 that what we call money is a subset of the entries on the *liabilities* side of bank balance sheets, namely the redeemable deposits. These funds are money precisely to the extent that they can immediately be transferred from one party to another, and therefore used to pay off other debts. It is in this sense that we can correctly say that "all money is credit" because, unless some entity in the banking system has extended credit in one way or another at some earlier time on the asset side of bank balance sheets, there could be no entries at all on the liabilities side (and hence no money). The opposite is not true, however. It is not the case that "all credit is money," because several of the other items on the liabilities side are not, in fact, money.

To illustrate further with an example from contemporary Canada, suppose that I have a total of six "bank" accounts in two different financial institutions. I put the term "bank" in quotes because these institutions do not actually have to be banks in the legal sense, as defined in the Bank Act. They simply have to be deposit-taking institutions. With "bank" A, I have a debit card but no chequebook. In this case, as already mentioned, when I use the debit card I will be given a choice of drawing funds from either a chequing account or a saving account. With "bank" B, I have neither a debit card nor chequebook, but I do have an electronic funds transfer (EFT) facility to be able to transfer funds to "bank" A. My accounts in the two financial institutions are listed in detail in Tables 3.2 and 3.3.

Table 3.2   List of Accounts in "Bank" A

1. An interest-bearing chequing/savings account denominated in US$. For the purposes of my debit card this is called a chequing account.
2. An interest-bearing savings account denominated in C$. For the purposes of my debit card this is called a savings account.
3. An interest-bearing savings account denominated in C$, embedded in a registered retirement savings plan (RRSP)

Table 3.3   List of Accounts in "Bank" B

1. An interest-bearing savings account denominated in C$.
2. An interest-bearing savings account denominated in C$, embedded in an RRSP.
3. An interest-bearing savings account denominated in C$, embedded in a tax-free savings account (TFSA).

What, therefore, is my individual "money supply"? I would say (if we have done our ontological spadework) that the answer is clearly A2 + B1 + B3. A1 is not part of the Canadian money supply, even though it is a chequing account, because it is denominated in US dollars. It will need to be converted into Canadian dollars if it is to be spent in Canada. A3 and B2 do not count because there are rules and regulations about how and when withdrawals can be made from an RRSP, and therefore the money is not immediately available. B1 and B2, on the other hand, *should* be included as part of the money supply because with a touch on the keyboard they can be transferred into A2 and then spent.

There is also little or no connection between the above and the so-called monetary aggregates reported by the statisticians, such as M1, M2, M2++, M3, M4, and so on. The collection and reporting of these statistics is really just a hangover from the heyday of monetarism, more than thirty-five years ago, when it seemed important to actually quantify the money supply. All of these series either omit items which are money, or include items which are not money. As the example shows, there is really no way to calculate the aggregate money supply without knowing the detailed financial circumstances of each individual and then adding them all up. On the other hand, even if we can never reasonably try to calculate the precise size of the money supply, we can certainly see the effects of money on the economy (in conjunction with other factors) by looking at what happens to interest rates, growth, inflation, exchange rates, and so on. It is also quite clear that in a banking system money demand must be equal to money supply at all times by definition (even if the exact quantity is unknown). At any given time someone, somewhere, *must* be holding the relevant deposits. Otherwise they would not exist. This circumstance can indeed therefore always be represented by an equation in the macroeconomic model.[6]

It is also true that all of the items that are part of the money supply, whether they can be counted or not, are theoretically convertible into the monetary base. The latter can, of course, be counted, as it just consists of the liabilities of the state central bank. Further, even though the total of the theoretical money supply cannot be counted precisely, we also know (just from the orders of magnitude of the published statitics) that it is certainly many times larger than the monetary base itself .This seeming disconnect has always been like the proverbial "red rag to the bull" to some groups of monetary reformers. It is what lies behind the proposals for 100 percent reserves and the like, as already discussed in previous chapters. Is there, therefore, a case to be made that fractional reserve banking simply *fraudulent*, in and of itself, as so many of the reformers like to claim? Not so, because we can always imagine or envisage a hypothetical pure credit system, in which the convertibility promises are always kept by making reserves available on demand. The red rag turns out to be a large "red-herring." As we have already seen in chapter 2, a real interest rule would be one way of achieving confidence in the convertibility of bank deposits in practice, as this does effectively make reserves available on demand (at the right price). Even in the real world situation where it cannot be guaranteed that central bankers will pursue a real rate rule (or even be aware of the possibility) there will usually be (a) deposit insurance, and (b) lender of last resort (LOLR) activity by the central bank. There are undoubtedly very many historical examples of actual culpable bank fraud by individual players in the financial markets, but this is quite beside the point. The claim that fractional reserve banking is "fraud" per se is simply hyperbole.

Money as a Social Relation

To continue in a similar vein, it sometimes bothers people to learn that money is created when financial institutions make loans, and "destroyed" when loans are called in. It seems as if money is just being created out of nothing. However, this is incorrect. The ability to create money actually derives from a concrete set of social and political relationships. Just because something is not defined by its physical properties, this does not mean that it is not "real," or that it cannot have causal effects in the physical world. This is the characteristic property of all social institutions, social relations, or social facts (Ingham 2004a, 2004b, 2005, 2018, Searle 2005, 2010). Social facts are altogether in a different category from the "brute facts" (the physical facts of nature) and money is a prime example. A social fact is what it is not by the laws of nature but because it is accepted as such by convention. It will involve such things as collective intentionality, the assignment of status function, and the adherence to rules and norms of behavior (Searle 2005, 19). A classic non-economic example of a social fact would be the proverbial "line drawn in the sand" (Smithin 2009a, 51), as a boundary between two warring factions, or even just two quarrelsome individuals on a beach. If all parties respect the boundary, it keeps the peace not by virtue of its physical properties (nothing actually prevents anyone from stepping over the line) but because it is respected as such. It nonetheless can be effective, and has a literal impact in the physical world (in this case specifically on spatial location) as long as its conditions of existence are in place. From this can be drawn some very obvious parallels with many important economic institutions including money itself, private property, firms, banks, mortgages, and pension plans. All these things rely on the same sorts of conditions of existence, and can be just as real and binding on the individuals participating in them. The example of the line in the sand also illustrates how easily social consensus can evaporate. The boundary may seem at one moment to represent a solid (social) fact of life and an unbreakable taboo. At the next, if someone steps over the line and no retaliation follows it simply crumbles. In the case of *social* institutions what needs to be explained is *both* why they can seem to be so solid and unbreakable at one moment, and then collapse the next. There is obviously a close correspondence between the example of the line and the typical sequence of events in the financial world in the event of a crisis.

It seems that, after all, there is really no mystery to be solved about money as a social relation once we recognize the truth of the familiar phrase "money is power." What does need to be elaborated, though, is precisely who has this power and how it can be exercised. In short, who has the right to make the decisive computer keystrokes? Whose liabilities really do count as money? Is there a hierarchy of promises to pay ranked by quality? And so on.

Confusion About the Functions of Money

In current textbooks the functions of money are usually given as something similar to the triad listed in Table 3.4:

Table 3.4   The Functions of Money as Given in Textbooks

1. Unit-of-account
2. Medium-of-exchange
3. Store-of-value.

What is meant by the expression unit-of-account is the abstract concept of a "dollar," a "pound," a "yen" and so on, in which prices are expressed, accounts are recorded, and profit is calculated. Keynes (1930, 3) had also introduced the notion of a "money of account" which he said was "the primary concept of a theory of money." Unlike Keynes, however, modern textbook writers apparently do not think that this function is very important. This is a serious mistake. If there were no unit-of-account, it would be impossible to conduct business on a rational basis by quoting prices, keeping accounts, and obtaining finance. On the other hand, we have seen already that the concept of the "medium-of-exchange" *is* regarded as somehow fundamentally important by the majority of economists. According to the adherents of the catallactic theory it is actually the quintessential function of money. Its prominence in textbooks seems to indicate that most contemporary economists still do believe in this set of ideas. However, this is also a mistake. A troubling implication is that mainstream economists must apparently also continue to believe that the characteristic economic transaction is a simple "spot" exchange of goods for money (Hicks 1989, 41) which is very far from being the case in today's complex society. In the standard academic theories of portfolio choice and the "demand for money" the store–of-value function also continues to be treated as important, but again the emphasis seems misplaced. To be sure, if money is indeed to constitute purchasing power it clearly must retain value, at least to some extent, from one period to the next. However, money is certainly not the only, nor necessarily the best, store-of-value in this sense. For example, in most circumstances a diamond ring, or a painting by a famous artist, can serve the same purpose much better.

Some sources have also suggested that there is yet another function of money, namely money as a means-of-payment. But, this term is often used simply as a synonym for medium-of-exchange which is why only three functions are usually mentioned. The idea of a means-of-payment simply gets lost. However, there is a key difference between the two concepts, and it is fundamentally important for a correct understanding of monetary theory to identify what the difference is. Interestingly enough Sir John Hicks (1989), in his posthumously published book *A Market Theory of Money*, broke entirely with the usual threefold classification, and one of his reasons for doing so had to do precisely with the meaning of means-of-payment versus medium-of-exchange. According to Hicks (1989, 43) money is always both a "standard-of-value" and a "medium[*sic*]-of-payment." Moreover, he does recognize that these two expressions at least roughly correspond to the more familiar locutions of unit-of-account and means-of-payment used above. Hicks's argument strongly implies that the two functions must be combined in the same instrument. On the other hand the store-of-value function is entirely downplayed. Therefore, according to Hicks, the key functions of money are the two shown in Table 3.5—not the three of Table 3.4.

How, though, does the idea of a means-of-payment actually differ from that of a medium-of-exchange? Hicks's answer is that in reality that the typical transaction is not a straightforward "spot" exchange of goods for money. In practice, and particularly for the more important transactions, some sort of agreement, a formal or informal contract, is required before trade can take place. The contract (explicit or implicit) comes first, then there is either delivery or payment, or vice versa. The timing of the actual payment for the goods and services is highly variable. Debts are continually being created and extinguished, but it is not possible to be dogmatic about when these debts are paid off. In some cases the buyer must pay "in advance," before delivery of the item, while at other times payment is made later "in arrears."[7] Spot payment is only a special case (Hicks 1989, 42). In all three cases, it is implicit that money, the thing offered in payment, is in a different category altogether from the goods and services being offered for sale. Otherwise, when trading an apple for an orange why not call *either* of them money? The concept of a means-of-payment also extends quite naturally to cover the case of purely financial transactions.

On this view the store-of-value aspect of money does not need be stressed. Indeed, historically money has very frequently continued to perform the unit-of-account and means-of-payment functions long after inflation rates have reached very high levels—making a mockery of the idea of "storing value." This experience shows that the twin functions of unit-of-account and means-of-payment functions are what really matters (Hicks 1989, 42–43). As argued by Smithin (2010, 56–57) to make this case is not to deny that money might be more "useful" in capitalism if its real value could be kept more stable. However, this does not necessarily mean that the inflation rate itself must be zero. As already shown in chapter 2, stable real values could be achieved via a real interest rate rule with the inflation rate at any level. (In this case money, does finally serve as a store-of-value, regardless of the rate of inflation.) De-emphasizing the store-of-value function completely undercuts the various narratives to the effect that money is about to be replaced by one or another innovative exchange media that outperform current money in this or any other dimension. The recent example of bitcoin has already been discussed in fn. 1 above. Here is what Mishkin (2015, 55–56), has had to say on this particular subject:

> Bitcoin . . . functions well as a medium-of-exchange . . . however it does not do well with respect to the other two functions of money . . . unit-of-account and store-of-value. The price of bitcoin [in money] is extremely volatile . . . over seven times that of the price of gold and eight times that of . . . [the] . . . stock market. . . . Because of this volatility [*sic*] . . . it . . . has not become a unit-of-account . . . bitcoin does not satisfy two of the three key functions of money. (Emphasis added)

Note, moreover, that Mishkin still takes the conventional view that the three functions of money are those listed in Table 3.4, rather than the two in Table 3.5. If we apply the correct list from Table 3.5 there is nothing left at all.

Table 3.5 The Functions of Money According to Hicks (1989)

1. Unit-of-account	("standard-of-value" in Hicks's own terminology)
2. Means-of-payment	("medium-of-payment" in Hicks's own terminology)

Money and the Method of Enterprise

If there has been confusion about the concept of money in mainstream economics, it has to be said that much the same is true even about the idea of an "economy" itself. The term economy is usually taken to refer generically to all possible methods of obtaining provisions. On this reasoning the seventeenth-century fictional character Robinson Crusoe for example, alone on a desert island, is supposed to be as much engaged in economic activity as anyone else. And, indeed, a fictional *Crusoe economy* is often a favorite starting point for conventional economic analysis (Robbins 1998, Robertson 1939, Rothbard 1998). Very frequently, the choices that Crusoe makes in this situation are presented as the paradigmatic example of the problem of resource allocation. In spite of its continuing popularity, however, this sort of discussion makes no sense whatsoever as social science. By definition, the decisions that Crusoe makes are not relevant to anyone but himself.[8] Crusoe may well decide to "build a shelter" today rather than "go out fishing," or vice versa, and these decisions always make perfect sense to him. Therefore, regardless of what the choices actually are they can always be said to represent an "optimal allocation of resources." However, Crusoe does not have to worry about competition in the market for new housing, what amount of *money* the fish will bring when offered for sale, the availability of credit financing, the cost of health care, or indeed most of things that are of serious concern to real people in a real economy. He is not participating in an economy at all in any mean-ingful sense.

Once we move beyond the isolated individual, and therefore have to make provision for more than one person, there are really only four other basic frameworks that have been identified in the fields of political economy and economic sociology potentially capable of achieving this. The first of these might be labeled a *traditional economy* of which there have been countless variations in historical practice, such as hunting and gathering, or traditional agriculture, for example. Whatever the practical details of how subsistence is achieved, the central organizing principle of a traditional economy is simply that decisions about what work should be done, when, by whom, and how the proceeds are to be shared, are going to be settled precisely by custom or tradition. The next broad generic type is that of a *command economy*. In this case, someone simply gives orders about what should be done, and about how the produce should be divided, and the others simply obey. The notion of a command economy also covers many historical and practical variants. It is the method of armies, for example, also of the various state socialisms that existed in the twentieth century before 1989, and of outright slavery and coercion of all kinds.

A third *potential* method (and here the emphasis should particularly be noted) is the notion of voluntary exchange in a free market. This is usually put forward as a normative ideal, rather than a historical case study, by such writers as libertarians, classical liberals, free market economists, and others. It is a regarded, by them, as a superior alternative to either custom or command, not only because of the material benefits that are supposedly achieved, but also because of the absence of any form of coercion. The basic idea is that individuals offering items for trade will either have made them by their own hands, or else have otherwise acquired undisputed property rights in the goods and services offered. Moreover, everything is done on a voluntary basis. In this way individual liberty will supposedly be maximized. The difficulty with this argument is not with the moral standpoint, but because the concept of the market employed in the narrative is purely abstract. It lacks any of the social structure necessary for actual markets to exist. It is significant that the most rhetorically persuasive theoretical accounts are those of a system of exchange portrayed as ideally functioning without the need for money, or financial accommodation of any kind, and possibly without even an abstract unit-of-account. Trade is assumed to be able to take place without any of the financial and monetary paraphernalia of a real system. According to the theory, identified earlier in this chapter as the "catallactic" theory, even if one of the commodities is chosen as simply a monetary *numeraire*, or somehow becomes a medium-of-exchange for convenience as already discussed, this is supposed to make no difference at all to the way in which the system operates. The lack of attention to social structure means that it can hardly be correct to identify the abstract pure exchange system as anything resembling the system called capitalism. Nonetheless, it is unfortunately very true that terms like market economy, the free market, capitalism, and so forth are often carelessly used as synonyms in both academic and political debate. To be sure, any system designated as capitalism must include the sale of goods for money in the marketplace. But, as we have already seen in previous chapters, it necessarily involves much more than this in the way of social structure (Smithin 2009a, 20–22, 2009b, 2011). Following Keynes (1933b, 408), the hypothesized pure exchange system of the textbooks should really be given its own separate label, and be defined as a *real exchange economy*, or similar. This label conveniently covers both the case of barter and that in which money is neutral and only serves as a medium-of-exchange.

Finally, there is the real world method of producing and delivery goods and services identified by the sociologist Max Weber (1927, 275–78) as part of his effort to decipher "the meanings and presuppositions of *modern capitalism*" (Emphasis added). This is therefore a system which does correspond to historical reality and, by implication, had reached something like its full maturity during Weber's own lifetime in the late nineteenth and early twentieth centuries. It is defined as follows (cf. Collins 1986, 21–22):

> The provision of human needs by the *method of enterprise,* which is to say by private businesses seeking profit. (Emphasis added)

It is significant that this definition quite sensibly avoids the insuperable problem of trying to pin down the vague and ambiguous concept of "capital" itself, much as discussed in chapter 1. At the same time, however, the use of the term "modern" in the definition also seems to indicate that in another sense Weber has cast his analytical net too narrowly. The method of enterprise, as here defined, and commercial society in general, have surely been recognizable, as such, in a wide variety of temporal, geographical, and cultural *mileux* both long before Weber was writing, and obviously also in the century that has passed since. It is true that there has never been a pure unmixed version of an enterprise economy. There have always been such things as government bureaucracy and regulation, the police and armed forces, nationalized industries, and so forth, to a greater or lesser extent. But this does not dilute the fundamental importance of the profit motive in keeping the whole thing going. Thus, in principle, what we should really mean by the enterprise economy is any system in which the profit motive plays a significant or leading role. As with the cases of the command economy and the traditional economy, it can be readily conceded that there have been a large number of diverse historical variants.

It is important to note that of the (altogether) five potential alternative methods for "obtaining provisions," mainstream economics in the academic world has seemed determined to focus exclusively on the two that are essentially hypothetical or conjectural. These are, namely, the Crusoe economy for an isolated individual, and the real exchange economy in the case of more than one person. To this extent, the economics profession can reasonably be accused of having very badly misdirected its efforts. By making such a statement I do not mean to suggest that no one has ever been stranded on a desert island, or that it has never happened that barter exchange has occurred between (say) different nomadic tribes, foreign explorers and native peoples, or between individuals in special situations such as the well-known example of the prisoner of war (POW) camp during World War II (Radford 1945). It is always possible for any two parties that come into contact to strike up whatever sort of bargain that they can reach on an ad hoc basis. The parties involved, moreover, can range from individuals, to social groups, to corporations, and to the state. Similarly, it is always possible for an individual to suddenly be placed in an extreme existential situation by accident, like Crusoe. However, unlike in the historical cases of tradition, command, or enterprise, what *is* in grave doubt is the idea that either of the other two modes of conduct has ever been the main principle by which any society has achieved its basic subsistence. That notion is entirely fanciful.

Two main issues arise in considering Weber's (much more realistic) idea of the method of enterprise. First, just by delineating this one particular method of providing for human needs compared to the others it immediately highlights the question about which of them the social scientist concerned with economic issues should be studying. Moreover (and in spite of the obsession with barter exchange by its practitioners) it is notable that economic analysis as a specialized field of study has itself only developed in connection with the rise of modern commercial society in the last few hundred years at most (Heilbroner 1992, 1999, Heilbroner and Milberg 1995, Smithin 2009a, 2–4). It therefore seems to be a very straightforward argument that it is the method of enterprise that economists should be studying, rather than institution-free mathematical theories of resource allocation (Lau and Smithin 2002, 6–7). Second, and crucially, what is this "profit" that provides the incentive for private firms to act? Most obviously it is a sum of money, implying that the system could not function in the absence of money, and ruling out any possibility of achieving the same results through nonmonetary methods.

The Hierarchy of Money

Stephanie Bell (2001, 505) reminds us of the important point that as money is a social relation involving indebtedness, there must be a hierarchy of money depending on the bona fides of the issuer. Debts are of different quality from the point of view of the creditor (Hicks 1989, 48) and some types of promises to pay are more acceptable than others. Strangely this point is often obscured or even ignored in textbooks, making it difficult for readers to understand even such basic things as why it is that central banks can conduct monetary policy by manipulating interest rates, or what is happening in a financial crisis.

Any individual or institution can issue promises to pay (IOUs) denominated in the unit-of-account and Bell (2005, 505–8) envisages a four-tier "debt pyramid" in ascending order of the acceptability of these IOUs. Generally speaking, the promises of households are regarded as being of the lowest quality, those of firms somewhat higher, those of financial institutions such as banks next, and the liabilities of the state, or government, ranked highest.[9] An IOU of a household or a firm will not necessarily be accepted at face value because it may not be reliable. To be able deliver the required number of units-of-account, a firm would have to make profits correctly denominated and in an acceptable form, a household would have to make wages (also correctly denominated) and so on.

Bell did not provide a graphical illustration of the ascending pyramid, but in Smithin (2013a, 19) I supplied a graph of an alternative "inverted" version by balancing the pyramid precariously on a point. The purpose of this device was to stress the idea that the most acceptable IOUs, those which support the whole structure, are also the most scarce. This diagram is reproduced in Figure 3.1. One way of making lower-quality IOUs acceptable might be a promise of conversion into the debt of an entity with higher quality (appearing here on a *lower* storey of the inverted pyramid). Alternatively, the less desirable securities may trade at discount or offer a higher rate of interest as a "risk premium" (Bell 2001, 506). In university classes on money and banking, I often carry out a simple experiment to illustrate this point about the different quality of promises to pay. I write out the following legend on a blank piece of paper, and then sign and date the document:

I promise to pay the bearer on demand one trillion dollars one hundred years from today's date, *if* I have not changed my mind in the meantime.

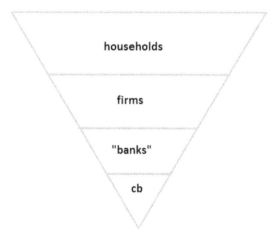

Figure 3.1 The Inverted Debt Pyramid. *Source*: Author.

What is the value of this promise to pay? Realistically it is zero. However, my students are always willing to humor me, and one of them will usually offer me, say, a one dollar coin (a "looney" in Canadian parlance), and I will gratefully accept. If the first student later decides to sell on this "asset," however, maybe the other students will not be as forgiving. Perhaps a second student will only offer a dime (ten cents). If, somewhat later, the second student then tries to unload the depreciating paper on a third student, maybe this student will only be willing to pay a nickel (five cents). These days this is the lowest denomination coin there is. The only place to go after that is zero.[10] The point is clear, the dubious promise to pay does not circulate at anything like its face value—and may well depreciate entirely and become worthless. Bell's argument was that this could well happen to the IOUs issued by any and all firms (including non-bank financial firms) and households. So, in general, the message is caveat emptor.

On the other hand, the obligations of the institutions that are called "banks"[11] in the second storey of the inverted pyramid frequently *will* be acceptable at face value. A main reason for this (there are others, as discussed below) is that they usually are in principle convertible into higher quality obligations, namely those of the state central bank. Finally, the liabilities of the central bank itself (i.e., currency in the hands of the public plus bank reserves) are the most highly ranked promises to pay (albeit at the base of the pyramid as drawn). They do not need to be converted into anything else, and even the term "promise to pay" itself becomes something of a misnomer. They are in fact payment.

The most plausible explanation for the special place of central bank liabilities is that given by the chartalist school (Bell 2001, Goodhart 1998, Knapp 1924, Wray 1998) which argues that the state has the power to levy taxes, but must also accept its own liabilities back from the public in payment of those same taxes. If the general principle is that the choice of the ultimate form of payment rests on collective acceptance by society, the chartalists have added that the specific social relation, that is decisive in practice, is the power of the state. Note also that the state will typically accept the liabilities of the commercial banks directly in tax payment (Bell 2001, 506–7). This then validates such obligations as money over and above any convertibility feature.

Thus, in any actual economy what is called the money supply consists mostly of a subset of the total deposit liabilities of financial institutions in the second storey of the inverted pyramid, such as commercial banks. The liabilities of the state central bank at the base of the inverted pyramid serve as the monetary base. Using a variety of financial techniques, the central bank directly controls the interest rate on loans of base money which we have earlier called the "policy rate" of interest. In turn, changes in the policy rate also affect the interest rates both charged and received by the commercial banks. This occurs because commercial banks need central bank base money to settle claims among themselves, and therefore no individual bank can afford to get too far out of step with its rivals in the composition of its portfolio. Changes in the policy rate this feed through to interest rates in general, and this is the main vehicle for the conduct of monetary policy.

Financial Assets, Financial Markets, and Financial Institutions

In the sort of terminology commonly used in textbooks on money and banking, and on finance, *financial assets* (i.e., bonds, stocks, and other debt instruments) and their *derivatives* (options, futures, etc.) are all ultimately nothing other than claims to sums of money. *Financial markets* are actual or virtual locations where financial assets are traded. *Financial institutions* are commercial firms which deal in financial assets (including money). Unfortunately, the descriptions of the different financial markets that one reads in textbooks, or online, typically make all of the methodological mistakes, and then some, that the reader was warned about in chapter 1. For example, the so-called money market actually deals in things that are *not* money on the definition given above. It relates to short-term debt instruments, such as T-bills, commercial paper, negotiable certificates of deposit, and so forth. Similarly, the capital market is not (as one might naively have thought looking at an introductory economics textbook) the market for physical capital goods, but simply for long-term debt instruments, such as long-term bonds, corporate and government, equities, mortgages, and so on.[12] Financial markets can be organized exchanges, like the stock market, or trades can take place in so-called over-the-counter (OTC) markets. The expression *primary market* is used when the shares or bonds are first issued. The term *secondary market* applies when the original bond or equity is sold on later to a third party for the market price at that time.

In orthodox financial theory the basic premise is that both financial markets and financial institutions exist merely to "channel funds from savers to borrowers" (to use a well-worn phrase), as well to participate in the payments system and to perform other types of financial service. However, this extremely limited perspective completely ignores the issue of credit and money creation, and therefore also the fundamental question about where the money comes from in the first place. Even the very terminology that is used in describing the various financial transactions is highly misleading. For example, when borrowers obtain funds by issuing debt instruments and selling them in financial markets, this is known in the textbooks as *direct finance*. When the borrowers get the funds from banks or similar institutions, however, this is known as *indirect finance* which definition (more-or-less deliberately) reduces these institutions to the role of intermediary. In reality, however, the central bank and commercial banks all combine in the process of *creating* the money that eventually will constitutes the total of whatever finance is available. There is nothing else that "finance" can be. Logically speaking, therefore, in the credit and money creation process, the terms direct and indirect finance from the textbooks could very easily be reversed.

The problems with the textbook approach may be further explained by looking at two alternative diagrams in Figures 3.2 and 3.3. Both of these diagrams purport to illustrate the flow of funds among and between financial institutions, financial markets, and agents. Figure 3.2 illustrates the conventional point of view that "deposits make loans." The starting point in this diagram is the group of "savers," that is, people who have refrained from spending all of their money on consumption, and therefore have saved some of it. The question of where the money came from originally is not addressed.

The savers can either lend out their money "directly" to borrowers via the financial markets (hence the term "direct finance" used above) or they can deposit the money with a financial institution or bank. The conventional wisdom is that based on the deposits the "banks" can then also make loans to the prospective borrowers. However, their ability to do so is (supposedly) restricted by the amount of the deposits.

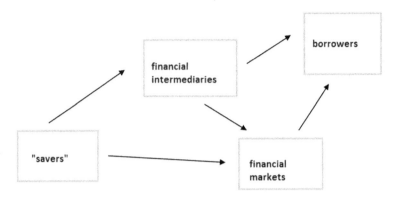

Figure 3.2   The Flow of Funds Starting with "Saving." *Source*: Author.

Figure 3.3, on the other hand, illustrates the far more realistic idea that "loans make deposits." In this case, for example as we saw in Table 3.1, the money cannot come into existence in the first place unless there has already been net credit creation by the banking system as a whole. The diagram in Figure 3.3 therefore adds a box in the top-left corner to represent the central bank's role in the process.

The money is actually created by the combination of the activities of the central bank and the commercial banks, and in the first instance gets transmitted to the borrowers in this way even before there are any deposits. Then, when the initial borrowers have spent the money, that is how it eventually gets into the hands of the savers, via the loop in the bottom right-hand corner. At this point, the savers can indeed then "recycle" the money they have saved in what is really only a *facsimile* of the orthodox theory of finance as this was described above. It is this second stage of the process that, in the past, has given a spurious credibility to the standard theory of banking—going back to well before the time of Keynes. Its survival to this day, however, clearly shows that Keynes, in his time, did not really do enough to effectively challenge the erroneous standard view.

In this chapter, as our primary interest in deciding what should "count as" money, and what should not, it is also important therefore to distinguish between three broad

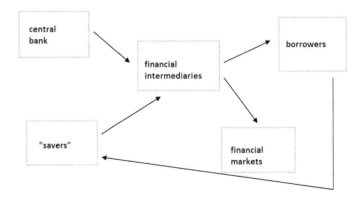

Figure 3.3   The Flow of Funds with a Central Bank and Endogenous Money. *Source*: Author.

classes of financial institution in the type of systems under discussion. These are (i) *depository* institution (banks and "near banks"), (ii) *non-depository contractual savings institutions* (pension funds, insurance companies, etc.), and (iii) *investment intermediaries* (finance companies, mutual funds). From this point of view taken here the depository institutions are clearly the most important. As already discussed, the other financial companies are less important from this point of view. They would be included among "firms" in general in the inverted debt pyramid.

Notes About Notation

To now try to summarize the above discussion, and to settle on a standard notation, let CU stand for currency in the hands of the nonbank public, D for the total of commercial bank deposits included in the money supply (defined as broadly as necessary), H for the monetary base, M for the money supply itself, and R for bank reserves. The definition of the monetary base will therefore be:

$$H = CU + R. \tag{3.1}$$

And the money supply itself is:

$$M = CU + D. \tag{3.2}$$

Currency in the hands of the non-bank public is included in both definitions. This is because even in the contemporary world it is still possible to pay for goods and services with actual cash—as when buying a cup of coffee. On the other hand and as already mentioned above it is certainly possible to envisage a future payments technology which makes no use of paper money or coins. In that case we would have $CU = 0$, $H = R$, and $M = D$. Bank reserves would consist only of commercial bank deposits with the central bank. There would be no vault and till cash held by the banking system. The whole of the money supply would consist of deposits in the commercial banking system.

The "purchasing power of money" is also known as the total of real money balances and (in principle, at least)[13] the value of real money balances may be determined by dividing the nominal money supply by the aggregate price index, P:

$$\text{Real Money Balances} = M/P. \tag{3.3}$$

A price index is a series which starts by defining the average/aggregate price level as $P = 100$ in an arbitrarily chosen base year, and then expresses the price level in every other year as percentages of that of the base year. In Table 3.6 the base is year 4. We can then get a series expressing changes in the average level of prices in the manner illustrated (with some arbitrary numbers) in Table 3.6.

Traditionally in macroeconomics the symbol Y stands for real GDP. Therefore, if the aggregate price level is P then, by definition, nominal GDP = PY and $Y = PY/P$. We might also usefully write the so-called expenditure breakdown of *nominal* GDP as:

$$PY = \$C + \$I + \$G + \$(EX - IM) \tag{3.4}$$

Therefore, dividing through by P, the breakdown of *real* GDP will be the familiar:

$$Y = C + I + G + (EX - IM), \tag{3.5}$$

where C stands for real consumption spending, I for real investment spending, G for real government spending, and $EX - IM$ for real net exports. In macroeconomic textbooks, so-called real GDP is taken to be the best measure of the total of real value-added (real output) in a modern economy. As a caveat to this, however, we have already made the point (in both chapters 1 and 2), that the numbers reported by the statisticians are not ideal from the theoretical point of view. There are a number of reasons for this in a specifically monetary economy—including the important issue of stock-flow consistency. It would be better if the figures used for real output, real consumption, real investment, and so on, were actual flows of funds divided by the appropriate price index. In our theoretical exercises (as was already done in chapter 2) we can simply assume that Y, C, I, and so on, are correctly calculated, and therefore that the theory is on the right track. However, the reader should again be warned that there may well be some discrepancies between this and the messy and unsatisfactory national income and expenditure accounts that are actually reported in each jurisdiction.[14] Assuming that we do have some confidence in the numbers the rate of economic growth, y, will be given by:

$$y = (Y - Y_{-1}) / Y_{-1} \tag{3.6}$$

Meanwhile, the inflation rate, designated by lower-case p, is simply defined as the rate of change of the aggregate price index. That is:

$$p = (P - P_{-1}) / P_{-1} \tag{3.7}$$

As we already have the series for the aggregate price index from Table 3.6, we can easily work out the corresponding inflation rate in each year as in Table 3.7.[15]

As also discussed in previous chapters, it is important to distinguish between real and nominal *interest* rates. Therefore, let r stand for the real rate of interest, i for the nominal rate interest rate, and p_{+1} for expected inflation rate. Thus the relationship between real and nominal interest rates is:

$$r = i - p_{+1} \tag{3.8}$$

Table 3.6   An Aggregate Price Index

Year	P
1	99.1
2	101.4
3	98.7
4	100.0
5	103.5

Table 3.7   An Aggregate Price Index and the Inflation Rate

Year	P	p
1	99.1	–
2	101.4	2.3%
3	98.7	−2.7%
4	100.0	1.3%
5	103.5	3.5%

Next, use the alternative symbol, $\underline{r}$ (r underscored) to stand for the "inflation-adjusted" or "ex post" real interest rate:

$$\underline{r} = i - p. \tag{3.9}$$

This is the nominal rate less the *currently observed* inflation rate (not the expected rate). In empirical work, this measure is often treated as a "proxy for" (approximation to) the true expected real rate of interest which is not itself directly observable. Although r is not exactly the same thing as r, we can therefore sometimes write:

$$r = \underline{r} \ \left(\text{approx.}\right) \tag{3.10}$$

Finally, given that this is a book about monetary macroeconomics, we should note that the *international* economy can usefully be viewed as a set of competing currency networks, each with its own central bank. As already described in chapter 2, the nominal exchange rate between the different currencies can either be floating (flexible) or fixed. Next define the symbol E as the nominal spot exchange rate where E = the foreign currency price of one unit of domestic currency. For example, if Canada is the domestic economy and supposing that US$1.00 is C$0.75, then $E = 0.75$. What is important for international competitiveness, however, is actually the real exchange rate, Q, where:

$$Q = EP/Pf. \tag{3.11}$$

Suppose that Canadian goods (say "widgets") cost C$12.00 per unit, so that $P = 12.0$. Also, that American widgets cost US$6.00 per unit, such that that $Pf = 6.0$ (where Pf is the price index in the foreign country).[16] Then the real exchange rate will be:

$$Q = \left(0.75 \times 12.0\right)/6.0 = 1.5. \tag{3.12}$$

As Q is greater than one, this means that Canadian goods are more expensive than US goods—though actually not *twice* as expensive, as might have seemed to be the case at first sight.[17] Nonetheless, they are less "competitive" and American widgets will outsell Canadian widgets. This is bad news for the Canadian balance of payments (BOP).

CONCLUSION

The title of a collection of essays that I edited some years ago was *What Is Money?* (Smithin 2000). At the time I chose this title, I was not aware that exactly the same ontological question had been asked, more than one hundred years ago, by the credit theorist Mitchell Innes (Innes 1913) in his very first article on the subject. That discovery seemed to me to make the original choice even more appropriate. This chapter has now addressed the same set of issues for the twenty-first century. In chapter 4, to follow, there will be a further development of these themes.

NOTES

1. For example, in recent years there has been much discussion of an electronic financial asset called "bitcoin" which can be acquired either by solving some sort of computer algorithm (in a process fancifully called "mining") or in exchange. This was the "money of the future" (du jour) in the second decade of the twenty-first century (Mishkin 2015, 55–56). It will be old news by the time anyone is actually reading this book, but it well serves as an example of the type of argument that has very frequently been put forward. The reasons why such types of payment innovation are not "money" per se will be explained in detail as the argument of this chapter proceeds. For now, we should simply note that the very use of such terms as mining, coin, and so on already indicates a certain naivety about what money is, and what money supposedly does.

2. Ingham (2004a, 12) elaborates "I shall argue that money is itself a social relation; that is say, money is a 'claim' or 'credit' that is constituted by social relations that *exist independently of the production and exchange of commodities*." (Original emphasis)

3. The final outcome, after all, was World War I.

4. The precise relationship between "credit and state theories of money" is explained in several of the contributions to the edited volume by Wray (Wray 2004).

5. The reader will no doubt be able to intuit from these figures that the author is a resident of the Greater Toronto Area (GTA).

6. In the late twentieth century it was a mistake on the parts of some Post Keynesian economists, and also the adherents of the new consensus, to try to construct models neglecting the demand for money. Recall the discussion about this topic from chapter 1.

7. In mainstream economics one of the methods of introducing money into neoclassical models that would otherwise reduce to barter exchange is by imposing a so-called cash-in-advance (CIA) constraint (Blanchard and Fisher 1989, Turnovsky 2000, Walsh 1998). The timing issue renders this method invalid (Smithin 2013a, 94).

8. In the seventeenth-century novel, Crusoe does eventually encounter a second person on the island whom he calls Man Friday. From this point in the narrative we do have a social situation and the Crusoe economy per se ceases to exist. Friday actually becomes a sort of servant to Crusoe, a situation which inevitably involves some degree of coercion.

9. There will, of course, always be some very wealthy households whose promises to pay actually rank higher than those of the weakest firms.

10. I should stress that at the end of the experiment all coins are returned to their original owners.

11. As mentioned earlier what is meant by "banks" is "all deposit-taking institutions." This includes banks as legally defined, but also the so-called near banks. Other types of financial institution are included among the "firms" in the third story of the inverted pyramid. There are both industrial firms and financial firms at this level.

12. Once again we find that it is impossible to give a concrete meaning to the concept of physical capital.

13. Recall that in practice the nominal money supply, as defined above, cannot really be counted.

14. This important question will also be taken up again in later chapters.

15. We do not have a similar set of numbers for real GDP (Y) in each year but, if we did, the series for the real economic growth rate, y, could be worked out in the same way.

16. For the sake of convenience in defining P and Pf the decimal point has been moved one place to the left.

17. This is because of the nominal exchange rate difference.

Chapter 4

The Mystery of Profit and the Enigma of Value

INTRODUCTION

The title of this chapter is a reference to Winston Churchill's famous comment about Russian intentions on the eve of World War II, in a radio broadcast in 1939. Russia, Churchill said on that occasion, "is a riddle wrapped up in a mystery inside an enigma." The discussions in chapters 1 to 3 have very probably stirred up much the same sort of sentiments about the concepts of "profit," "value," and the like, in the monetary production or enterprise economy.

A central problem in such a world, one that has often been mooted but never stated perfectly clearly, is the deceptively simple question of whether, or not, in a real money-using economy (as opposed to a barter economy or real exchange economy) there is ever enough money in existence to purchase the full value of the output. As shown by Smithin (2009a, 2013a, 2013b, 2016b) this is indeed a real problem, but seems never to have been successfully posed by would-be monetary reformers. Orthodox economics has therefore always been able to elide the issue, in both the macroeconomic and microeconomic contexts, by such devices as the concept of the velocity of circulation. In previous chapters we have seen that the enterprise economy is supposed to be one in which the pursuit of profit by the private sector is the main principle guiding economic activity, and providing incentives to engage in economic activity. But, by definition, that "profit" must in the first instance literally be a sum of money. Therefore, if there is no money, there is no profit and no incentive. This is one of the points that needs definitively to be established in this chapter.

At this stage, we now also need to ask the further question of what is actually meant by the term "value." Suppose, for example, that the value of a good or service is interpreted as being equal its costs of production. In that case, even if there does happen to be enough money in existence to cover the money value there is still not going to be enough to generate any profit. Alternatively should profits themselves be included as part of value? In this chapter it is going to be necessary to investigate a variety of these types of question.

In a recent paper (Smithin 2016b, 1259) I discussed what I there called "three puzzles about money and finance," the answers to which bear directly on the current topic. The first puzzle was about the velocity of circulation of money and, as a reference point, I quoted from a book written by Keynes's opponent Robertson (Robertson 1922) written nearly a hundred years ago. (The reader will recall that some of Robertson's other work has already been discussed in chapters above. His name will also come up again in later chapters.) The second puzzle concerned the idea of the monetary circuit which, as mentioned in chapter 1, was originally due to Marx, briefly interested Keynes, and was revived in the late twentieth century by the Franco-Italian circuit school. The reference point for this discussion was an even older book than that by Robertson, namely Vol. II of Marx's *Das Kapital* (Marx 1885).[1] The third puzzle was derived from my own work and involved what I have previously called "the widget problem" (Smithin 2013b, 2016b). This deals with the question of how it might actually be possible to "make money by making widgets"; that is, more generally, how it is possible to receive monetary compensation by engaging in production. The present chapter will once again try to explain the various arguments that were made about all three of these puzzles in Smithin (2016b).

Robertson (1922) on the Velocity of Circulation

As already suggested, the notion of the velocity of circulation has been the means by which classical, neoclassical, and mainstream economists have tried to avoid the issues raised in circuit theory and similar types of discussion. Long ago, in the short textbook *Money* (1922), the pre-Keynes Cambridge economist Robertson[2] tried to explain the idea of the velocity of circulation to his readership by means of a "parable," that is, a simple scenario. In my view, however, he succeeded only in demonstrating the emptiness of the concept. A reconsideration of Robertson's failure is therefore a useful way to show exactly why a theory of the monetary circuit is necessary. Robertson's parable about the velocity was set out succinctly in the following passage from *Money* (Robertson 1922), as previously quoted by Smithin (2009a, 57). Naturally enough, given its age, there several archaisms in the text and these are explained by way of footnotes.

> On Derby Day,[3] two men Bob and Joe, invested in a barrel of beer, and set off to Epsom with the intention of selling it at retail on the racecourse at 6d[4] a pint, the proceeds to be shared equally between them. On the way Bob, who had one three-penny bit left in the world, began to feel a great thirst, and drank a pint of the beer, paying Joe 3d as his share of the market price. A little later Joe yielded to the same desire, and drank a pint of the beer, returning the 3d to Bob. The day was hot, and before long Bob was thirsty again, and so, a little later, was Joe. When they arrived at Epsom, the 3d was back in Bob's pocket, and each had discharged in full his debts to the other, but the beer was all gone. One single three-penny bit had performed a volume of transactions which would have required many shillings[5] if the beer had been sold to the public in accordance with the original intention.

Old as this text is, the situation it presents could well be a case study in business school even today. If we treat it as such, most non-economists reading this passage would surely immediately sense that something is wrong. What is it? It is that from the purely business point of view the episode seems (and *is*) disastrous. The entrepreneurs have literally "drunk the profits." The strange thing is, however, that Robertson does not seem even to notice this. His point is to illustrate the idea of the "transactions velocity of circulation" which means how rapidly the money (in this case the coin) changes hands. In reality, however, as I have just said, the story only shows up the emptiness of the concept.

The reason that Robertson misses the most obvious feature of the situation (that he has himself created) is simply that according to the theory of neoclassical economics there is actually nothing "wrong" with it. From this point of view, the beer has been produced and drunk, and has given utility or satisfaction. It really does not matter to whom the satisfaction accrues. In the economics jargon it can easily be argued there has been an "optimal allocation of resources," "utility is maximized," and so forth. It becomes apparent, therefore, in spite of what is still taught in colleges and universities every day, that the neoclassical theory of utility is not, and cannot be, an accurate theory of capitalism. There is no mechanism within it for the realization of profits in money terms. The theory therefore fails—because the pursuit of money profit is precisely how the system does work in practice. Note also that exactly the same sort of criticism could be made of the rival "Austrian" subjective theory of utility, and indeed of all such similar approaches to the question of economic value.

Interestingly enough, there seems also to be nothing amiss in this story from the perspective of either Marxism or of classical economics. Marx, for example, had an alternative labor theory of value based on quite different principles from those of utility theory. Nonetheless, the labor theory does have *one* thing in common with utility theory in that it is also, in some sense, a real theory of value, as opposed to a monetary or social theory (Ingham 2004a, 204). In the Marxian view, so-called exploitation is a "real" phenomenon (in the economists' sense of the term) which occurs when the value of the working capital (or variable capital) needed to sustain the workforce, and as measured in labor time, is less than the value created (also measured in labor time) during the working day. During an eight-hour day, for example, the time necessary to produce the equivalent in goods and services of the wage bill may be only five hours. In this case, what is produced in the remaining three hours is the "surplus value," and accrues to the employer as profit. Joan Robinson (1962, 46) probably had the best answer to this type of argument, at least from a Keynesian point of view, when she cleverly wrote that:

> the misery of being exploited by the capitalists is nothing compared to the misery of not being exploited at all.

Be that as it may, it can plausibly be argued that the issue does not even arise in Robertson's scenario. Consider the meaning of the term "invest" as it appears in the text. This is an expression that is always highly ambiguous when used by professional economists. Does this mean simply to put down money, or does it mean to *invest* in the sense of putting in time and effort? If it is the latter, Robertson's scenario actually becomes a case in which the original producers consume all their output and, therefore, there is no exploitation in the Marxian sense. Moreover, even if Robertson really did mean to convey the former idea there is nothing to stop the reader from independently working out the implications of a similar case in which the entrepreneurs are indeed the original producers.

The important takeaway from this discussion is that the realization of profits, in a specifically monetary form, is much more important in reality than it is ever allowed to be in most types of economic theory. Indeed, one of the crucial advantages of thinking about such things as credit creation, the financing of production, debt service and retirement, and so forth in terms of a circuit is that it brings out this essential point inescapably. The main problem in our example is the simple fact that there is *not* actually enough money in existence to purchase the full money value of the output. The idea of the velocity of circulation is simply an attempt to avoid the issue. To be sure, the old quantity theory of money was usually only explicitly invoked at the macroeconomic level, either in the transactions form $MV = PT$ or the income form $MV = PY$. Nonetheless, it is possible also to work out a "microeconomic" transactions velocity of circulation for Robertson's Derby Day story. In the traditional notation this would obviously be:

$$MV = PT; \tag{4.1}$$

where M is the money supply (in our microeconomic example the single coin), V is transactions velocity, P is the price per transaction, and T is the total number of transactions. In the beer scenario, Robertson does not actually say how many transactions there are. However suppose for the sake of argument that there are twenty of them (20 pints of beer). Then we would have $M = 3$, $P = 6$ and $T = 20$. Velocity can then be calculated follows:

$$V = (6 \times 20)/3 = 40. \tag{4.2}$$

This relatively rapid velocity of circulation is thus supposed to save the day for neoclassical economic theory. All such sophistry is bound to collapse, however, as soon as anyone asks the entrepreneurs to "show me the money." The single coin is all there is.

When teaching university level courses in money and banking, monetary theory, political economy, and so on, I find it useful to supplement the discussion of Robertson's case study with a simple classroom experiment involving role-playing by the students. The experiment reinforces all of the points just made, and at the same time provides some further insight into the meaning of the concept of "value-added," a term which has already been used several times in previous chapters and will recur later in this one. The idea is to simulate a money-using market of some kind in the classroom setting. I begin by taking from my wallet a C$20 bill, bearing the likeness of Queen Elizabeth II. Perhaps a student in the front row has (e.g.) some blank notebooks and some pencils. I will offer to buy them as a job lot for $20, and the student agrees. Next, maybe a second student in the row just behind has a packed lunch and flask of coffee which the first student would like to have, and they also agree to a price of $20 for the meal. The second student may then use the $20 to buy (say) an old cell phone from a third student. This third student, though, may by now have become thoroughly puzzled as to what is happening in class, and offers a fourth student $20 for an explanation (an informal tutorial) about what is going on. Having done this, the fourth student can then buy a used textbook from a fifth student. There is clearly a lively trade going on in all kinds of things. If the fifth student then buys the original lot of notebooks and pencils from me, we can bring the whole process to an end. The $20 bill will be back where it started in my wallet. (At the end of the class all the physical goods traded will be returned to their original owners at no charge—assuming that the first student has not yet eaten the lunch.)

We seem to have had a highly successful trading session. However, if we ask the question how much money has actually been made during the session the answer is precisely zero. I already had the $20 bill in my possession to start with, and now have it back again. We *seem* to have done a total of $120 worth of business, but have nothing financially to show for it. Appeals to the concept of the velocity of circulation will do nothing to change the arithmetic. It might be argued (e.g., by neoclassical economists) that even if no money has been made something useful has indeed been achieved as people have acquired the goods that they wanted, and there is certainly some force in this argument from the sociological point of view. Even so, however, if we further inquire not how much money has been made but how much has actually been produced in the mini economy (how much output has been added to what we had to start with), the answer is still much less than $120 worth. Most of what has been traded are simply existing assets which were *already* part of the economy's total wealth (e.g., the book, the lunch, and the cell phone). The only new production that has occurred is the *service* represented by the tutorial given by the fourth student to the third student for $20. The theoretical total of value-added in the "economy" is just that, $20. Moreover, it *still* has not been possible to realize that value in money terms (which is the point of capitalism) and therefore to report an accounting profit. At the end of the day, if we were ever to try to translate these classroom ideas into a real economy in which the main principle for organizing production is by Weber's "private firms seeking profit," this is clearly going to be an insuperable problem.

Marx (1885) on the Monetary Circuit

If Robertson's text is archaic Marx's is still older by thirty-seven years but, nonetheless, remains highly relevant to our present concerns. As Marx was the inventor of the concept of the monetary circuit, it is clearly still pertinent to ask how the original Marxian version of the circuit was supposed to work. The starting point for an answer is to write out the scheme from *Das Kapital* Vol II in full (Marx 1885, 109), and then to try to explain precisely what the various terms in that scheme are meant to represent. According to Marx, the circuit can be written as:

$$M - C \ldots P \ldots C' - M' \tag{4.3}$$

The entrepreneurs are thus supposed to start the circuit with a sum of money or "money capital" on hand, equal to M. With the money they acquire the commodities, C, that are needed for the production process (including "labor power" itself). Next they engage in production, P, to make more (i.e., *more valuable*) commodities C'. The term $(C' - C)$ thus corresponds to the real value-added in the economy. The entrepreneurs then sell the enhanced commodities C' for more money M'. The difference $(M' - M)$, or ΔM, is the resulting increase in their money capital at the end of the process (Mosley 2016, 28). So, this is what capitalism is all about according to Marx. Moreover, at the descriptive level at least, the argument seems to be not dissimilar to the views of Weber, Schumpeter, Keynes, and others.

But to proceed any further with the discussion we would first need to define what is meant by the expression real value, a very old question in economics. As already mentioned, in Marx and also in some versions of classical economics there was a labor theory of value.[6] On the other hand the later neoclassical economists, the Austrian school, and modern mainstream economics, all fell back on the nebulous concept of utility. Regardless of the value theory eventually adopted, however, from the point of view of a Schumpeterian monetary analysis[7] there still seems to be something missing in Marx's account—just as there was in Robertson's utility-based theory. Once again, the problem arises of how can it ever be *possible* for M' to be greater than M, and hence for money profits to be realized? This is the crucial question but neither Marx, nor the classical economists, nor the neoclassical economists, ever seemed to get around to either asking or answering it. As we have already seen in chapter 1, in addition to a labor theory of value Marx had a commodity theory of money. The "money commodity" was supposed to be gold. Therefore, it might perhaps be argued that more or additional money is produced by mining. If so, however, that would only turn the whole argument into a real theory of production completely, rather than anything resembling a monetary theory. The supposed "money" has to be produced by human effort, and the value of this money is presumably the labor power that goes into digging it up from the ground. There would be no meaningful distinction to be made between M and M' and C and C'. One of these pairings simply becomes redundant (Smithin 2018). Alternatively, even if M is a non-commodity money but the money supply is also supposed to be fixed—as was the case both Robertson's scenario[8] and our classroom experiment—the difficulty in trying to make $M' > M$ is obvious. It cannot be done.

Perhaps the essence of what is at stake in this discussion is contained in a question that economic sociologists (e.g., Collins 1986, 122) do sometimes ask, but economists almost never, namely "where do profits come from?" Once again, the point being made is that the enterprise system as a whole must surely be able to first generate positive aggregate profits, in money terms, *before* any "real" profit or surplus can even come into existence for the different parties to dispute. The only way for this to happen is if there is sufficient credit and money creation. Granted, even with the money supply constant so that aggregate M' is equal to aggregate M at all times, it could still be argued that it is possible for *some* firms to make profits while others make losses. Indeed, this has been the usual meaning of the term "competition" in standard economics. However this cannot be the answer to the systemic problem. It is still impossible for firms, on average and in aggregate, to be profitable. The system as a whole simply cannot function on this basis. The expectation of success in any particular business would be zero and there is no genuine incentive for anyone to act. The only feasible solution is that there must always be sufficient credit and money creation by the banking system.

In modern economics real value-added is no longer thought of as either "embodied labour time," nor even as "utility" in practice.[9] Instead it is calculated along the lines of the standard definition of real GDP in the national accounts. That is:

$$Y = C + I + G + (EX - IM), \tag{4.4}$$

where Y where stands for real GDP, C for real consumption expenditure, I for real investment spending (firm spending), G for real government spending, and $(EX - IM)$ for real net exports.

I say "along the lines of" because—as we saw in all three previous chapters—the published GDP statistics leave a lot to be desired from the point of view of monetary theory. For example, the reported GDP numbers are not stock-flow consistent, a theoretical requirement now widely endorsed by very many writers in the various heterodox traditions (Godley and Lavoie 2007, Palley 2015, Tymoigne and Wray 2015, Wray 2012). It was mentioned earlier that for theoretical purposes this problem may be solved by assuming that the various magnitudes in equation (4.4) be taken as referring to real "flows of funds" (i.e., money flows deflated by a Fisher "ideal" price index),[10] rather than the imputed values provided by the statisticians. However, there would still remain the problem of relating the theory to the imperfect statistics that are available. In practice, the GDP numbers are all that we have for empirical work, but in no way are they 100 percent consistent, or accurate from the point of view of monetary theory. At this stage the importance of this theoretical qualification is that if the flows of funds statistics were somehow to be accurately compiled, this might be able to provide a basis for an alternative theory of value to either utility theory or labor theory as, for example, in Ingham's (2004a, 204) "social theory of value." This important topic will be further discussed in of both chapters 6 and 11 to follow. For now, with this caveat in mind, we should simply note the Marxian circuit can reasonably be rewritten in more-or-less standard economic notation as:

$$M - Y - M' \tag{4.5}$$

where the symbol Y (rather than C' – C) now stands for real value-added. The problem with equation (4.3), however, is that if M' is always equal to M, there will be no Y forthcoming. Why is this so (no pun intended)? Because, as already established, in the context of an enterprise economy there is no real incentive to produce value-added, or to engage in the production process at all, if the value cannot be realized in terms of money profit. Even in the case where there has been positive credit creation (and therefore M' is greater than M), it would still be quite possible for there to be no Y. This would happen when the borrowed money is *not* actually used for the financing of new production. Then, the circuit degenerates to:

$$M - M'. \tag{4.6}$$

This, therefore is, the case where all of the borrowed money goes for financial and other speculation, and nothing gets produced. The possibility of this occurring seems always to have been a major worry for economists of all political persuasions. Both the "right" and the "left" seem to completely agree on this point—as already discussed in chapter 2.[11]

If, on the other hand, $(M' - M)$ is greater than zero, and is also roughly equal to Y (or at least is consistently not much greater than Y) then there clearly *has* been sufficient profit incentive for firms to undertake production. And moreover, in these circumstances, prices will also either be roughly stable, or at least the inflation *rate* will be "low and stable." Alternatively, if Y is greater than zero, but at the same time $(M' - M)$ is now much greater than Y, then although there obviously still has been some incentive for production and the economy will still be functioning, in this case prices will be rising. There will be a high inflation rate. It seems clear, therefore, that both macroeconomic policy and financial regulation should be working toward making the first of these last two outcomes a reality as far as possible.

Smithin (2013b, 2016b) on the "Widget Problem"

I originally introduced the so-called widget problem in a contribution to a *Festshrift* for Professor Alain Parguez, one of the co-founders of the circuit school (Rochon and Seccareccia 2013, Smithin 2013b). That discussion presented a numerical example of the realization problem and how to solve it. It was thereby possible both to illustrate, and clarify, in a fairly straightforward way, a number of the issues that have arisen in the development of the monetary theory of production and of circuit theory. What follows, however, is an alternative numerical example to the one presented in the 2013b paper. There are a number of changes, and additional nuances, designed to ask and answer some quite specific questions. This version was published three years later in Smithin (2016b), and I there set out an alternative scenario for the numerical exercises, as follows:

> Suppose . . . that an entrepreneur borrows $1,000,000 to make "widgets." The widgets take one year to produce, but the entrepreneur pays the workers "in advance" (right at the start) and pays out the whole sum of money. There is a "Wicksellian bank" in the system that is, a single bank representing the financial system as a whole, whose liabilities count as money. . . . Suppose that this bank has simply been given a "charter" (a Canadian legal term) to make it legitimate . . . [but] . . . starts out with zero reserves and zero capital. The bank charges 10 percent simple interest on loans, but does not insist on repayment of either principal or interest until *after* the production period is complete (emphasis added). We further assume that *whenever* goods are available all deposit holders among the "non-bank public" will try to spend 80 percent of their money holdings at that time and save . . . [only] . . . 20 percent (original emphasis). No other transactions (financial or otherwise) occur in this economy. All bank profits will be retained by the bank owners to build up their "capital."

Evidently, immediately after the charter is granted, this bank's balance sheet will not be very impressive. There will be zeros all round as shown in Table 4.1.

As soon as the first loans are made, however, at the beginning of year 1, the balance sheet will begin to look a bit more meaningful. It will be as shown in Table 4.2.

At the next stage the widgets are actually finished and sold, at the end of year 1. At this point, however, it already becomes clear that, given our initial assumptions about

Table 4.1   "Wicksellian Bank" Balance Sheet #1[13]

Assets		Liabilities	
Loans:	0	Deposits:	0
	---		---
	0		0

behavior, there is a big problem with the financial arithmetic. The widget-maker will actually make a loss on the sale of the widgets amounting to $300,000. This is shown in Table 4.3 which is an income statement rather a balance sheet. There is an economic and financial crisis. Both the firm *and* the bank will be likely to fail.

Is there any way of solving this crisis? The answer is yes, there is. In general, the solution is simply that one sector, or another, of the economy must continuously be willing to become indebted (as the net aggregate result of the decisions of everyone in that sector) in order that *current* producers can make money profits. We can think of a number of possibilities as to how this might be achieved in a real economy. For example, other domestic firms may borrow, either to make more widgets or to start some other product line. In Keynesian terminology, this would be a case of positive "animal spirits." In Smithin (2013b), for example, I used the device of positing different firms each with a longer production period than the original widget-maker. These firms were supposed to be producing "super widgets," "extra super widgets," and so on. Another possibility is that domestic consumers will borrow, in order to buy consumer goods. Recall that in chapter 2 above we there looked at a case in which there was borrowing by *both* firms and consumers in excess of the aggregate wage bill. Alternatively the foreign sector can borrow, in order to be able to pay for domestic exports with domestic currency. A final possibility is that the domestic government could borrow (i.e., they can run a budget deficit). In each of these cases, it is clear that if our solution is to work that the new borrowers would have to receive their loans at some time before the original widgets come on the market. However, they must not be obliged to pay them back until later in the process.

To save the situation in our numerical example we will therefore have to let some other borrower become active sometime before the original widgets come on sale. This will solve the crisis. The simplest way out is actually to let a second widget-maker (a "second-mover") fortuitously become active, just before the end of the production period of the first batch of widgets. The second-mover will therefore borrow a further $1,000,000 before the original widgets come to market (just before the end of year 1). At this point, the bank's balance sheet will momentarily look like that shown in Table 4.4.

From Table 4.4, it is clear that the first-mover will now be able to make a profit. Now, when the first batch of widgets comes on sale, there will be a profit of $500,000—not a loss. The details of this are provided in the second income statement in Table 4.5.

Table 4.2   "Wicksellian Bank" Balance Sheet #2[14]

Assets		Liabilities	
Loans:	1,000,000	Deposits, Nonbank Public:	1,000,000
	------------		------------
	1,000,000		1,000,000

Table 4.3   Income Statement #1[15]

Receipts:	$(0.8) \times (1,000,000)$	....	800,000
(minus)			
Repayment of Principal and Interest:	$1,000,000 + 100,000$	....	1,100,000

		(Loss)	**−300,000**

It is important to note, however, that as the ultimately successful producer (the first-mover) has now paid off the first loan at this stage the overall amount of the money supply left over (the total of bank deposits remaining) must have fallen. The question therefore immediately arises, for the future, whether there is going to be enough money around in the economy for the second-mover to be able to make a profit when the time comes. Another point to note is that the bank itself is now starting to build up its capital reserves (which were zero to start with). The increase in capital arises from the interest payments (profits to the bank) it has now received. Both of these points are illustrated in Table 4.6. From Table 4.6 it is clear that both the ratio of bank capital to total assets and the level of the money supply itself are actually endogenous variables. They are evolving over time as can easily be seen by comparing Tables 4.1, 4.2, and 4.4 with Table 4.6

As noted, the fall in the money supply inevitably raises the issue of how it is going to be possible for the second-mover also eventually to be able to "cash in," and make a profit. The answer has to be the same as before. In general, one sector or another of the economy must be continuously willing to become indebted so that current producers can make a profit. In our example, there would have to be a third "player." Therefore, let a third widget-maker become active and borrow a further $1,000,000, just before the second batch of widgets is brought to market (just before the end of year 2). The bank balance sheet will then look as it does in Table 4.7.

Given the figures in Table 4.7, we can see that the second-mover will now be able make a profit. This turns out to be $420,000 as shown in the income statement in Table 4.8. We must now sound another cautionary note, however. There are still positive profits at this point, but the profitability of widget-making seems to be falling over time. It has fallen from $500,000, in the first round of production, to $420,000 currently.

Further, the bank itself will now have received a second repayment of principal, and a second interest payment, and its capital holdings will again increase. The bank's balance sheet will now appear as in Table 4.9.

Clearly, we will next be faced with the question of how the third-mover (who has just bailed out the second-mover) will also be able to eventually make a profit. There must be a fourth player and so on. It is then very natural to ask the question how long can this process go on?

Table 4.4   "Wicksellian Bank" Balance Sheet #3[16]

Assets		Liabilities	
Loans:	2,000,000	Deposits, Nonbank Public:	2,000,000
	------------		------------
	2,000,000		2,000,000

Table 4.5 Income Statement #2[17]

Receipts:	$(0.8) \times (2,000,000)$	....	1,600,000
(minus)			
Repayment of Principal and Interest:	$1,000,000 + 100,000$	....	1,100,000

		(Profit)	**+500,000**

Table 4.6 "Wicksellian Bank" Balance Sheet #4[18]

Assets		Liabilities	
Loans:	1,000,000	Deposits, Nonbank Public:	900,000
		Bank Capital:	**100,000**
	-------------		-------------
	1,000,000		1,000,000

Table 4.7 "Wicksellian Bank" Balance Sheet #5[19]

Assets		Liabilities	
Loans:	2,000,000	Deposits, Nonbank Public:	1,900,000
		Bank Capital:	**100,000**
	-------------		-------------
	2,000,000		2,000,000

Table 4.8 Income Statement #3[20]

Receipts:	$(0.8) \times (1,900,000)$	....	1,520,000
(minus)			
Repayment of Principal and Interest:	$1,000,000 + 100,000$	....	1,100,000

		(Profit)	**+420,000**

Table 4.9 "Wicksellian Bank" Balance Sheet #6[21]

Assets		Liabilities	
Loans:	1,000,000	Deposits, Nonbank Public:	800,000
		Bank Capital:	**200,000**
	-------------		-------------
	1,000,000		1,000,000

Table 4.10 "Wicksellian Bank" Balance Sheet #7[22]

Assets		Liabilities	
Loans:	2,000,000	Deposits, Nonbank Public: Bank Capital:	1,800,000 **200,000**
	-------------		-------------
	2,000,000		2,000,000

To cut this potentially very long story short, the next two balance sheets in Tables 4.10 and 4.12, and the income statement in Table 4.11, will simply illustrate a further iteration of the process, in order to make clear the trends already discussed. At the end of year 3, if there is again some more borrowing before the end of the year, the bank balance sheet will be as shown in Table 4.10.

The third-mover is now able to makes a profit of $340,000 (thanks to the fourth-mover), as shown in the income statement in Table 4.11. However, note that the level of money profit achieved is again lower than was in the previous year. In the previous year profits were $420,000 and have now fallen to $340,000.

At the beginning of year 4 the bank balance sheet turns out as shown in Table 4.12. Notably, the bank owners' capital continues to pile up. Inevitably, therefore, in each year there will be less and less money available in the form of redeemable deposits (i.e., for actually spending on goods and services), than there was before.

By this time, it should be quite clear to the reader how the sequence of events will continue to unfold. The time will eventually come when there will actually be losses once more, and the system will collapse. In the next section of the chapter we will move on to discuss how these numerical results may be used to highlight some of the key implications for our understanding of such things as monetary production, the importance of bank credit creation, and the role of endogenous money

Implications of the Numerical Results

In summarizing the lessons that may be learned from the above numerical examples the first, and most obvious, question to be asked is whether or not the original proposed solution will provide a permanent resolution? That is, does it eventually lead to a positive steady-state equilibrium for money profits? To be clear, when using the term "equilibrium" in this context, I do not mean a full *macroeconomic* equilibrium of the type studied in chapter 2. That would require a situation in which none of the agents involved has any incentive to change their behavior. The numerical examples and anecdotes discussed in this chapter are clearly not "economic models" in that sense. In the present context steady-state equilibrium simply means a solution in which (if

Table 4.11 Income Statement #4[24]

Receipts:	$(0.8) \times (1,800,000)$	....	1,440,000
(minus) Repayment of Principal and Interest:	$1,000,000 + 100,000$	....	1,100,000

		(Profit)	**+340,000**

Table 4.12   "Wicksellian Bank" Balance Sheet #8[23]

Assets		Liabilities	
Loans:	1,000,000	Deposits, Nonbank Public:	700,000
		Bank Capital:	**300,000**
	------------		------------
	1,000,000		1,000,000

the assumed behavior of the agents continues indefinitely) the same level of *money* profits will be realized period after period. It has to do with the logical and arithmetical consequences of a certain assumed pattern of behavior rather than investigating the motivations for that behavior.

In any event, the original solution is not a permanent fix because holdings of the bank's capital keep piling up unused. As we have seen, after first recovering to some extent money profits will then gradually fall off again in each succeeding period. If nothing changes there will eventually be another serious crisis after only a few more iterations. In effect, what is happening is that the bankers are not spending enough money on Keynes's famous "riotous living" (Keynes 1930, 125). To get an equilibrium with positive money profits, in this particular case, we would actually have to let the bank owners spend (or dissipate) their capital at the same rate as everyone else, that is, at 80 percent. Another possibility would be to set the nominal interest rate at zero.[12] However, this last suggestion simply reaffirms the point that a solution with positive money profit is not necessarily a full macroeconomic equilibrium, We have already seen, in chapter 2 for example, that a nominal interest rate peg (whether of 10 percent as we started with here, or 0 percent, or any other number) will *not* lead to macroeconomic stability. A general lesson for economic theory and policy is that it is always necessary to set out the exact conditions under which equilibrium states of various kinds may be achievable—as we did in chapter 2. Then, in order to translate this into practical policy advice, the next step is to try to establish exactly what sort of policy framework is going to allow these conditions to occur in the real world.

Another question that can be asked is what do the numerical examples have to say about the usefulness, or otherwise, of banking regulation? Would the imposition of reserve requirements on the banking system, for example, be able to solve the potential problem? Reserve requirements are a type of banking regulation designed to affect the composition of the asset side of the bank balance sheet, and thereby restrain lending. For instance, the bank might be required to keep a certain percentage of their total assets on hand in the form of cash reserves. In our example, however, the only bank in the system is a single "Wicksellian Bank." There is no cash in the system, reserves are not required, and such regulation would be irrelevant. To deal with the same question more generally, we must go on to ask the further question of what actually *is* the "potential problem" here. In fact, the problem is not *enough* lending. Even if they could be applied, therefore, reserve requirements would actually be worse than irrelevant in this case. They would exacerbate the fundamental difficulty.

In a similar vein it could alternatively be asked whether imposing ex-ante capital requirements on the Wicksellian Bank would solve the problem. Once again, however, the answer is a definite no. Capital requirements are another form of bank regulation, in this case designed to affect the composition of the liabilities side of the bank balance sheet. The banking authorities, for example, may set a minimum ratio of bank capital to total liabilities (or assets) that the bank must keep. This will supposedly make the bank "sound." Once again, however, the problem is not the theoretical soundness of the bank but, to repeat, that there is not enough lending going on. In this particular case, if the bank had had to conform to a 10 percent or 12 percent capital requirement to start with, the very business of banking would never have got off the ground in the first place. The numerical examples have clearly shown that the capital-asset ratio of the bank is actually an endogenous variable. It depends exclusively on how the bank performs. In the case discussed here, we have already noted that as the situation develops the bank actually becomes *over*-capitalized. Bank capital keeps piling up as time goes by and there must *inevitably* be another crisis sooner or later—even if the bank passes every imaginable "stress test" at a given point in time.

The numerical examples studied here have deliberately been kept very simple, involving only three type of financial asset or liability, namely, loans, deposits, and bank capital. Other types of financial instrument have not been considered. But does this matter for the purposes of illustrating the main point we have making? Is there, for example, or could there be, any role for bond financing in these sorts of scenario? It would be possible, in fact, to complicate the argument in any number of ways. However, there seems to be nothing that could be added which would affect the basic conclusions. Our examples have, in effect, drawn attention to what circuit theorists have usually called "initial finance." This means the financing of the working capital, or variable capital, whereby the production process initially gets off the ground. This is achieved by bank lending. To close the circuit, however, there must also eventually be a supply of "final finance." According to Graziani (2003, 69–70):

> The liquidity collected by firms *either* selling final commodities or issuing securities can be denominated final finance. (Emphasis added)

In the widget problem the final finance obviously comes from the former source. The quote from Graziani, however, also makes clear that the two types of final finance are equivalent. Evidently, therefore, it would be quite feasible to set out another scenario, or scenarios, in which the firms also issue securities. More importantly, the process of working through the complete circuit with numerical examples has had the advantage of making it crystal clear that the ultimate source of final finance (to be obtained by either selling goods or by issuing securities) must be exactly the same as that of initial finance. It is still the case that some third party, somewhere in the system, must always continuously be willing to incur debt. Otherwise, there could be no money (bank deposits) in existence for anyone to be able for anyone either to pay the wage bill, or to buy securities or final commodities.

A further important question within the circuit theory framework—as Graziani (2003, 149–50) has also explained—is about the source of interest payments. In the widget problem it has been made clear that the genesis of the fund for making interest payments is also purely *monetary*. The funds from which interest payments were made arose, or rather created, in the course of the circuit itself. The rate of interest is once again shown to be an entirely monetary phenomenon (as Keynes had said), and not a "real" phenomenon supposedly derived from such things as the rate of time preference, or the marginal product of capital.

CONCLUSION

One thing that needs to be stressed in this conclusion is to reiterate the point, made above, that the numerical examples and anecdotes discussed in this chapter have been deployed for a specific arithmetic purpose. They do not constitute a complete macroeconomic analysis. Ever since I have started publishing articles on this topic, in the last few years, I have received several interesting communications and comments to the effect that, "if you change the assumptions of your *model,* the *results* would be . . . different . . . [in one way or another]" (my emphasis). There have also been several suggestions for *extensions* or *modifications* to the *model.* But, as I have said these exercises are not models, they are simply numerical exercises to make a specific point about the arithmetical logic of the system. In particular, about the necessity for continuous credit creation if there are ever to be monetary profits. It has not been possible in this chapter, for example, to discuss the relation between nominal money profit and real profits. The relation is indeterminate as it stands because in this chapter, unlike in chapter 2, we have not modeled a closed system with an exact theory of price determination. (On the other hand, various possibilities were briefly sketched out in the section on the Marxian monetary circuit above.)

Therefore, the most important lesson to be learned from the numerical examples does not have to do with alternative theories of inflation or economic growth but rather with the idea—essentially a question of economic sociology—that nominal or money profits must always be available *before* there can be any question of working out the total of real profits to be distributed. If, in the real world (as has so often been the case in practice) policy-makers are nonetheless tempted to try to reduce inflation via policies which will have the effect of reducing nominal profits, this is bound to lead to trouble.

Given that the numerical and other examples discussed in this chapter do not constitute a complete macroeconomic model further analysis would be required to be able to make specific recommendations about monetary or fiscal policy. The important outstanding issue in that field is clearly the monetary policy necessary to promote macroeconomic stability. In the widget problem nominal interest rates were set arbitrarily but, in chapter 2, it has already been shown that in a complete model a nominal interest rate peg leads to instability. Moreover, the instability can go in either direction. There could either be an "inflationary boom" or a "Great Depression" depending on the circumstances. Stability requires a "real interest rule" (Smithin 1994, 2003, 2009a, 2013a), To the contrary, and again as already noted in chapter 2, one of the most popular and widespread interpretations of the actual global financial crisis (GFC) of the early twenty-first century is that it was a consequence of the inherently unstable nature of the financial system, along the lines of Minsky's (1986, 1992) "financial fragility hypothesis." The latter stresses the changing incentive structure facing private-sector bankers as a boom proceeds, and the economy seemingly becomes more and more prosperous, leading to excessive credit creation. In this type of discourse there seems to be no rule which could potentially save the situation. It is simply thought that, eventually, a stage will be reached at which "what goes up must come down." This is a quite different point of view to the one that has been taken here, focusing on the structural weaknesses of the system, and also on the simple arithmetical logic that applies when there is not enough credit creation.

NOTES

1. In Smithin (2016b) I wrongly gave the date of publication of Marx's Vol. II as 1884. I must have been half thinking of Vol. III the publication date of which was 18*94*. I suppose that another intriguing possibility for, so to speak, "Freudian" error, given that we are discussing Marx, would have been the Orwellian *1984*. It is uncanny to me how all these dates fit seem to fit neatly together. Indeed, Orwell's date of writing was in 1948, exactly one hundred years after the *Communist Manifesto*.

2. In reality, Robertson started out as Keynes's student. "Pre-Keynes" here means pre-*General Theory*.

3. The "Derby" is a horse race in England, held at Epsom racecourse in June (it goes on to this day).

4. The symbol *d* means a "penny," from the Roman "denarius."

5. A "shilling" was another coin in circulation at the time (1922) worth 12 pennies.

6. Other classical commodity theories include Ricardo's original "corn model," and Sraffa's (1960) modern neo-Ricardian approach.

7. Recall the discussion of real versus monetary analysis (specifically with reference to Marx) in chapter 1 above.

8. In 1922, when Robertson was writing, the three-penny bit was already merely a token coin.

9. As discussed in chapter 1, economic theorists contributing to the "microfoundations of macroeconomics" literature do, of course, continue to favor the utility maximization approach (see also King 2012). However, there is a large and obvious disconnect between that theory and the methods by which the statistical national accounts data are compiled.

10. Irving Fisher was an American economist of the early twentieth century who did a great deal of work on the index number problem, with the objective of finding a valid aggregate price index that could serve as a guide for monetary policy. For this, he was much criticized by the "Austrian" economists of the time, such as Hayek, who did not believe that stabilization of the aggregate price level was a viable policy objective. There was, however, never any real objection to Fisher's technical work (Kresge 1995, 2). The supposed "ideal" index was the geometric mean of two other indices differing in their assumptions about the choice of base year, weights, and so on, and was therefore arguably more "efficient" or accurate than the original indices taken separately.

11. Recall, for example, the similarities between the Austrian theory of the business cycle and Minsky's financial fragility hypothesis that were discussed in that chapter. See also Smithin (2013a, 243–45).

12. I am indebted to Shakeb Abdul-Hakim for pointing out this possibility to me. There may also be other solutions which we have not yet seen.

13. When the charter is granted, just before the start of year 1.

14. At the beginning of year 1, after the first loan has been made.

15. After the first year, when the output has been sold.

16. Just before end of year 1, when there has been new borrowing.

17. With additional borrowing before the end of year 1.

18. At the beginning of year 2, when there has new borrowing before the end of year 1, but after the original widgets have been sold and the first loan is paid off.

19. At the beginning of year 3, when there has been new borrowing just before the end of year 2, but before the second batch of widgets is sold.

20. At the beginning of year 3 after the second batch of widgets has been sold.

21. At the beginning of year 3, when there has been new borrowing before the end of year 2, but after the second batch of widgets is sold and the second loan is paid off.

22. At the end of year 3 when there has been new borrowing just before the end of year 2, but before the third batch of widgets is sold off.

23. At the end of year 3 after the third batch of widgets has been sold.

24. At the beginning of year 4, after there has been new borrowing before the end of year 3, and after the third batch of widgets is sold and the third loan paid off.

Chapter 5

Interest Rates, Liquidity Preference, and Endogenous Money

INTRODUCTION

It has been made clear, in previous chapters, that one of the main collective contributions of the various heterodox schools of monetary thought has been to stress the importance of the endogeneity of money via bank credit creation (see also Smithin 2016a, 65–66). This issue was hardly discussed at all in mainstream economics after Keynes's death, not until the very end of twentieth century and the beginning of the twenty-first. Even then the model put forward by the so-called new consensus which emerged as the orthodox theory over the turn of the twenty-first century (and did allow for endogenous money), tended to obscure rather than clarify the issues at stake. This was probably inevitable given that Wicksell (1898), whose own work was more than a century old by this time, was explicitly or implicitly the inspiration for the new consensus (Woodford 2003). Neo-Wicksellian models are bound to carry a heavy load of intellectual baggage such as the bogus concept of the natural rate of interest. They also suffer from a failure to recognize that there can be multiple sources of inflation and deflation which is fatal once the idea of endogenous money has been admitted.

The common ground between recent neo-Wicksellian models and some of the earlier Post Keynesian theory is the idea that monetary policy is conducted via changes in the policy rate of interest set by the central bank, rather than by quantitative restrictions on the money supply. Although there was never any acknowledgement on the part of mainstream economic theorists, this change in the basic premises of the textbook model certainly validated the focus on interest rate behavior in the intramural debates among Post Keynesians in the 1980s and 1990s.[1] Those debates were particularly concerned with the relationship between the policy rate of interest and other interest rates in the system. However, there any similarities between Post Keynesian thought and that of the new consensus come to an end. By definition, a neo-Wicksellian model retains the concept of a natural rate of interest, and hence long-run neutrality with respect to both monetary and fiscal policy changes. As already argued in chapter 2, however, in reality neither monetary policy changes nor aggregate demand changes (from whatever source) are neutral. They affect real economic variables in both the short-run and the long-run.

As soon as the idea of endogenous money has been introduced, the other central issue in monetary theory is the question of what determines the rate of interest (Smithin 1994, 2003, 2009, 2013b), and particularly what determines the inflation-adjusted or "real" interest rate. The purpose of this chapter, therefore, is to explore the interaction between monetary endogeneity and interest rate determination in some detail. The chapter begins by addressing the myths surrounding the natural rate of interest which have prevented mainstream economics from ever being able to develop a viable financial theory. It then goes on to distinguish the invalid concept of the natural rate from the valid notion of the real rate of interest. Next, we review the main existing competing theories of the *nominal* rate of interest, namely, loanable funds theory, liquidity preference theory, and horizontalism, and also inquire how the traditional theory of the demand for money needs to be modified for the twenty-first century. The final sections of the chapter explain how the notions of liquidity preference and endogenous money may be reconciled, and will present a simple two-equation model of *real* interest rate determination able to take into account the all relevant factors.

The Myth of the Natural Rate of Interest

For two hundred and seventy years or more, at least since Hume (1752, 295–307) the bedrock of the mainstream/orthodox approach to the question of interest rate determination has been that the rate of interest is *not* primarily a monetary or financial phenomenon. Instead, it is supposed to be determined by the ubiquitous real forces in the economy of "productivity and thrift" (Humphrey 1983, 35). Wicksell himself famously wrote of the "natural rate" of interest in this vein, and provided a definition. According to Wicksell (1898, xxv):

> This natural rate is roughly the same thing as the real interest of actual business. A more accurate, though rather abstract, criterion is obtained by thinking of it as the rate which would be determined by supply and demand if *real* capital were lent in kind without the intervention of money. (Emphasis added)

It should immediately be clear from this wording, however, that the idea of the natural rate—influential though it has been throughout the history of economics—is untenable. Even in the basic definition Wicksell invokes an entirely hypothetical world which has no money but which nonetheless supposedly has a fully fledged market economy, presumably conducted by barter. In spite of its perennial popularity with those seeking a purely materialist and reductionist explanation of social phenomena, this notion is really little short of an absurdity. For the reasons set out in chapter 3 and 4 above (which discussed the nature of money) these are conditions which have never existed in the past, do not exist in the present, and could not possibly exist in the future (Ingham 2004, 2018, Searle 2010, Smithin 2013a, 2013b, 2016b, Weber 1927, Wray 2012). In a recent book entitled *Debt: The First 5000 Years*, the anthropologist David Graeber (2011, 21–41) has provided another explanation of why this is so with a chapter *explicitly* entitled "The Myth of Barter." But, if barter is a myth then, according to Wicksell's definition, it follows that the concept of a natural rate of interest must also be a myth.[2] It is sometimes argued to the contrary that the likes of Menger (1892), Wicksell (1898), and even Adam Smith (1776) in *The Wealth of Nations* were simply making thought experiments about exchange, and had no obligation to be historically accurate. However, if the objective is understand "actual business," in Wicksell's own unambiguous words, this is clearly not so. To put the point as straightforwardly as possible, how can there be actual business without a money of account and credit creation?

Keynes (1936, 167) in the *General Theory* (*GT*) had a much more common-sense definition of the rate of interest than that which typically appears in (either) microeconomic or macroeconomic textbooks:

> [It is]. . . (n)othing more than the inverse proportion between a sum of money and what can be obtained for parting with control over that money for a stated period of time.

Moreover, to his great credit Keynes, in the *GT*, explicitly repudiates the notion of the natural rate. Writing about his own earlier *Treatise on Money*, Keynes (1936, 242–43) frankly admits that:

> it was a mistake to speak of the natural rate or to suggest . . . [it] . . . would yield a unique value for the rate of interest irrespective of the level of employment. . . . I am no longer of the opinion that the concept of the natural rate of interest has anything useful or significant to contribute to our analysis.

This seems quite definitive. However, frequently commentators on Keynes have not taken these remarks as seriously as they might have done, or should have done. A prominent example is to be found in the work of Leijonhufvud (1981, 164–69) who argued at some length that Keynes should have adopted an intermediate position. This sort of response entirely misses the point about what Keynes was apparently trying to do whether or not he actually succeeded in persuading his colleagues in the economics profession at that time, or later (Smithin 2013b).

Real and Nominal Interest Rates

In reality there is no such thing as a natural rate of interest. However, the concept of the *real* rate of interest is still very important. As explained in chapter 3, in standard economics the strict definition of the real rate of interest is that it is equal to the nominal rate of interest (the percentage rate actually charged in the marketplace) less the expected inflation rate over the period of the loan. That is:

$$r = i - p_{+1} \tag{5.1}$$

Also, however, according to the prominent mainstream economist, Taylor (e.g., in his famous short paper on "Rules versus Discretion"), we can often use the simple inflation-adjusted interest rate as a "proxy for" (approximation to) the real interest rate itself (Taylor 1993). The inflation-adjusted real rate in this sense, also called the ex-post real rate, may be defined more straightforwardly. It is simply the nominal interest rate less the currently observed inflation rate;

$$\underline{r} = i - p, \tag{5.2}$$

Therefore, the level of $\underline{r}$ may be sometimes used as an approximation or "guesstimate" of what r itself is going to turn out to be. Contrary to Taylor and Wicksell, however, and also to the vast majority of professional economists right down to the present day, it must continue to be stressed that the real rate of interest on *either* definition can take on any value. It is not tied down by any natural rate.

Alternative Theories of Nominal Interest Determination

Strangely enough, in university level textbooks on money and banking and on finance, and in spite of the very well-known distinction between real and nominal interest rates just discussed, the treatment of interest rates is usually restricted to a few chapters about how the nominal rate is determined. This is a very telling omission. Moreover, although as explained by Hicks (1989, 102) there have historically been three broad classes of such theories debated, only one of the three ever makes an appearance in the contemporary classroom. We can identify the three historical theories as (i) loanable funds theory, (ii) liquidity preference theory, and (iii) Post Keynesian horizontalism. It is only the loanable funds theory that ever sees the light of day in current university courses.

Loanable Funds Theory

This was the name originally given to the theory put forward by Keynes's opponent Dennis Robertson in the 1930s (Robertson 1934, 83–91) and which, to this day, remains the only theory of interest rates deemed worthy of discussion in the textbooks. Keynes seems actually to have had the better of the argument with Robertson when they were both still living (Fletcher 2001, 2007). However, posthumously at least, Robertson's revenge in the classroom has been almost complete. The loanable funds theory simply postulates that there is a demand by borrowers for the soi-disant "loanable funds," denominated in the unit-of-account, that depends inversely on the nominal interest rate. Also, that there is a supply of such funds, from lenders, that depends positively on the nominal rate. The market interest rate, and the total sums lent and borrowed, are then supposedly determined by demand and supply equilibrium in the usual way, as illustrated in Figure 5.1.

It is clear that the standard predictions about interest rate behavior made by most economists emerge directly from an analysis of this type. If, for example, there is an increase in the willingness to save, that is, something causing a shift of the supply curve down and to the right, the interest rate will fall. If there is an increase in the willingness to borrow (causing a shift of the demand curve up and to the right), interest rates will rise. And so on.

Liquidity Preference Theory

This was the theory put forward by Keynes (1936) in the *GT*. In the version elaborated in that book, it depends on one of the most basic principles of asset pricing in financial economics, namely, that there is an inverse relationship between the price of bonds

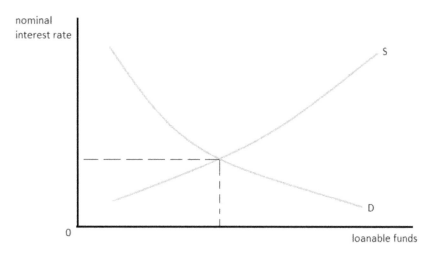

Figure 5.1   Loanable Funds Theory. *Source*: Author.

and current interest rates. The annual "coupon" payment on the bond, as it used to be called, is always based on the interest rate prevailing when the bond was first issued. Therefore, if current interest rates rise the price of the bonds must fall to make the yield competitive, and vice versa. Keynes would actually have put this point the other way round. Suppose that there is a fall in confidence about the future course of asset prices (a worry that asset prices may fall). Such circumstances imply an increase in the demand for money (an increase in the demand for *liquidity*), and a sell-off of financial assets (generically called bonds) to obtain the money. Keynes (1936, 196–97) called this the "speculative demand" for money. The price of bonds will therefore fall, and interest rates will rise. In short, an increase in liquidity preference leads to an increase in the interest rate. On the other hand, a decrease in liquidity preference in the same context implies the contrary belief that asset prices are likely to rise. This would cause a fall in the demand for money, an increase in the price of bonds, and a fall in the interest rate.

Consistent with Keynes's basic worldview note the appeal to psychological concepts such as "confidence," and implicitly to genuine uncertainty in the financial markets as opposed to probabilistic risk. There also seems to be a strong element of "self-fulfilling prophecy" in the argument. Worry that bond prices may fall actually does make them fall, and interest rates rise. Robertson (1939, 25) strongly objected to this, on the grounds that in Keynes's theory:

> the rate of interest is what it is because it is expected to become other than it is . . . [but] . . . there is nothing left to tell us *why* it is what it is. (Emphasis added)

Robertson is clearly looking for some sort of sheet anchor for the rate of interest similar to the old natural rate, but there is no such thing in Keynes.

It seems clear therefore that the liquidity preference theory in its *GT* version was Keynes's attempt to break with both natural rate theory and loanable funds theory. One weakness of his exposition, however (in addition to those to be discussed below), was that he mostly failed to make the distinction between real and nominal interest rates. This was admittedly true of most of the economics literature prior to the final quarter of the twentieth century and, as already mentioned, is still seemingly (deliberately?) so in textbooks on financial economics. But such vagueness makes it impossible to discuss the concept of the natural rate of interest in any serious way. Figure 5.2, therefore, attempts to provide a graphical illustration of Keynes's argument about nominal interest rates only. This was the argument actually made in the *GT*.

Starting from the putative loanable funds equilibrium, the diagram in Figure 5.2 shows what is supposed to happen to the rate of interest in the case of an increase in the speculative demand for money. The increase in liquidity preference causes a sell-off of bonds, and a fall in the price of bonds. Therefore, at least temporarily, there will be an increase in the rate of interest. In the diagram, the new higher level of interest is shown by the bold broken line.

The same graph, however, also shows how difficult it is to provide an overall evaluation of the effectiveness of the theory as presented in the *GT*. There is no doubt that Keynes's ideas about financial markets had great heuristic value in the turbulent environment of the 1930s and continue to do so to this day. From the point of view of technical economics, however, there was unfortunately a serious problem with the way in which the argument was expounded. As explained below, this problem does not actually confirm the intuitions of Robertson and Keynes's other contemporary critics on the matter. However, it certainly gave the critics *plausibility* at a crucial juncture in the debate, and arguably was an important factor leading orthodox economists eventually to repudiate Keynes's ideas.

The point being made here is that the diagram in Figure 5.2 also illustrates that the interest rate will not permanently stay at the new higher value desired or imposed by the "bears" in financial markets. Sooner or later, the interest rate will return to the original level shown by the fine broken line. The reason for this is that, specifically in the *GT*, but interestingly enough not in the earlier *Treatise on Money*[3] Keynes had conducted his analysis of the demand for money on the assumption that the money supply itself was fixed. This was a theoretical mistake sufficient to undermine the

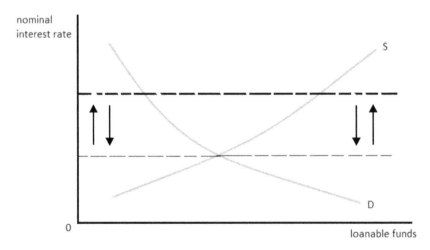

Figure 5.2 Liquidity Preference Theory. *Source*: Author.

whole basis of the formal theory, no matter how insightful and well informed were Keynes's other observations of real-world financial behavior. In the assumed circumstances of a fixed money supply, the problem is that if interest rates do indeed temporarily rise because of an increase in liquidity preference, then this is very likely to put deflationary pressure on the economy. Output prices are likely to fall. However, a fall in the aggregate price index, P, automatically has the effect of increasing the real value of the fixed nominal money supply, M. As P goes down, M/P goes up. The increase in the real value of money holdings can ultimately proceed to such an extent as to satisfy the original increase in liquidity preference altogether. This removes the upward pressure on interest rates and returns the nominal rate of interest to its original level.

This point was never properly understood by orthodox economists. Nonetheless, it so happened that in the decade or so after the publication of the *GT* certain variants of the theorem were stumbled onto by orthodoxy and used as weapons to challenge the theoretical bona fides of Keynesian economics. The general idea came to be known as the "Pigou effect" after Pigou (1943), or the "real balance effect" as in Patinkin (1948). The challenges were generally successful, tactically speaking, although the really important point about exogenous versus endogenous money was not appreciated. This is well illustrated, for example, by the highly inconclusive argument in Friedman's (1968) famous article in the *American Economic Review*.[4] This exercise was supposed to provide the coup de grace to Keynesian economics, but in the long-run ultimately failed to do so, at least from the rigorously theoretical point of view. In Friedman, as elsewhere, the real balance effect was interpreted as an argument in the consumption function, that is, as an argument in the Hicksian "IS curve" (Hicks 1937, 134).[5] A fall in prices was therefore supposed to directly increase consumption spending via some sort of wealth effect. However, this was by no means such as decisive argument as would have been the (correct) one outlined above. Only Hicks (1967b, 146–47) himself, to the best of my knowledge, in a paper that was originally a review of Patinkin's (1956) *Money, Interest and Prices* tried to make the argument that the real balance effect also applied to the "LM curve" and he was roundly criticized by his fellow neoclassical economists for doing so.[6] Nonetheless, even if orthodox economists did not understand the reason why, there was indeed a genuine theoretical problem with the exposition in the *GT*. The only way it could have been avoided was if the nominal money supply itself had been allowed to fall endogenously as the deflation proceeds, as described. It can therefore certainly be argued that Keynes's omission in this respect greatly facilitated the restoration of the loanable funds theory to pride of place in the textbooks, and in academia generally.

Post Keynesian "Horizontalism"

The name for this last approach derives from the title of Basil Moore's famous book *Horizontalists and Verticalists* (1988). Another work frequently cited as foundational for this point of view is Kaldor's *The Scourge of Monetarism* (1982). Marc Lavoie (1992), himself a well-known horizontalist, has also pointed out that these ideas were anticipated some twenty years earlier by the French economist Jacques Le Bourva in 1962.

The basic idea of horizontalism is simply the observation that central banks typically conduct monetary policy mainly by setting the policy rate of interest, essentially the rate at which commercial banks can borrow central bank money in the overnight market. As explained in chapters 1 and 2, I have chosen the generic term "policy rate" because this very short-term interest rate goes by many different names (or aliases) in the different institutional settings. In the United States it is called the federal funds rate, in Japan the overnight call rate, in the Euro-zone the main refinancing rate, in Canada the overnight rate, and so on. Historically, monetary theorists also used to write about such things as "bank rate" or "discount rate." (These were rates of interest at which the central bank would lend directly to the commercial banks.) Whatever the exact terminology or precise institutional arrangements, however, the idea is that the central bank usually accommodates the demand for commercial bank reserves at the policy rate. The given setting of the policy rate is then thought simply to feed through to interest rates in general. Ultimately, the argument is that the supplies of both credit and money become infinitely elastic at the market rate thus established.

For example, let i_0 be the nominal policy rate of the central bank (as mentioned, it is called the overnight rate in Canada), and i_L stand for the nominal commercial bank lending rate. Similarly, let i_D stand for the nominal commercial bank deposit rate. The commercial bank deposit rate is usually a "markdown" from the policy rate.[7] Therefore, we can write:

$$i_D = m_1 i_0, \qquad 0 < m_1 < 1 \tag{5.3}$$

Thus, if m_0 stands for the markup between commercial bank deposit and lending rates:

$$i_L = m_0 + m_1 i_0, \qquad m_0 > 0 \tag{5.4}$$

The expression in equation (5.4) therefore explains commercial bank nominal lending rates. It is essentially the transmissions mechanism of monetary policy. Furthermore, as i_L must be competitive with the general rate of interest on loanable funds, i, we can also write $i_L = i$, and:

$$i = m_0 + m_1 i_0, \tag{5.5}$$

The supply curves of both money and credit become horizontal lines at this rate. Figure 5.3 shows how this situation might be graphed in the loanable funds diagram, where the total amount of lending is "demand-determined" along the horizontal supply curve. (The same would be true of the quantity of money in an alternative money demand and supply diagram.)

As suggested, the term horizontalism was originally associated with certain members of the Post Keynesian school in the 1980s and 1990s. However, other Post Keynesians of the time were actually more concerned with the preservation of Keynes's insights about liquidity preference as discussed in the previous section. This latter group came to be known as structuralists. Hence, this gave rise to debates between the "horizontalist" and "structuralist" factions among Post Keynesians during the 1980s and 1990s. And, recall that the structuralist position was there could

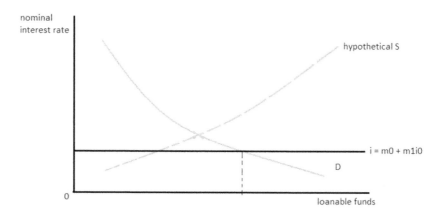

Figure 5.3 Horizontalism. *Source*: Author.

indeed be slippage between the policy rate and the other interest rates in the system. An important question, therefore, is whether or not it is possible to reconcile these two Post Keynesian positions in any way? I would argue that the answer to this is yes, and that the key to the reconciliation is, once again, the treatment of endogenous money.

The Demand for and Supply of Endogenous Money

It was mentioned earlier that one point of common ground between the neo-Wicksellian models of the new consensus and some Post Keynesian theory was the assumption of endogenous money—but not much else. Actually, this is not quite right. There was one other thing, namely, the relative neglect of the demand side of the money demand-supply nexus. In the mainstream literature at the end of the twentieth century papers began to appear with titles like "Doing without Money" (Woodford 1998), "Keynesian Macroeconomics without the LM curve" (Romer 2000), and so forth. On the heterodox side another name for the horizontalists was "accomodationists" (see, for example, Pollin 1991, Rochon 1999), also implying that the supply of money, *Ms*, would always passively adjust to the demand for it, *Md*. It nonetheless remains true that holdings of bank deposits at any point in time must, by definition, be equal to the supply of bank deposits in existence at that time. Somehow, deposit holders have to be willing to hang on to these sums rather than spend them, and contrary to most of the fin-de-siècle literature this fact should surely always be taken into account in macro-economic modeling. In short, even with an endogenous supply of money it continues always to be true that;

$$Md = Ms. \qquad (5.6)$$

And thus, as soon as there is any "voluntary" element to the demand for money (Hicks 1967a, 15–16), the idea of purely passive adjustment is untenable. Therefore, in some recent work (e.g., Smithin 2013a, 228–30, 2016a) and also in chapter 2 above, I have put forward a simple theoretical framework to discuss these issues of endogenous money supply *and* demand. In these exercises, the voluntary demand for money is expressed as a fraction of nominal GDP and the supply of money as a multiple of the lagged nominal wage bill. That is:

$$Md = \psi PY, \qquad 0 < \psi < 1 \tag{5.7}$$

$$Ms = \phi W_{-1} N_{-1}, \qquad \phi > 1 \tag{5.8}$$

where M stands for broad money supply, consisting primarily of commercial bank deposits, and WN stands for the nominal wage bill. It was explained in chapter 2 that the supply function in (5.8) originally derives from circuit theory (Graziani 2003, 29) and also, that if the economic system is to be *viable* in the sense of being able to generate positive money profits, the coefficient ϕ must be greater than unity.

Note that the expression for money demand in (5.7) is fairly straightforward. On the other hand, the history of money demand theory in the textbook macroeconomics of the second half of the twentieth century was very convoluted. (This may, perhaps, have been one reason why both Post Keynesian horizontalists and neo-Wicksellian economists were eventually happy to ditch the idea of money demand altogether.) However, this was a serious mistake on both their parts. What seems to have occurred is that over time Keynes's original expression "liquidity preference" gradually lost much of its meaning. It came to be used merely as a synonym for the demand for money, rather than as an alternative theory of interest rate determination. The well-known journal article by Tobin (1958) was very influential, negatively, in this respect. Its title was "Liquidity Preference as Behavior towards Risk," that is, as opposed to fundamental uncertainty. Tobin's stochastic theory of money demand was fairly complicated and, as already argued in chapter 1, made a number of strong (and frankly unwarranted) assumptions about the applicability of statistical probability theory to the problem. The typical textbook theory was somewhat more straightforward than this, but nonetheless also argued that the demand for real money balances, M/P, depends positively on real income, Y, and negatively on the nominal interest rate, i. That is:

$$M/P = L(Y,i). \qquad L_y > 0, L_i < 0 \tag{5.9}$$

This formulation tries, not very successfully, to combine the notion of a "transactions demand" for money with that of "speculative demand," where both terms are originally due to Keynes in the *GT*. In spite of these impeccably Keynesian origins, and in a very strange twist to the narrative of the history of economic thought, the approach was actually common to both the so-called Keynesians and so-called monetarists during the famous debates between these two schools in the mid-twentieth century (Leeson 2003a, 2003b, Smithin 2004). Students of the period were led to believe that there was somehow a great theoretical divide between the two groups although in reality they were all mainstream/neoclassical economists. Their approach to the theory of money demand was identical.

The most significant thing about the shared theory was that in order to bring in the interest rate argument it had to be assumed that money is not interest-bearing. Money was thus taken to consist of only notes and coins plus any non-interest-bearing bank deposits. In the modern era, however, in which almost all money does consist of bank deposits which all (at least potentially) do bear interest, there is really no justification for this. Hicks (1989, 103–4) put the point in this way:

> We are well on the way to a credit economy in which any money that does not bear inter-est has become no more than small change or petty cash. It is surely as least a tolerable simplification to which an economic theorist is accustomed to take it that this has already happened.

Hicks is pointing out that in principle a bank deposit is effectively a loan from the depositor to the bank and that there is no reason why it should *not* bear a market-determined interest rate. This passage was written in 1989, at a time of high interest rates, but the point is not affected by the observation that in a period of low interest rates in general, such as the present, the interest rate on bank deposits may again fall to very low levels. This will change quickly enough as soon as the overall of level interest rates has risen sufficiently once more The quote from Hicks thus suggests that whenever we think about the demand for broad money in the modern credit economy, the relevant bank deposits should be treated in principle as interest-bearing. Reverting to the Keynesian terminology used above it therefore seems that we are left with only a "transactions demand" for this type of money. The demand for money function must once again become something similar to the expression in equation (5.7).

In chapter 2 above we already noted that the combination of equations (5.6), (5.7), and (5.8), repeated in the present chapter, implies that the value of the aggregate price level, P, must satisfy (that is, be consistent with):

$$P = (\phi/\psi)(W_{-1}/A). \tag{5.10}$$

This expression includes the ratio of two terms, ϕ relating to the supply-side of the money market, and ψ which relates to the demand-side. Also in chapter 2, a proposed specification for the behavior of the ratio ϕ/ψ was as follows:

$$\phi/\psi = [(\phi_0/\psi_0)]e^{-\lambda(r-r_{-1})}. \qquad 0 < \lambda < 1 \tag{5.11}$$

This contains a version of Keynes's (1936, 196) "speculative demand" for money, as well as a speculative *supply* of money (unlike in Keynes) arising from bank loans for things other than the wage bill.[8] Note also that as the two relevant monetary magnitudes, ϕ and ψ, are themselves real variables (dollar values divided by some relevant price index) the speculation must always be supposed to about real asset prices and real interest rates. This is a different argument altogether from the textbook idea that the demand for real money balances depends on nominal interest rates as in equation (5.9).

Another important result from chapter 2 was that this particular type of speculative behavior might actually be eliminated altogether provided that the central bank fol-lows some sort of real interest rate rule (Smithin 2007, 2016a, 2016c). The specific rule that was suggested in chapter 2 was as follows:

$$r_0 = r'_0 + \left[(1 - m_1)/m_1\right](p - p_{-1}), \tag{5.12}$$

where r'_0 is the chosen target for the real policy rate. If the central bank is indeed pursuing such a rule equations (5.10) and (5.11) will reduce to:

$$P = [(\phi_0/\psi_0 W_{-1}]/A \tag{5.13}$$

Thus, in the lowercase notation introduced earlier, we can derive an equilibrium theory of inflation as follows:

$$p = p_0 + w - a, \tag{5.14}$$

where lowercase a stands for the natural log of labor productivity, w is the natural log of the equilibrium average real wage rate (such that $w = w_{-1} = w_{-2} \ldots$ etc.), and p is the inflation rate.

However, from the point of view taken in this chapter, although the real rate rule is stabilizing to some extent this does not eliminate the problems of changes in liquidity preference entirely. It only deals with those changes which come about from rationally speculating about the future course of real interest rates. We should recall from chapter 2 that the term p_0 (equal to $ln\phi_0 - ln\psi_0$) is also a sort of inverse measure of the overall state of liquidity preference—not in the sense of the speculative demand of the *GT* but rather the more generic "bullishness" and "bearishness" of the *Treatise on Money*. The point is that monetary policy may be able to remove or dampen the strictly "rational-speculative" element in interest rate forecasts, but cannot deal with changes in sentiment inevitably arising from fundamental uncertainty.

As p_0 is an inverse measure of liquidity preference, this implies that when liquidity preference *increases* (an increase in "bearishness") p_0 goes *down* and vice versa. As was the case with speculative demand (and supply), the p_0 measure of liquidity preference is also relevant to both sides of the money market. It involves both the willingness to hold or absorb money balances (illustrated by the $ln\psi_0$ term), on the one hand, and a reluctance to borrow for whatever reason (illustrated by $ln\phi_0$) on the other. An increase in bearishness, for example, implies simultaneously an increased willingness to hold commercial bank deposits and a reduced willingness to borrow from those same banks. It causes a fall in the p_0 term and ultimately via equation (5.14) in the inflation rate. Conversely, a reduction in liquidity preference will mean both a reduced willingness to hold commercial bank deposits and an increased willingness to borrow to acquire securities. In this case, there will be an increase in the p_0 term and therefore in the inflation rate.[9]

Thus far, we have seen only how changes in liquidity preference broadly defined may affect the inflation rate. We have not yet discussed the effect on interest rates which was the original point of Keynes's argument. This topic is taken up in detail in the next section.

Liquidity Preference and the Real Rate of Interest

The debate between the horizontalists and structuralists in the 1980s and 1990s was about the need to reconcile the notions of endogenous money, central bank "interest rate operating procedures" (Lavoie and Seccareccia 2004, 4), and the intuitive idea from Keynes that liquidity preference also matters for the determination of interest rates. In fact, all of these things are entirely compatible.

In the absence of a natural rate of interest, however, it is important to move beyond the strict terms of reference of the twentieth century debate, to recognize that the most important point at issue is really about the determination of real interest rates, not just nominal interest rates. If, as suggested above, the central bank can target the real policy rate then they will certainly also have much influence over the real interest rates that will actually be paid by borrowers, including those paid by business firms making investments. That said, however, it is by no means a contradiction to suggest that liquidity preference considerations can also separately influence the effective real rate of interest paid by borrowers.

The shift in emphasis from nominal interest rates to real interest rates is highly significant from the point of view of both monetary theory and social ontology. The argument is ultimately that it is the real rate of interest that can properly be described as a "monetary phenomenon," in every sense of that term. We would have a "*monetary* theory of the *real* rate of interest" (Burstein 1995, emphasis added), as opposed to either a real theory of the real rate of interest, or a monetary theory of the nominal rate of interest. To see the force of the argument we can use the device of subtracting the observed inflation rate, p, from both sides of equation (5.2) above. This will give:

$$i - p = m_0 + m_1 i_0 - p. \tag{5.15}$$

Rearranging, the operation will yield;

$$r = m_0 + m_1 r'_0 - (1 - m_1) p, \tag{5.16}$$

where r'_0 is the target for the real (inflation-adjusted) policy rate of interest, as defined in chapter 3 above. As already mentioned, out of equilibrium $i - p$ is a "proxy for" the true real rate of interest, and in equilibrium $i - p$ and $r = i - p_{+1}$ coincide.

Therefore, if the central bank is following a real interest rate rule for the policy rate, equation (5.14) shows that there is a *negative* relationship between the inflation rate and the general level of real rates of interest in the marketplace. Historically, this kind of relationship was known as the "forced saving effect," or similar, reflecting the idea that the saving, supposedly necessary for more investment, is brought about involuntarily by higher inflation. As explained by Smithin (2013a, 185–88) a more accurate term would have been "forced investment" and, in the "Austrian" business cycle theory of the 1930s, due to Mises (1934) and Hayek (1935), the term "overinvestment" was actually used—albeit in an entirely pejorative sense. The Austrians thought that investment brought about in this way could *not* ultimately be successful in increasing the per capita capital stock and per capita output, because it violated their theoretical notions of economic equilibrium. They thought that the "overinvestment" would merely cause an inflationary boom, and then have to be painfully undone in a subsequent recession or depression. Later in the twentieth century, the forced saving effect was revived and dubbed the "Mundell-Tobin effect" after the work of Mundell (1963a) and Tobin (1965). In that literature, the opposite argument to that of the

Austrians was made, that inflationary finance might potentially succeed in increasing output. Needless to say in all periods these types of results have been subject to much debate (Blanchard and Fischer 1989, Hayek 1932, Kam 2002, 2005, Kam and Smithin 2012, Smithin 2013a, Walsh 1998). The reason for this is that if the forced saving effect was actually seen to work, it would go completely against the grain of almost the entire corpus of classical, and neoclassical, economics (Humphrey 1983, Smithin 2013a).[10] With this background, the importance of equation (5.16) is that it shows up the existence of a negative relationship between inflation and the real rate of interest in a fairly simple and straightforward way against which there can hardly be much argument. This is an important finding in its own right whether or not the Mundell-Tobin effect actually does causes *forced* saving (note emphasis), or indeed has any bearing at all on the ethics of income distribution.

As we have seen, the inflation rate p depends on p_0, the inverse measure of the state of liquidity preference. Therefore, an increase in liquidity preference (for example) must cause a fall in p_0, then a fall in p, and via equation (5.16) an increase in the real rate of interest. On the other hand, a decrease in liquidity preference (an increase in bullishness) causes the real interest rate to fall. The results therefore turn out to be very similar to Keynes's original arguments, but with the emphasis shifted to real rather than nominal interest rates and without the theoretical flaws of Keynes's own approach. This, therefore, is the solution to the problem of reconciling the different views on interest rate determination in the endogenous money environment. The central bank is undoubtedly in a position to set the real policy rate, if it chooses to do so, and the level of this real policy rate does feed through to affect the average level of real interest rates in general. At the same time, changes in liquidity preference may also affect the differential between the real policy rate and real interest rates in the market. There is no contradiction.

A Simple Two-Equation Model of the Real Rate of Interest

It is now possible to put together a simple formal model with two equations jointly explaining the determination of the real interest rate and the inflation rate. From equations (5.14) and (5.16), above this will be:

$$p = p_0 + w - a \tag{5.17}$$

$$r = m_0 + m_1 r_0 - (1 - m_1) p. \tag{5.18}$$

Next, solving explicitly for real rate of interest rate, we have;

$$r = m_0 + m_1 r_0 - (1 - m_1)(p_0 + w - a). \tag{5.19}$$

The real rate of interest, therefore, depends positively on the real policy rate, positively on liquidity preference (bearishness), negatively on the (natural logarithm of) the average real wage rate, and positively on the (natural logarithm of) average labor productivity.

The equilibrium can also be depicted in graphical form as in Figure 5.4. The symbol r_0 stands for the real policy rate of the central bank, and it has already argued that if the central bank behaves sensibly it will be trying to stabilize that rate at some given level, r'_0. However, if the central bank neglects this advice and either makes a deliberate change in the real policy rate, or passively allows such a change to happen, these "policy errors" (Collis 2018) will always be reflected in changes in real interest rates generally.[11]

An increase in the real policy rate, illustrated by a vertical upward shift of the downward-sloping line in the diagram, will increase the overall level of real interest rates while leaving the inflation rate unchanged. A reduction in the real policy rate will cause the overall level of real interest rates to fall.

In addition, something like the original Keynesian argument about liquidity preference continues to have relevance. An increase in liquidity preference (a fall in the p_0 term), shown by a shift to the left of the vertical line in the graph, will both increase the real interest rate and cause a fall in the inflation rate. The opposite is true for a fall in liquidity preference (an increase in "bullishness").

Changes in labor productivity, in this context shown by changes in the term a, also cause changes in the real rate of interest. An increase in a (which is the natural logarithm of average labor productivity) shifts the vertical line in Figure 5.4 back, and to the left, reducing the inflation rate and raising the real interest rate. A fall in labor productivity has the reverse effect. To be sure, arguments to the effect that changes in productivity cause changes in real interest rates are not uncommon in the mainstream literature. However, we should be careful to explain exactly what is happening in this particular case. There is quite a different mechanism at play than is assumed in orthodox theory. It involves not only the changes in productivity themselves but also, in a major way, the attendant financial considerations. In the case of an improvement in productivity, there is first a fall in the inflation rate via equation (5.14). Then there will be an increase in the real rate of interest via the Mundell-Tobin effect in (5.16).

An increase in real wages with no change in productivity, shown by a shift of the vertical line in Figure 5.4 to the right, has the opposite effect to a productivity

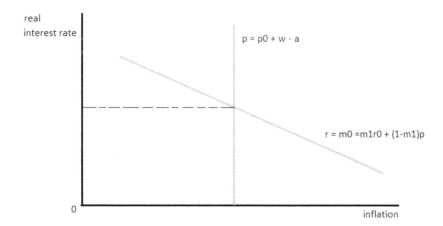

Figure 5.4   Real Interest Rate Determination. *Source*: Author.

improvement. It will cause inflation to rise, and real interest rates to fall. Conversely, a real wage cut, shifting the vertical line to the left, causes inflation to fall and the real rate of interest to rise. Interestingly enough, many years ago Hicks (1935, 65) had already addressed this question of the effect of real wage changes on interest rates, and found it something of a puzzle. He could come up with both an argument to the effect that a rise in wages leads to a fall in interest rates—and also the opposite. Hicks reconciled these two positions, somewhat unconvincingly, by suggesting that one effect applies in the short-run and the other in the long-run. In the present case, however, the final answer is quite definitive. There is a negative relationship between real wages and real interest rates in both the short-run and the long-run.

CONCLUSION

According to Keynes (1936, 408) capitalism is best described as a monetary production economy. In such an economy, the money supply must be an endogenous variable if the system is to function at all. However, it is not clear that Keynes himself sufficiently recognized this point, or took it fully into account in developing his version of the liquidity preference theory of interest rate determination. In a system of "capitalist credit money" (Ingham 2004a) the money supply is endogenous almost by definition. The central bank sets the nominal policy rate of interest (i.e., the rate of interest that must be paid to obtain reserves of base money), and can also (if they have the administrative/political will) set the real policy rate, simply by following a rule which adjusts the nominal policy rate for inflation. The level of the real policy rate, however determined, is then passed through to a greater or lesser extent to real interest rates in general. At the same time, liquidity preference considerations also have a considerable effect on the overall level of real interest rates. In an endogenous money environment there is no contradiction between these positions.

APPENDIX: HOW DOES THE CENTRAL BANK
SET THE POLICY RATE OF INTEREST?

Although the overall demand for interest-bearing money cannot reasonably be thought to depend on the level of nominal interest rates as such, nonetheless we can still continue to argue that the demand for base money (or bank reserves) does depend negatively on a *particular* nominal interest rate. Specifically it will depend upon the central bank policy rate of interest, as illustrated in Figure A5.1.

Why is this? In the first place much of the monetary base, for example the currency itself, clearly does not bear interest. Moreover, even for that part of the monetary base which is interest-bearing (such as, in some jurisdictions, commercial bank deposits at the central bank) the relevant interest rate, the policy rate itself, is effectively set by the central bank.

As can be seen in the diagram horizontalism therefore does "work," in a quite precise sense, in the analysis of the overnight market for "federal funds" (the American term), if not for interest rates in general. The central bank itself sets the interest rate

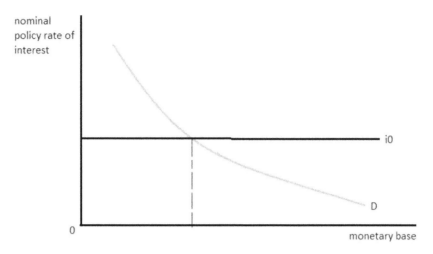

Figure A5.1   Demand and Supply in the Overnight Market. *Source*: Author.

relevant to that particular market, and the actual level of the monetary base is demand-determined by the position of the demand curve for central bank money, given the interest rate.

Figure A5.2 is a useful diagram to illustrate precisely how the central bank might go about setting the nominal policy rate.

The horizontal axis in Figure A5.2 depicts the levels of "settlement balances," S, of the commercial banks in the clearing house. For any individual bank these will be positive or negative—on either side of the line vertically above zero in the diagram.

If a bank has positive settlement balances they will receive the deposit rate paid by the central bank, or i_{CD}. If they have negative balances, they will have to borrow in the overnight market to make up the deficit. To set the policy rate, the central bank arbitrarily fixes the rate at which they will lend directly to the commercial banks (sometimes known as the "bank rate," or i_B), and also the band between this rate and the rate the central bank pays the commercial banks on positive balances. Very often

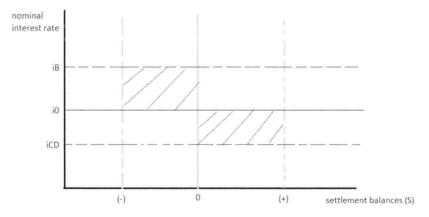

Figure A5.2   Setting the Overnight Rate (Policy Rate). *Source*: Author.

the band will be something like 0.5 percent. The policy rate therefore always comes in somewhere inside the narrow band between bank rate and the central bank deposit rate. In fact, the policy rate will end up at whatever level the central bank wants it to be, within the band.

To explain, look at the matter first from the point of view of those institutions that are in a deficit position. If they can borrow funds at a lower interest than bank rate they will do so. Similarly, if a bank in a surplus position can get a higher interest rate by lending those funds in the overnight market at i_0, rather than by leaving them on deposit with the central bank at i_{CD}, they have every incentive to do so. The sums saved and gained respectively are shown by the shaded areas in the diagram, and the market will therefore settle at i_0. In addition to this, note that there is a wide range of financial techniques at the disposal of the central bank to push the whole market into a surplus or deficit position, if they so decide. These include open market operations, drawdowns and redeposits, purchase and resale agreements, and so on.[12] In the limit, therefore, the overnight rate could be pushed as high as the bank rate, or as low as the central bank deposit rate, or anywhere in between.

NOTES

1. See the comprehensive work by Rochon (1999) entitled *Credit, Money and Production* which describes the state of play in this debate between "horizontalists" and "structuralists" at the end of the twentieth century.

2. As discussed in chapter 1, this is far from being a question of historical importance only. The same idea, under different names, has survived and thrived in twenty-first century "micro-based" macroeconomics, albeit by various sleights of hand. In the ubiquitous dynamic stochastic general equilibrium (DSGE) model, for example, an unobtrusive device that does the trick is the assumption of a constant rate of time preference. This simply fixes the real rate of interest rate for all time. However, this sort of argument falls apart as soon as it is allowed that time preference can change (Kam 2000, 2005, Smithin 2013a). A recent paper by Kam, Smithin, and Tabassum (2016) sums up the technical details of this issue in a mathematical idiom accessible to contemporary graduate students and young PhD economists, a group who most likely will not have had the requisite training to follow the arguments from social ontology and the history of economic thought.

3. For further discussion of the changes in Keynes's theory of money and banking between the *Treatise* and the *General Theory* see Smithin (2013e).

4. This was Friedman's Presidential Address to the American Economic Association (AEA).

5. The letters IS stand for "Investment-Saving" that is, the real side of the economy (including real consumption, $C = Y - S$). Hicks actually put these letters the other way round (SI).

6. LM = "Liquidity-Money." This came to be the generally accepted lettering in the literature. For some reason, and as is well-known, Hicks himself used the notation LL which was less appealing to most of his readers.

7. This used to be called the "two-for-one rule," as explained by Rogers and Rymes (2000, 259) implying that the markdown was exactly 0.5. However, that idea was based on the assumption that commercial bank expectations of being "out of the money" at the clearing house are normally distributed. This is implausible in the extreme. In reality, the markdown is larger than 0.5 but still less than 1.0.

8. For example, literal financial speculation, consumer spending, capital expenditure, and so on. All of these things have a forward-looking aspect to them.

9. The p_0 term actually turns out to a flexible tool for the discussion of both monetary policy and also other macroeconomic changes. It is possible, for example, to discuss the (supposedly) new or "unconventional" policy of quantitative easing, introduced in the early twenty-first century, by considering changes in p_0. In its current usage the expression "quantitative easing" implies the purchase of government bonds of varying maturities by the central bank in an effort, quite literally, to increase the quantity of the monetary base. In the context of equation (5.14) these actions would bring about an increase in p_0, and hence in the inflation rate, through its impact on the $ln\phi_0$ term. In the actual experience quantitative easing did not work implying an offsetting change in $ln\psi_0$, leaving p_0 unchanged.

10. However, Kam (2000, 2005), Kam and Smithin (2012), and Smithin (2013a), have shown that the various and sometimes ingenious arguments that have been made against forced saving effect, or Mundell-Tobin effect, do not hold up theoretically.

11. In chapter 2 it has already been argued that current central bank policy, of setting the nominal policy rate of interest rate at periodic intervals, essentially *guarantees* that the central bank will continuously be making such errors.

12. The details may be studied in any textbook on money and banking.

Chapter 6

Interest, Profit, and Wages

INTRODUCTION

In monetary macroeconomics it is crucially important to distinguish between the real rate of interest on money and the profitability of business enterprise (Smithin 2012, 2013a). The former is a monetary phenomenon, as claimed by Keynes,[1] whereas the latter is in the nature of a "surplus" over and above the costs of production, including financing costs.[2] There must therefore be an inverse relationship between the real rate of interest and the average or aggregate business markup. Income distribution is the primary channel through which monetary policy affects the economy, and higher real interest rates, for example, will have a direct negative impact on both real wages and entrepreneurial profit. Interest on money is something that is in a different category altogether from profit. Therefore, there must be a three-way split in the functional distribution of income—between interest, profit, and wages—rather than the simplistic two-way split, between the "wage share" and the "capital share" that is most often discussed in the literature.

In the standard or mainstream approach to economics, however, the rate of interest is often simply identified with the "rate of return to capital," or some such, so that a high rate of interest means the same thing as a high rate of return to capital. For policy-makers and market participants this is bound to be confusing when applied to practical discussions of monetary policy. In the latter context, the more usual (common-sense) argument is that higher interest rates will tend to reduce profitability by causing an economic downturn. The reason for these inconsistencies seems to be a combination of both ontological uncertainty about the two concepts, interest and profit, as well as the reflexive use by most economists of competitive marginalist analysis even in the macroeconomic context in which demand constraints are pervasive, and the existence of large imperfectly competitive firms cannot be ignored (Kaldor 1983, 1985). And, in fact, there really is no theory of profit as such in neoclassical economics. Therefore, in the first instance we must turn to either the old Marxian theory, or the still older classical theory, to find any real attempt at the explanation of profit. The older theories, however, are also very far from completely satisfactory. The overall purpose of the present chapter, therefore, is to present a synthetic theory of profit and of the functional distribution of income in general to illustrate these points, and in an attempt to avoid the problems found with all of the earlier theories.

It should always be remembered that there are two aspects to a theory of profit. As already discussed (in chapter 4 for example), the first aspect is the "technical" *monetary* question of how it is possible for monetary profits that are denominated in the unit-of-account actually to be realized. In terms of the discussion in chapter 4, how can it be true that M' is numerically greater than M? As we have seen, this requires a theory of endogenous money and credit creation. The second aspect, however, is the issue of "real" profit, and this is the domain of the present inquiry. How does the system generate a surplus in the form of goods and services that is greater than the amount of goods and services used up in production? This is the question of the distribution of real income. In modern terms it would typically be posed as the question of the distribution of real GDP. For example, what determines the "profit share" in real GDP?

A main conclusion of the analysis is that profit is essentially in the nature of what used to be called "differential rent." We should be careful however, to note that this highly ambiguous term (rent) should be applied to the specific characteristics of each business *firm*, including demand conditions, rather than (say) to plots of land or individual pieces of machinery. The outcome of the "struggle over income distribution" is then ultimately determined by, (a) considerations of effective demand (as Keynes did try to argue in the 1930s), and (b) the bargaining power of the main players, including business itself, labor, and the financial interests. In a further complication, having just suggested that profit is essentially differential rent to the firm, we must recall that the financial interests themselves have also, confusingly, often been called the "rentier" interests.[3] So to be clear about terminology, in what follows profit is considered to be that which accrues to entrepreneurial business, wages accrue to labor, and interest accrues to the holders of financial capital (the soi-disant "rentiers").

Alternative Theories of Value and Distribution

As already suggested the orthodox neoclassical theory of economics provides little or no help in discussing profit. In the supposedly "best developed model of the economy" in that tradition (Hahn 1983, 1), that is, the Walrasian general equilibrium (GE) model, there is no profit at all in equilibrium. Total income is distributed between wage earners and a sort of "rental return" (again note the awkward terminology) to each of the different types of purely physical capital. Nothing remains as a surplus over and above the costs of production, and nothing is left that is recognizable as profit in the accounting sense. It is allowed that short-run profit may accrue to a firm in disequilibrium, that is, if it gets into a temporary position with some sort of monopolistic advantage before other competing firms can enter the market. In fact, it is only such fleeting situations that are (improbably) supposed to provide the incentive for firms to engage in productive activity at all. In the long-run, all short-run profits are competed away, allowing the firm only to cover the costs of production.

As neoclassical theory is silent on the question of profit, it is necessary to turn back to older sources, such as the Marxian and "classical" theories. More than sixty years ago these three different approaches were usefully compared to one another in an important, but now neglected article, by Kaldor (1955–56)[4]. In that same paper,

Kaldor also put forward what he described as a "Keynesian" (i.e., a demand-side) theory of income distribution, and this Kaldorian construct must also be discussed. It will be argued, however, that the genuinely Keynesian credentials of Kaldor's approach are dubious.

Classical and Neoclassical Theory

Kaldor used Ricardo's famous "corn model" of rent, profit, and wages, to illustrate the pre-Marxian classical theory.[5] In this picture of the world, labor is applied to agricultural land to yield "corn" (i.e., grains such as wheat or barley), supposed to be the only product available in the economy. Production is subject to diminishing returns, and both the average product (AP) and marginal product (MP) of labor are falling. Total employment, however, is not determined by any sort of marginalist principle. The real wage, also measured and paid in corn, is taken to be a constant close to the subsistence level. The demand for labor is thus actually predetermined each period by a previously accumulated "wage fund" of stored-up corn. This fixes the amount of labor demanded at each real wage, and therefore also the amount of labor actually employed, and the level of output. Kaldor (1955–56, 85) provided the following simple diagram, now reproduced in Figure 6.1, to illustrate the "corn model" as well as to exemplify the classical theory in general.

The only role played by marginalism in this analysis, a concept that later on came to dominate economics completely, is to determine the total of ground rent (once again, note the multiple meanings of this confusing term). This is given by the cumulative difference between the average product (AP) and marginal product (MP) of labor as applied to intra-marginal land, multiplied by the amount of employment, and accrues to the landowners. Profit is then whatever is left over for the organizers of production, who are basically tenant farmers. It is equal to the difference between the MP of

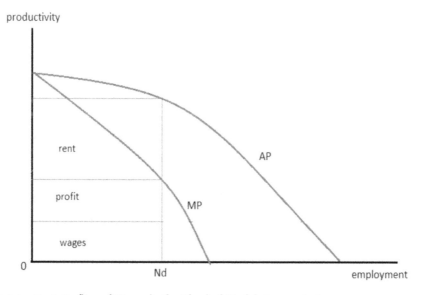

Figure 6.1   Rent, Profit, and Wages in the Classical Model. *Source*: Author.

labor and the real wage, again multiplied by the amount of employment. In the era of classical economics, this basic theory of profit and rent was made the centerpiece of a whole series of theoretical propositions about the causes of growth, tax incidence, the merits of free trade versus protection, and so on.

The later neoclassical economists certainly would not have accepted the implicit demand constraint that fixes the amount of the employment of labor at *Nd* in the diagram. Indeed, one of the main tenets of late nineteenth-century neoclassical economics was the supposed refutation of the wage fund argument. The underlying idea of demand constraints which can limit the amount of employment was abandoned. It did not re-emerge until advent of Keynesian economics in the mid-twentieth century, when it took a completely different form. Then, with the resurgence of the neoclassical school to total dominance in academia in more recent times, the notion of demand constraints was promptly dropped once again. There matters rest.

The original neoclassical argument, still very much alive in the theory of "perfect competition" a century-and-a-half later, was that the firm is so small in relation to the market that it simply *believes* that it can sell all it wants to at the going price. Such firms need not be (and are not) constrained from employing more people by any sort of demand restriction, either in terms of an a priori wage fund, or any other demand constraint. Wages are, ultimately, thought of as simply a share in the output produced and are received ex-post, not in advance. This is basically an underlying "pay as you go" argument, the idea being that the incomes created can always be shared out after the product has been sold.[6] Therefore, the position taken by the neoclassical economists, and by all of their successors in orthodox or mainstream economics down to the present day, was that employment should be pushed to the point where the real wage equals the MP of labor. This is the level of employment *Ne* in Figure 6.2.

In this vision of the world profit disappears entirely, and the whole distribution of income is ultimately only between the two primary factors of wages and ground rent. Nor is there any room for interest on money. These highly abstract and unlikely

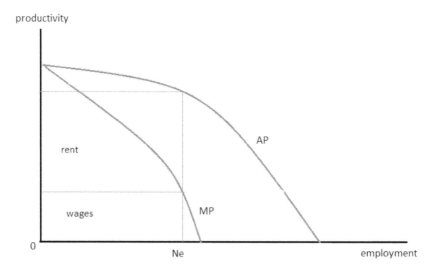

Figure 6.2 The Real Wage Rate Equals the Marginal Product of Labor. *Source*: Author.

ideas have somehow survived to dominate economic discussion down to the present day. Moreover, interestingly enough, they also correspond precisely to the picture of the orthodox theory painted by Schumpeter (1934, 3–56) back in the early twentieth century, in Chapter 1 of his *Theory of Economic Development* entitled "The Circular Flow of Economic Life." Schumpeter was ahead of modern economists, however, in that, although paying obeisance to this type of construction on the grounds that it is a "useful starting point," Schumpeter was also one of the first to recognize that it would hardly do as a theory of *capitalism*. This is why he found it necessary go on to develop his own theory of "creative destruction" the purpose of which was to give some sort of account of where it is that profits actually *come from*. Common sense, after all, dictates that the profit motive should a prominent role. Moreover, and as already suggested in earlier chapters if, as we must) we take into account the role of the banking and financial sector in financing of production, it is simply not credible that real interest rates will automatically fall to zero in equilibrium. This could actually only happen as the result of a deliberate episode of central bank policy. Failing this, even in a static circular flow there must always be an interest charge on the wage bill. This is because, as shown in chapter 4 above, credit creation and the monetary circuit must continue to be in play for even the most routine circulation of commodities to occur.

The current mainstream theory of distribution, ruling the textbooks, simply generalizes from the picture of Figure 6.2. Instead of having one variable factor, labor, and one fixed factor, land, the more modern neoclassical theory dispenses with land altogether and adds an alternative variable factor, the so-called capital whose reward is also determined by marginal productivity. The result is the standard theory of distribution that informs the literature on the "aggregate production function" and the many variants of the "neoclassical growth model" descended from Solow (1956)—a construct that still appears in the opening chapter of many current undergraduate textbooks. In Walrasian GE theory, the same basic idea is generalized to include multiple variable factors.

The Marxian Concept of Surplus Value

Aside from Kaldor's paper, there are clear expositions of Marx's theory of surplus value in such sources as Sweezy (1942, 56–71) and Rima (1996, 220–43). The reason it is now worth reexamining the Marxian view or some features of it, in spite of the obvious anti-capitalist bias, is that it does at least address the question of the existence and origins of profit. This is a subject that orthodox economics, supposedly the staunch defender of capitalism, studiously avoids.

Marx used the term value in a specific sense. He put forward a version of the labor theory of value whereby the value of any commodity is given by the amount of "socially necessary labor time" that went into its production. Using the notation that appears (for example) in Sweezy (1942, 63–71) recall that, in Marx, the expression for total value is given by a formula such as:

$$value = s + c + v \tag{6.1}$$

where s stands for "surplus value," c for "constant capital," and v for "variable capital." The meaning of so-called constant capital is that it is supposed to account for the amounts of physical capital equipment and raw materials that are "used-up" in the production process, again measured as "stored-up labor time." It is the value of the combined total outlay on depreciation plus raw materials. *Variable* capital, meanwhile, is "the value of the outlay on wages and salaries" (Sweezy 1942, 63). As already discussed (in chapter 4 above) a main argument in Marxian political economy is that the value of variable capital needed to actually sustain the workforce will be less than the total value created during the working day. In an eight-hour day, for example, the time necessary to produce the equivalent in goods and services of the wage bill may be only five hours. What is produced in the remaining three hours is the surplus value. This is the term *s* in equation (6.1) and accrues to the employer as profit.

In many ways equation (6.1) is just an accounting identity, similar (for example) to the modern concept of GDP, or to the income statement of an individual firm. This is one of its strengths as compared to marginal analysis. It simply adds the wage bill *v*, depreciation *c*, and the profit or surplus *s*. It is true that from the perspective of a pre-Marxian classical economist there is one obvious omission. No allowance is made for the ground rent. But Marx was well aware of this and made the explicit assumption that ground rent is zero (Sweezy 1942, 67).

There is another omission, however, this time from the standpoint of a modern monetary economist which seems more serious on general theoretical grounds. This is that, in the formula $s + c + v$, no account seems to be taken of interest on money as anything separate from, or different to, the profit or surplus itself. In effect, as noted by Moseley (Moseley 2016, 389), Marx's analysis is based on the assumption that the original split between labor income and the total of non-labor income is pre-determined by the theory of value set out in *Capital* Vol. I. Later on, in Marx's Vol. III, there then has to be a *further* discussion of the distribution of the given total of non-labor income between interest and profit. It is posited that ex-post there must be some kind of intramural dispute between the two types of "capitalist," within the broader class struggle, over the distribution of the pre-determined total surplus. A major disadvantage of this procedure is that it rules out any useful discussion of a three-way split as in the classical theory just discussed, or as one later finds in Keynes (1923, 1936).

In any event, in Marx the overall rate of profit, *p*, including interest, is given simply by the ratio of surplus value to total capital:

$$p = s/(c + v) \tag{6.2}$$

Equation (6.2) defines profit as a percentage of the total value of capital used-up in the production process, rather than as a percentage of the total value of capital employed. The latter is probably the more usual definition, but Marx can get around this with no real loss of generality by assuming that all capital turns over exactly once during the production period (Sweezy 1942, 67–68). In other words, and presumably for the purposes of the exposition only, the depreciation rate is assumed to be 100 percent.

The point at which Marx does get into difficulties, however, is not in defining the average markup for the economy as a whole, or in working out a rate of profit for each individual enterprise, or each industrial group, but in the simultaneous insistence that

Table 6.1   Examples of Value Calculations

Firm	c	v	s		Value
1	80	20	20	=	120
2	50	50	50	=	150

the process of competition must equalize the rate of profit across all industrial sectors. This is what causes confusion, in the standard interpretation of Marxian scheme, between values as defined in terms of their labor inputs and the prices observed in the actual economy. It thus gives rise to the so-called transformation problem (Bortkiewicz 1907, Moseley 2016, Steedman 1977, Sweezy 1942). The argument is that the ratio of constant capital to total capital $[c/(c + v)]$, a ratio Marx calls the "organic composition of capital," is bound to differ between industries depending on their technical requirements. Therefore, if the rate of profit is to be equalized between those same industries, the prices charged by each of them must differ from their supposed values. The following numerical example is perhaps the simplest way to understand the point being made.

For the sake of simplicity, suppose that we have a world consisting of just two "industries," with just one large "firm" in each, whose value calculations work out as in Table 6.1.

For both firms/industries the rate of surplus value the ratio of the surplus value to the wage bill (s/v) is 100 percent. However, the organic composition of capital $[c/(c + v)]$ in each case is different. Firm 1 has an organic composition of capital of $[80/(80+20)] = 0.8$ but, in Firm 2, the organic composition of capital is $[50/(50+50)] = 0.5$. If the goods are to be exchanged at their values, the rate of profit in Firm 1 will be $[20/(80+20)] = 20$ percent, and in Firm 2 $[50/(50 + 50)] = 50$ percent. For the economy as whole the aggregate value calculation is as shown in Table 6.2:

Table 6.2   The Economy-Wide Value Calculation

C	v	s	Value
130	70	70	270

In the overall economy the organic composition of capital is $[130/(130+70)] = 0.65$, and the economy-wide rate of profit is $[70/(130+70)] = 35$ percent. If the rate of profit is be equalized across the two firms/industries, therefore, the rate of profit must somehow rise from 20 percent to 35 percent, in the case of Firm 1, and fall from 50 percent to 35 percent in Firm 2. This will require a redistribution of the total amount of surplus value between them. Thus, comparing the prices actually received to their theoretical values, the results are as in Table 6.3:

The beginning value of firm capital is 100 in both cases. Thus, the conclusion is that price has to be increased by 15 units from putative value in the case of Firm 1, and reduced by 15 units in the case of Firm 2, to generate a uniform rate of profit of 35 percent. Simple and stylized though the above example may be, it nonetheless suffices to illustrate the basic issue debated in the academic literature on the transformation problem in Marx.

As already suggested, however, from the point of view of a workable theory of profit the main problem is actually not with the logic of the calculation of the organic

Table 6.3   Deviations of Price from Value Required to Equalize the Rate of Profit

Firm	Value	Price	Deviation of Price from Value
1	120	135	+15
2	150	135	−15

composition of capital, but with the further assumption that rates of profit between the different industries should be "equalized." How is this supposed to happen? The usual answer, as noted by Rima (1996, 234–35), is that:

> economy-wide equalization is brought about by inter-industry capital movements. If the rate of profit is above average in . . . (some) . . . industries . . . capital will tend to be attracted from industries . . . where the rate of profit is lower than average, until the average is . . . (the same) . . . for all.

This is clearly not an idea unique to Marxism. It was taken directly from classical economics, and continues to live on in mainstream/neoclassical textbooks to this day. Of exactly what, however, is this "capital"—flowing from one place to another—supposed to consist (Smithin 2009, 95–96)? If the notion of capital involves specific items of physical plant, equipment, and machinery, then the image of these things being attracted to, or flowing from, one industry to another is a problem. It is true that devices such as Marx's labor theory of value itself (or even merely using a common unit of account) are able to solve the problem of heterogeneity from the purely accounting point of view (Moseley 2016, 296). However, this does not dispense with the physical reality. It may be possible to imagine an individual machine being unbolted from one location, sold secondhand, and moved to another, but even then it would have to be used for a purpose somewhat similar to its original function. It is simply not possible to visualize a broad mass of physical things being switched effortlessly from one entirely different purpose to another. It is really only capital in the sense of money itself that can really move from one industry to another with any degree of fluency. But constant capital, in particular, *is* supposed to consist mostly of physical things such as materials and machines. This in itself therefore casts serious doubt on the existence of any smooth mechanism to equalize industrial profit rates. The same sort of argument also applies to the sociological concept of human capital things like expertise and experience gained in a particular field. Thus a world of generic imperfect competition, and therefore inevitably some sort of demand constraint for at least some individual firms and in aggregate—combined with the imperfect mobility of physical capital—the transformation problem would be made redundant (Smithin 2012, 311). There would be an individual version of equation (6.3) even down to the level of each enterprise, defining the rate of profit in that enterprise. There would also be aggregative versions for each industry and for the economy as a whole summing up all the individual equations. The result would be conceptually similar to Kalecki's notion of the "degree of monopoly" (Kalecki 1971, 45). From the aggregative equations it would still be possible to make meaningful macroeconomic statements about changes in the overall profit markup and, from the point of view of political economy at least, nothing essential would be lost in terms of the vision of capitalism that can be achieved.[7]

"Keynesian" Theory?

According to Kaldor (1955–56, 95):

> Keynes, as far as I know, was never interested in the problem of income distribution as such. One may nevertheless christen a particular theory as "Keynesian" if it can be shown to be an application of the specifically Keynesian apparatus of thought and if evidence can be adduced that at some stage in the development of his ideas Keynes came near to formulating such a theory.

In my view, however, the theory that Kaldor then put forward was not really very Keynesian at all—at least not in the sense of closely following the leads set down by Keynes. In the first place, Kaldor assumed just two categories of income (wages and profits) which, as we have just seen, is clearly a Marxist rather than a Keynesian or classical assumption.[8] On the other hand, when Keynes does talk about income distribution, for example, in the *Tract on Monetary Reform* (Keynes 1923, 5–32), there were usually three rather than two categories, namely the "the investing class,"[9] "the business class," and the "earner." As mentioned, the soi-disant investing class are also sometimes called "rentier[s]" (Keynes 1923, 40), and the very same language recurs thirteen years later in the *General Theory* itself, as in the discussion of "The Euthanasia of the Rentier" (Keynes 1936, 374–77) in chapter 24. Another problem with Kaldor's distributional theory from a strictly Keynesian point of view is that he specifically assumes full employment (Kaldor 1955–56, 95). On the face of it, coming as it did some twenty years after the first publication of the *GT*, this assumption seems quite un-Keynesian.[10]

The basic idea in Kaldor's theory was that each of the two remaining categories of income recipient have different "propensities to consume" out of their respective incomes. Specifically, he assumed that the propensity to consume out of wages is much higher than out of profits. The most extreme version of this is to assume workers do not save at all and that the only saving is done by capitalists. In that case the share of profit Π, in income Y, is given by;

$$\Pi / Y = (1/s_\Pi)(I/Y), \tag{6.3}$$

where I is investment spending, now in the modern economist's sense of this term (i.e., spending on physical capital equipment), and s_n is the propensity to save out of profits. Kalecki, who earlier had put forward a somewhat similar theory of profit (Kalecki 1937, 35–42), is reputed to have characterized this situation as "workers spend what they get and capitalists get what they spend" but (apparently) did not actually record this statement anywhere in his published work (King 2016, 11, Toporowski 2013).

One thing, however, that Keynes, *contra* Kaldor, did say about income distribution (in a discussion in the *Tract*—having to do with the effect of inflation on income distribution between the *three* categories of income recipient) was that "the same man may deal, earn, and invest" (Keynes 1923, as quoted by Smithin 1994, 182). If so, this must pour cold water on the idea that qua consumers the "earners," "investors," and "dealers" would have dramatically different proportional consumption/saving propensities out of their respective incomes. And later on in Keynes's writings, for example in the *General Theory*, for the most part they do not seem to do so. Moreover, also in the GT itself, the entrepreneurs (to give this group a more reputable label than Keynes's original "dealers")[11] are taken to be the ones who typically undertake *additional* spending, over and above their consumption needs, on investments in fixed and circulating capital. Logically, therefore, this would seem to imply that, under capitalism, an increase in profits at the expense of the other two income categories would actually increase the total of effective demand (Smithin 2009, 2013a).[12] Admittedly there is one passage in the *General Theory* in which Keynes (1936, 262) does raise the *possibility* that workers may have a higher consumption propensity than the other "factors of production" (i.e., presumably the entrepreneurs). However, the allusion is not made in the context of a theory of income distribution, and does not take into account the additional investment spending by the entrepreneurs. It appears only in a discussion about whether or not wage flexibility can restore full employment, and seems altogether tentative and exploratory. No claims are made about magnitude, and there is no suggestion that this effect would ever be enough to offset the profit incentive for investment. Moreover, the remarks are made explicitly in the context of a return to Keynes's original three-way distribution between wages, interest, and profit from the *Tract*, in which current rentiers, by definition, must have been saving to some extent when they themselves were workers and/or entrepreneurs. Otherwise how did they ever get to be rentiers? Keynes's brief treatment of this issue in Chapter 19 of the *General Theory* does not therefore seem to affect the validity of the broader statement made above—that an increase in profits at the expense of other income shares will tend to increase overall effective demand. It should finally be noted that Kaldor's original reference to Keynes coming "near to" his (Kaldor's) own theory of income distribution does not actually refer to the relevant passage from Chapter 19 of the *GT*, just discussed, but rather to the chapters on the "Fundamental Equations" in the *Treatise on Money* (Keynes 1930, 120–53) which were later superseded by the *General Theory* itself (see Smithin and Kam 2018).

The upshot of the argument is that probably the most representative interpretation of Keynes's final or mature position on income distribution would be to retain the idea of a threefold distribution of income between entrepreneurs, workers, and rentiers but, also, not to let the several changes in distribution between these three groups have very much effect on the macroeconomic propensity to consume. This, after all, was the working assumption throughout most of the theoretical exposition of Keynes's major book.

An Alternative Theory of Profit

The objective of this penultimate section of the present chapter is to put forward an alternative synthetic theory of profit to summarize the basic arguments made above. However, this theory will need to be "more general," in three separate senses, than the discussion thus far. First, there is no reason why it should rest on the classical and neoclassical premise of diminishing marginal productivity or, a slightly different point, on any marginal principle at all. Secondly, as in Keynes (1936), it should indeed allow for the presence of demand constraints that limit the output of each individual firm, and also in aggregate. Thirdly, there should be three basic categories in the functional distribution of income, wages, profit, and interest—rather than just two.

The synthetic theory can be derived from the following two equations:

$$PY = \Pi + \left(1 + i_{-1}\right)W_{-1}N_{-1} + (1 + i_{-1})P_{-1}U_{-1} \qquad \left(\text{nominal revenue}\right) \qquad (6.4)$$

$$Y = AN_{-1} \qquad \left(\text{production takes time}\right) \qquad (6.5)$$

Here Y stands for real output produced in the last period and sold in the current period, and P for the price level. Therefore PY stands for nominal revenue in the case of an individual firm, or (say) for nominal GDP in aggregate. As already discussed several times in previous chapters, for theoretical consistency in the aggregative version the symbols should be taken as referring to flows of funds rather than the imputed values provided by the statisticians. Recall, for example, that the GDP numbers reported in the national accounts are not "stock-flow consistent" (Godley and Lavoie 2007, Palley 2015, Tymoigne and Wray 2015, Wray 2012). Although in practice the GDP numbers are all there is for empirical work, the theoretical development will need to be much more precise.

With this qualification, the money value of variable capital can be identified with the nominal wage bill $W_{-1}N_{-1}$ (in this case the lagged nominal wage bill), where W_{-1} is the lagged nominal wage rate and N_{-1} is the lagged level of employment. The term U_{-1} is meant to be a concept similar to Keynes's (1936, 66–73) "user cost" (from which the symbolism is derived) or, alternatively, to Marx's "constant capital." It represents the starting money value of the amounts of raw materials and physical capital equipment "used-up" in the production process. The nominal interest charge levied on both "variable capital" and "constant capital" is i_{-1}. Following tradition, the Greek uppercase symbol Π stands for the net profit (surplus value in Marx). Evidently equation (6.4) does have a mathematical structure somewhat similar to the Marxian value equations discussed above. It is crucially important to note, however, that it is expressed in money terms only.

Equation (6.5) allows for the basic fact that production takes time (and, hence, the need both for the interest charge and the necessity for entrepreneurs to form expectations) via the device of a one-period production lag—the simplest possible. Although this specification only shows explicitly the relation between output and labor inputs, it by no means ignores the constant capital component. As we have seen, this is carefully accounted for in the definition of profit. In effect the contributions of the various machines, technical knowledge, raw materials, and so forth, are rolled up in the term A. What emerges is perhaps best described as a "*virtual* labour theory of *production*" (Smithin 2012, 225, emphasis added) rather than a labor theory of value. It is a rival, or antidote, to the familiar "*AK*" model of contemporary neoclassical growth economics (Jones 1998, 148–50) and accepts without reservation Keynes's (1936, 41) view (as discussed in chapter 1) that it is best to restrict attention to "quantities of money-value and quantities of employment" rather than to attempt the quixotic task of trying to attaching a concrete meaning to the notion of the capital stock.

Next, introduce two more definitions:

$$s' = \Pi / \left[W_{-1} N_{-1} \left(1 + i_{-1} \right) \right], \tag{6.6}$$

$$k' = P_{-1} U_{-1} / W_{-1} N_{-1}. \tag{6.7}$$

The first of these is similar to the rate of surplus value in Marx but with the addition of the explicit interest charge on the "variable capital." The second relates to Marx's notion of the organic composition of capital or the more familiar capital-labor ratio from neoclassical economics. Therefore, equation (6.5) can be rewritten as:

$$PY = (1 + s' + k')(1 + i_{-1}) W_{-1} N_{-1}. \tag{6.8}$$

Finally, let the symbol k (different from k') stand for the "gross entrepreneurial markup," such that $k = k' + s'$. The newly defined markup factor, k, includes an allowance both for depreciation on physical capital and for the rate of surplus value. It is a "gross" markup in that sense but note also that it is "net" of the nominal interest charge. Thus, equation (6.9) becomes:

$$PY = (1 + k)(1 + i_{-1}) W_{-1} N_{-1} \tag{6.9}$$

This therefore expresses money value as a multiple of the original investment in variable capital (also measured in money terms). The multiplying factor covers the three main elements in the accounting scheme, that is, the interest charge, depreciation on fixed capital, and net profit.

We can now employ the mathematical technique of taking natural logarithms of each variables, employing the widely used approximation that $ln(1+k)$ and $ln(1+i)$, for example, may be represented by k and i respectively. This gives:

$$lnP = k + i_{-1} + lnW_{-1} - lnA. \tag{6.10}$$

Next, subtract lnP_{-1} (the natural log of the lagged price level) from both sides of the equation and rearrange. The result is:

$$k = lnA - \left[i_{-1} - \left(lnP - lnP_{-1} \right) \right] - \left(lnW_{-1} - lnP_{-1} \right), \tag{6.11}$$

where the term in square brackets, $[i_{-1} - (lnP - lnP_{-1})]$, is simply the lagged nominal interest rate minus expected inflation at time t_{-1}. (In other words, it is the lagged real interest rate, r_{-1}.) Also, let lowercase w stands for the natural logarithm of the real wage rate, such that $w_{-1} = lnW_{-1} - lnP_{-1}$, and lowercase a for the natural logarithm of labor productivity, $a = lnA$. Then from (6.11) the basic theory of profit can more simply be written as:

$$k = a - r_{-1} - w_{-1}. \tag{6.12}$$

This is an "adding up" theory expressed in terms of logarithms or percentages. It states that the gross markup is equal to the natural logarithm of labor productivity minus the lagged real interest rate, and minus the natural logarithm of the lagged average real wage rate.

From a behavioral perspective it is a great advantage that k is the *expected* markup as this (obviously) is what is relevant for actual economic decision-making, both at the level of the individual firm, and in aggregate via summation. In equilibrium, actual and expected k will coincide. But, also, both in equilibrium and out of it, there always exists a subjective value of k, at both the firm and aggregate levels (Kalecki 1943, 47–48). To be clear, however, k is not an expected profit *rate*. As explained, the latter concept is difficult to define and, moreover, is hardly meaningful at the aggregate level. There is a closer analogy to the Marxian concept of the rate of surplus value—albeit in this case with an allowance for depreciation. To be sure it remains possible for each firm to define for themselves either an expected, or (eventually) an ex-post, accounting rate of return in the course of individual business decision-making. Presumably each of them will be doing so. In specifying an aggregative *behavioral* model, however, the k term itself is by far the more useful concept, and is the most appropriate specification for use as an incentive variable—for example, in an aggregate investment function. This is because an increase in the k term is a prerequisite both for an increase in the rate of surplus value and also overall (on average) for increases in the various ex-ante rates of return that are used as individual decision metrics. Each firm is also individually aware of the depreciation allowances that must be set aside under alternative business plans.

In equilibrium the theory of income distribution becomes simply:

$$k = a - r - w. \tag{6.13}$$

Therefore, when expressed in terms of logarithms or percentages, the natural logarithm of labor productivity resolves into *three* components, not just two, profit, real interest, and the real wage.

Graphical Illustrations

We now turn to a graphical analysis in order to illustrate some implications of the theory set out in equation (6.13). Suppose in the first instance, that labor productivity can be taken as given, determined by whatever stage of technological development the society has reached. The term a will therefore be a constant. This does *not* mean, however, that the "capital stock" itself, regardless of how this is defined, is supposed to be held constant.[13] Similarly we will take it that the real interest rate is determined in the financial sector (ultimately by the policy of the central bank), and that real wages have been determined by some sort of bargaining process reflective of the socio-political conditions. In these circumstances, the profit markup k will be the residual component of income after the other shares have been decided. This is the situation depicted in Figure 6.3 which graphs the natural logarithm of output per head against the natural logarithm of the level of employment.

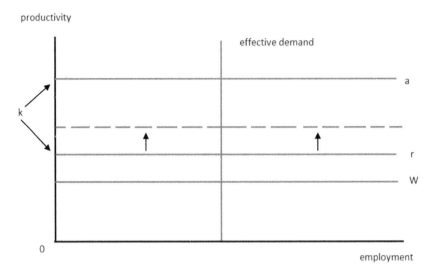

Figure 6.3   Distribution of Income between Wages, Interest, and Profit. *Source*: Author.

Taking a cue from Keynesian economics, the actual level of employment is determined by a demand constraint—depicted here as a vertical line. As simple as this diagram is, it immediately answers the original question about the relation between interest and profit. If there is an increase in real interest rates this will cut into the profit share, and vice versa.

Meanwhile an increase in aggregate demand itself (a relaxation of the demand constraint) increases output and employment in an essentially Keynesian manner. In Figure 6.4, we note that output and employment are indeed increased as a result of an increase in effective demand. However, because the income shares are pre-determined by assumption, there is no change in the distribution of income between interest, profit, and wages.

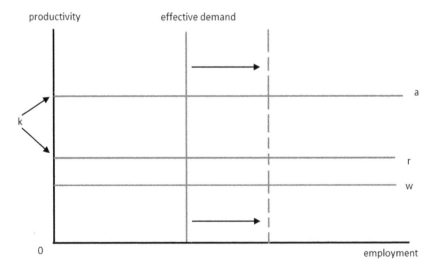

Figure 6.4   An Increase in Effective Demand. *Source*: Author.

A More Interesting Diagram?

The graphical analysis in Figures 6.3 and 6.4 suffices to make the main points about income distribution and effective demand that were advertised in the introduction. However, a more interesting, and informative diagram would (for example) put the rate of real GDP *growth* on the horizontal axis instead of employment. This would make the income distribution theory commensurate with the alternative monetary model (AMM) of Smithin (2013a) that was discussed in chapter 2 above. It will also be interesting to add an explicit wage function. For the closed economy AMM, for example, recall the wage function was specified as follows:[14]

$$w = t + h_0 + h_1 y, \qquad 0 < h_1 < 1 \tag{6.14}$$

These changes will yield the graphical illustration depicted in Figure 6.5. This is a more sophisticated construct than was shown in Figure 6.2, but evidently, the basic result about the inverse relationship between interest and profit, derived earlier, remains unchanged.

Finally, Figure 6.6 shows the effect of an increase in the rate of demand growth in the new circumstances. Once again, the fundamentally Keynesian result from the static case carries though to the growth context. However, with this specification of the wage function, although a demand expansion continues to improve the overall economic situation, it also *reduces* the aggregate markup. This may not, therefore, seem like much of an "improvement" from the point of view of entrepreneurs. The reason for this result is that real wages are rising as employment rises and the growth rate is increasing, but productivity and the real interest charge are assumed to stay constant.

It would not, however, be correct to describe the situation in Figure 6.6 as a "falling *rate* of profit" as in Marx. It is not the rate of profit but the average markup that is falling, as demand increases and the economy expands. Nonetheless the falling markup

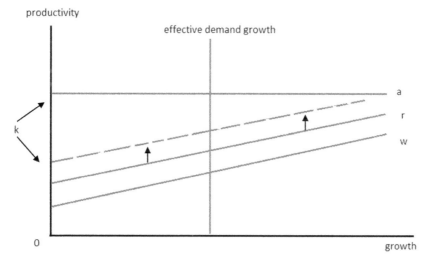

Figure 6.5   Income Distribution and Economic Growth. *Source*: Author.

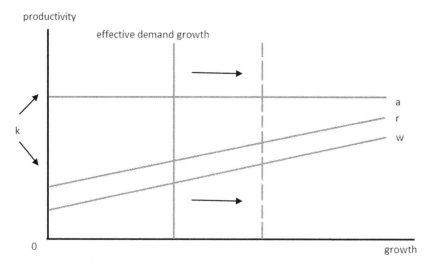

Figure 6.6   The Effect of an Increase in Demand Growth. *Source*: Author.

will presumably have very similar effects on the political economy of the system taken as a whole (see, for example, Smithin 1996).

It would clearly be possible to go on to examine a large variety of other cases—each with different technical assumptions about the behavior of the variables. However, the exercises already completed suffice to establish that the basic point that the simple expression, $k = a - r - w$, provides a flexible tool of analysis for dealing with questions of income distribution between the three key groups of recipients in capitalist economic systems.

CONCLUSION

Recall that Max Weber's definition of capitalism was "the provision of human needs by the method of enterprise, which is to say, by private businesses seeking profit" (Collins 1986, 21–22). The profit motive is the main principle of capitalism. Every business strives to make profit and if they fail to do so they literally go out of business. It is clear, therefore, that neoclassical theory which focuses mainly on market exchange rather than business enterprise, and in which there are no profits, or profits tend to zero, cannot be an adequate theory of capitalism.

Profit is not the same thing as interest on money. Profit is the surplus, whether measured in money or real terms, over and above the costs of production including the necessary interest and financing costs. It is unlikely that this "surplus" will be the same in every firm or industry. It will differ according to a variety of circumstances, such as demand conditions, the specialized nature of the physical capital already invested, and the competence and different expertise of the management and workforce. It is therefore unreasonable to expect to see the equalization of the rate of profit among industries, or even among different firms in the same industry, in any finite state of the world. There is no effective mechanism to achieve this. The economy-wide profit share is therefore nothing other than simply the aggregate of all of the individual surpluses. On the other hand interest rates on money can, in principle, be equalized across a monetary economy as money itself can flow freely. The implication of all this is that, in the presence of a demand constraint, there is always an inverse relation between the general level of interest rates and the aggregate markup.

It perhaps goes without saying that to identify the profit or surplus in practice is bound to be complicated by the different accounting rules and regulations in place in different jurisdictions. It is also complicated by different systems of corporate governance. If, for example, the shareholders of a company are the same persons as those controlling the firm then the dividend payments that they receive may genuinely be counted as part of profit. If, on the other hand, the shareholders are purely passive, then the real managers of the firm will surely see the dividends they have to pay out as just another element of cost, similar to interest payments (albeit with a different contractual status and the addition of some sort of "risk" premium[15] to the sums disbursed). In this case, we would have to look for the surplus or profit in such areas as retained earnings, the salaries, bonuses and prerequisites of the top management, and possibly also consumption-type spending by the firm itself (Smithin 2009a, 107). These, however, are basically empirical rather than theoretical issues. For them to come up for discussion at all, for there to be any debate about how the surplus is distributed, there must be a profit surplus in existence in the first place.

NOTES

1. And, I would argue, later proven by Smithin (2009, 2013a, 2016a, 2016c), and in chapter 5 above.

2. The term "surplus" is in quotes because of the implicitly pejorative implications of this which are unnecessary at this stage. However, see also the discussion later in this chapter about the original Marxian theory.

3. The problem is that since the early twentieth century, influenced by Keynes (1923, 1936) himself, this expression has come to mean, more-or-less exclusively, the recipients of income from financial assets.

4. See also the remarks by Polyani-Levitt (2017) about Kaldor's earlier teaching on this subject at the London School of Economics (LSE).

5. Another prominent contemporary "classical" commodity theory is Sraffa's (1960) "neo-Ricardian" approach. This, however, only appeared in a work published some four years after Kaldor's paper.

6. Notice the difference between this sort of arrangement and the more detailed discussion of numerical examples of the production process in chapter 4.

7. This sort of argument would not, of course, satisfy those Marxian scholars who wish to reinstate the labor theory of value according to Marx's original logic. See, for example, Moseley (2016) who argues that the transformation problem can be eliminated even in the context of long-run competitive equilibrium by adopting an entirely aggregative and sequential approach. See also the review by Smithin (2018).

8. Piketty's (2014) recent best-selling book on income distribution also used the two-class framework. It's title was *Capital in the Twenty-First Century,* an explicit reference to Marx.

9. "Investment" here evidently means financial investment.

10. A later Post-Keynesian (or Post-Kaleckian) literature relaxed this full employment assumption and thereby constructs an argument that the distribution of income is also a determinant of the level of employment and/or the growth rate. On this topic see the survey by Lavoie (2014, 3–7).

11. In the context Keynes in which Keynes first used this term he seems to have been thinking mainly of war profiteers (from inflation) and the like. Elsewhere, he does refer more positively to the business class as the "active group," and as "entrepreneurs" (Keynes 1923, 33, 39).

12. The reader will recall that this was the assumption of the model (the AMM) put forward in chapter 2 of the present volume.

13. This was an assumption that Keynes (1936, 246)—misleadingly—made in the *General Theory*. However, it is not the case in the present analysis. If the firms are indeed to expand production at their planned rates, with labor productivity constant, they must assumed to be always be making just sufficient investment in actual physical capital (and also new management techniques and so forth) to keep the *a* term constant at the same level in each period. The real money cost of any such investment is certainly included *within* the term *I* in the national income and product accounts As pointed out, however, given that *I* includes many other things which have no impact on productivity, the cost will never be equal to *I*. There is, therefore, literally no way of relating the real money cost to any (supposed) measure of the physical capital stock. Examples of "firm spending" that are included in *I*, and do add to demand, but have no impact on productivity, might be such things as redecorating the boardroom, holding a "sales conference" in Hawaii, hiring a corporate jet, and so on. The assumed constancy of labor productivity in the theoretical exposition is thus simply a *behavioral* assumption made for the purposes of this specific piece of analysis. It is not tied to, or dependent on, any arbitrarily chosen accounting conventions.

14. If we were trying to empirically estimate the parameters of this expression for a "real-world" open economy the specification would also have to include the effect of the (natural logarithm of) the real exchange rate, q. For example, $w = t + h_0 + h_1 y - h_2 q$, where $0 < h_1 < 1$ and $h_2 > 0$. On this point see Collis (2016, 2018).

15. The term "risk" is once again put in quotes for the reasons first mentioned in chapter 1.

Chapter 7

Alternative Approaches to the Theory of Economic Growth

INTRODUCTION

The purpose of this chapter is to develop two generic growth equations both of which include the trade balance as percentage of GDP, the primary budget deficit as a percentage of GDP, and the domestic investment/savings balance also as a percentage of GDP.

The first of these illustrates a "Keynes's-type" growth theory which is to borrow (and perhaps slightly misuse) a terminology employed by Hicks (1985, 108) in *Methods of Economic Dynamics*. Hicks's purpose was to discuss a particular method. In the present case, however, the reference is rather to a growth equation that validates a number of familiar Keynesian *ideas*. These include, for example, the notion that fiscal expansion leads to growth. Also, that investment drives saving, a proposition which was one of the main points made by Keynes (1936, 372–73) in the *General Theory*, and later came to be called the "paradox of thrift." The same equation also suggests that an increase in the trade surplus as a percentage of GDP will lead *directly* to growth. This is part of a process that in chapter 2 and in Smithin (2013a, 263–66) I ventured to call monetary mercantilism.[1] Another term for this general attitude toward economic policy might simply be "economic nationalism." The Keynes-type growth theory is, of course, the same theory as that employed to good effect in the development of the Alternative Monetary Model (AMM) in chapter 2.

The so-called classical economists had very different opinions on how the "Wealth of Nations" might be achieved. They were died-in-the-wool globalists. The second growth equation therefore, again by analogy to Hicks's discussion, can be called a "classics-type" theory of growth. This attempt at theory, however, yields some highly anomalous results and turns out not to provide a solid foundation for the classical, neoclassical, or contemporary mainstream approaches to trade, savings, and public finance—quite the opposite.[2]

To first define terms, recall that the conventional breakdown of real value-added (or "real GDP") in the aggregate and over a given time period such as a quarter of a year, is as follows:

$$Y = C + I + G + (EX - IM) \tag{7.1}$$

where C stands for real consumption spending, I is real investment spending, G stands for real government spending, and $EX - IM$ is real net exports. This identity has already been discussed on several occasions in previous chapters. In this chapter, we are interested primarily in the rate of growth rate of the real GDP concept (lowercase y) defined as:

$$y = (Y - Y_{-1}) / Y_{-1} \tag{7.2}$$

Although something like equation (7.1) is familiar from every contemporary economics textbook, we have already made the point (e.g., in chapters 2 and 6) that the relationship between equation (7.1) and the numbers actually reported in the national income and product accounts of the various countries is not straightforward. From the point of view of monetary theory the numbers in the national accounts are much less than ideal. This is because, in compiling the accounts, there is frequently much "imputation" involved in the calculation of the final value of goods and services even in cases where *no money has actually changed hands* (note particularly the emphasis). For example, the figures quoted for "investment" may include an imputed value for the accumulation of inventories, planned or unplanned, covered by an epithet such as the "value of physical change in inventories" or similar. This type of thing is of little or no use for the purpose of devising a monetary theory. There is no money flow corresponding to this piling up of unsold merchandise. It would be much better if terms like consumption, investment, and so on could be taken as referring to actual flows of funds (Wray 2012, 37). Consumption, for example, would more reasonably be defined simply as actual *household spending* on final goods and services and, in the same way, so-called investment should be defined as *firm spending*. It is also by no means clear that all (or even most) of what is labeled investment spending ever really does add anything to the productive capital stock. A great part of it either misfires, or is simply disguised consumption spending on behalf of the firm itself or its managers (Smithin 2009a, 2012). The important point is not whether either of these things, on the household side or the firm side, adds to capacity, but that they all most certainly do increase effective demand.[3] Therefore, even though this is *not* the case in the published accounts, for theoretical purposes the working assumption in what follows will be that the various magnitudes do indeed all represent flows of funds, regardless of on what they are actually spent. In the end the most significant difference between C, I, and G, and so on, is who is doing the spending (either households, firms, or government) and not what the money is spent on.

A "Keynes-Type" Theory of Growth

The Keynes-type growth theory can be derived quite simply by adding a lagged consumption function to the formulation in equation (7.1).

This is another idea originally due to Hicks (1949, 179). To explain how Hicks arrived at this argument recall that the original so-called Keynesian consumption function, such as that which appeared in the many editions of Samuelson's (1964) ubiquitous textbook and its several clones, was usually something along the lines of $C = C_0 + c_1(Y - T)$. Here the symbol T stands for total tax collection, and therefore the term $(Y - T)$ is equal to disposable income. The symbol C_0 is then simply the vertical intercept of the "consumption function," and c_1 is the "marginal propensity to consume" a term originally coined by Keynes (1936, 114) himself. The "average propensity to consume" is thus given by $C/Y = C_0/T + c_1(1 - t)$, where lowercase t stands for the average tax rate, T/Y.

Hicks's idea was simply to suggest that, in reality, household consumption was more likely to depend on lagged disposable income than on current disposable income, as in:

$$C = C_0 + c_1\left(Y_{-1} - T_{-1}\right), \qquad 0 < c_1 < 1 \tag{7.3}$$

In this new formulation, c_1 has thus become the marginal propensity to consume out of last period's disposable income. Using (7.3) in (7.1), we can therefore obtain:

$$Y - I - G - \left(EX - IM\right) = C_0 + c_1\left(Y_{-1} - T_{-1}\right) \tag{7.4}$$

Next, define the total "autonomous spending" of the private sector as:[4]

$$X = I + C_0 \tag{7.5}$$

Lavoie (2014, 347–416), in common with several other writers, has recently called the I term in (7.5) "capacity-creating autonomous expenditure," and labels C_0 as "non-capacity-creating autonomous expenditure." To use this sort of language obviously does buy into the assumption that the items recorded as investment spending (what we have been calling firm spending) in the national income and product accounts do, in fact, add to physical productive capacity in some measurable sense. I think that Lavoie and other like-minded authors would certainly agree, on the one hand, that equation (7.5) shows that the autonomous component of investment spending as well as that of consumption spending does indeed represent effective demand. On the other, they also wish to stress the possible difficulties that may arise as and when the supposed capital spending (which also admittedly adds to effective demand when first made) increases the future supply of goods and services because of the (assumed) increase in the capital stock. Strangely enough this seems to be quite similar to Austrian worries about "overinvestment" as discussed in previous chapters. To put the point as simply as possible, the concern is about whether or not there will be enough demand to pay for the higher levels of output supplied in the future. As we have seen, however, the basic answer to this question boils down simply to whether or not there will be enough credit and money creation in future. Moreover, as already discussed in chapter 6 above, it is plainly false to assume that all firm spending will actually succeed in adding to productive capacity, realistically only some fraction of it will ever do so.

The set of issues at stake here are well illustrated by Keynes's own famous passage on "banknotes in bottles" which appeared in chapter 10 of the *General Theory* on the "Marginal Propensity to Consume" (Keynes 1936, 128–29).

> The above reasoning shows how "wasteful" loan expenditure may nevertheless enrich the community on balance. Pyramid building, earthquakes, even wars may serve to increase wealth, if the education of our statesmen on the principles of the classical economics stands in the way of anything better. . . . It is curious how common-sense, wriggling for an escape from absurd conclusions, has been apt to reach a preference for *wholly* "wasteful" forms of expenditure rather than *partly* wasteful forms, which, because they are not wholly wasteful tend to be judged on strict business principles (original emphasis). For example, unemployment relief financed by loans is more readily accepted that the financing of improvements at a charge below the current rate of interest; whilst the form of digging holes in the ground known as gold-mining, which not only adds nothing whatever to the real wealth of the world but involves the disutility of labour, is the most acceptable of all solutions. . . . If the Treasury were to fill old bottles with banknotes, bury them at suitable depths in disused coalmines which are then filled up to the surface with town rubbish, and leave it to private enterprise on well-tried principles of *laissez-faire* to dig up the notes again (the right to do so being obtained, of course, by tendering for leases to the note-bearing territory), there need be no more unemployment, and, with the help of the repercussions, the real income of the community, and its capital wealth also, would probably become a good deal greater than it actually is. It would indeed, indeed, be more sensible to build houses and the like; but if there are political and practical difficulties in the way of this, the above would be better than nothing.

The point is that so-called non-productive expenditure, just because it does represent an effective demand for *something*, can nonetheless cause employment to increase, or set off an increase in the growth rate, just as well as the supposedly productive expenditure. At the same time the worry that many writers have had about this, that any expenditure which actually does add to physical productive capacity may be storing up trouble for the future, did not seem to bother Keynes. He would have been quite happy to "build two railways from London to York"[5] instead of just one, if only that would reduce unemployment. He was also obviously well aware that in practice it is difficult, indeed impossible, to make any clear-cut distinction between supposed capacity-creating and non-capacity creating autonomous expenditure.

Perhaps an even more important consideration than the above is simply that *any* argument based on capital-theoretic concepts, such as the capital stock itself, the capital-output ratio, the rate of capacity utilization and so forth, is inherently problematical. Keynes was also aware of this last point as discussed at the beginning of this book, in chapter 1. Later on, in chapter 6, we also saw how it is possible to completely avoid these issues and nevertheless still determine the profitability of production within a consistent accounting scheme, but without attempting any spurious measurement of the physical capital stock.

The short answer to the question of where the future demand for any increase in supply will come from is simply credit creation by the banking system. It can also be shown that in the Keynes-type theory of growth it is unnecessary to try to determine ex-ante whether any particular component of effective demand does, or does not, have an impact on productivity per se. The argument stresses the importance of the total amount of autonomous spending, that is, the total of the X term from equation (7.1) rather than its composition. To see this, substitute equation (7.5) into (7.4), and then divide through by Y_{-1}. The result will be:

$$Y/Y_{-1} - \left(Y/Y_{-1}\right)\left[X/Y + G/Y + \left(EX - IM\right)/Y\right] = \left(1 - s_1\right)\left[1 - \left(T_{-1}/Y_{-1}\right)\right] \tag{7.6}$$

Symmetrically with the earlier definition of the propensity to consume, the term s_1 is the marginal propensity to save from lagged disposable income. Also, let $g = G/Y$, $x = X/Y$, $ex - im = (EX - IM)/Y$ and so on, and recall that lowercase y is the symbol for economic growth. This therefore implies:

$$\left(1 + y\right)\left[1 - x - g - \left(ex - im\right)\right] = \left(1 - s_1\right)\left(1 - t\right) \tag{7.7}$$

Taking natural logarithms, and using the approximation that $\ln(1 + z) = z$ and so on, equation (7.7) therefore becomes:

$$y = \left(x - s_1\right) + \left(g - t\right) + \left(ex - im\right) \tag{7.8}$$

The expression in equation (7.8) is, in fact, the Keynes-type growth equation we have been looking for. It suggests that growth occurs when:

1. **The *total* of autonomous private sector spending (on "consumption"—household spending, and "investment"—firm spending) both as a percentage of GDP, is greater than the *marginal* propensity to save (also a percentage).**
2. **There is a primary budget deficit as a percentage of GDP.**
3. **There is a trade surplus as percentage of GDP.**

I have put these statements in bold type to stress the fundamental importance of each of the three propositions. To avoid misunderstanding, it should immediately be stated that the argument obviously does not imply that growth cannot occur either in a putative high-saving economy, or when there is a trade deficit, or when the primary budget is in surplus. It would still be possible for growth to occur when a minimum of only one of the three terms on the right-hand-side (RHS) of (7.8) is positive, but also outweighs the combined total of the two negative terms. However, the equation does definitely assert that in addition to the basic Keynesian idea of the "paradox of thrift," an increase in either the primary budget deficit as a percentage of GDP, or in the trade balance as a percentage of GDP, each taken in isolation, will always lead to a one-to-one increase in the economic growth rate. Therefore, this leads us directly back to the notions both of so-called fiscal stimulus, and to what we have been calling either "monetary mercantilism" or "economic nationalism."

Reconciliation of the Growth Equation with the Sectoral Balances in the National Accounts

The next question to ask is how the growth equation in (7.8) relates to the alternative "injections and withdrawals" version of the national income identity, often seen in textbooks. Also, how does it relate to the notion of "sectoral balances" that inevitably arises from the latter approach? To answer these questions, first note that equation (7.1) is clearly equivalent to:

$$I + G + EX = S + T + IM \tag{7.9}$$

This is the injections/withdrawals approach. Next, divide through by Y and let the symbols *inv* stand for the ratio of investment spending to current income ($inv = I/Y$) and *s* for the average propensity to save out of current income ($s = S/Y$). This will yield:

$$0 = (inv - s) + (g - t) + (ex - im). \tag{7.10}$$

Equation (7.10) thus illustrates the basic accounting identity stating that the sectoral balances, the domestic investment/saving balance, the primary budget deficit, and the trade balance, must all sum to zero. Now compare this to the growth equation from (7.8) above, repeated as equation (7.11):

$$y = (x - s_1) + (g - t) + (ex - im) \tag{7.11}$$

The difference between these two expressions is simply that equation (7.11) can have either a positive or negative magnitude. There can be either positive growth, a boom, or negative growth, a recession. Therefore equation (7.11) need not sum to zero whereas equation (7.10) must do so. The two equations are therefore quite consistent with one another. The x and s_1 in equation (7.11) are not the same things as *inv* and *s*.

The "Harrod-Domar" Growth Formula

In order to derive the alternative classics-type growth equation, it will be useful first to remember the so-called Harrod-Domar growth formula from the 1940s (Sen 1970, 9–14) which was named for the independent contributions of Harrod (1939) and Domar (1946). These authors probably did not think that they were contributing to the revival and rehabilitation of the pre-Keynesian classical approach. Almost certainly they would have believed that they were contributing to the then fashionable "neo-classical Keynesian" model. Nonetheless, there can be little doubt that this literature and all that descended from it actually represented a major step backward from what Keynes achieved, or at least was trying to achieve. In any event, the Harrod-Domar formula can easily be derived using the procedure shown in equations (7.12) through (7.21) below. For the sake of simplicity, we will initially work with a truncated version of the GDP identity (with no government sector and no foreign sector) thereby following the original sources in this respect. The GDP identity is thus reduced to:

$$Y = C + I \tag{7.12}$$

The next step is to add a somewhat simplified consumption (or savings) function of the form:

$$C = (1 - s)Y, \tag{7.13}$$

where s is the average propensity to save. As compared to the Keynesian-type consumption function discussed earlier this differs by setting the intercept at $C_0 = 0$, and also by replacing the concept of the marginal propensity to consume with that of the marginal propensity to save, where $s = 1 - c$.[6]

The key move made by Harrod which was quite different in spirit from Keynes's own approach, was to specify an "aggregate production function" of the form:

$$Y = AK \tag{7.14}$$

where A stands for the average product of capital.[7] Given our discussion of methodological problems in chapter 1 above, this specification should probably immediately set off warning bells about the Keynesian bona fides of Harrod's analysis. He is doing something which Keynes (1936, 41) had actually had said could not, and should not, be done. The very idea of a production function involving a supposed physical measure of the capital stock is something which is clearly firmly in the domain of classical economics rather than that of Keynes's intuitive ideas about effective demand. Indeed, in the event, fifty years after Harrod the mainstream theory of economic growth came full circle when the original neoclassical growth theory, due to Solow (1956), finally morphed into the "AK" model of the so-called new growth theory (Jones 1998, 148–50). Ironically, this turned out to be identical to the approach of Harrod and Domar.

The dynamic element in "Harrod-type" models (again, see Hicks 1985, 110–30) comes in because, by definition in this sort of literature, the level of investment spending recorded in the national income and product accounts is supposed to accurately measure the increase in the physical capital stock (an assumption which really goes against all common-sense, as previously pointed out). Thus, ignoring depreciation, it is assumed always to be true that:

$$K_{+1} - K = I \tag{7.15}$$

Thus, the literature following Harrod and Domar took quite seriously the notion of being somehow able to measure the physical capital stock and any increments to it. No account, at all, was taken of the many and various possible pitfalls of this procedure that were discussed in detail in previous chapters. This being the case a final concept that is used in deriving the Harrod-Domar growth formula is the (otherwise dubious) notion of the capital-output ratio, O. Once again, if we assume counterintuitively that the units of the measured capital stock, K, and the rate of output, Y, can somehow be made commensurate, the capital/output ratio will be:

$$O = K/Y \quad (= 1/A) \tag{7.16}$$

And, then, given (7.14), equation (7.16) can be re-written as:

$$O(Y_{+1} - Y) = s/Y \tag{7.17}$$

Next, using the definition of the growth rate in (7.2), the formula that Harrod (1939, 47) called the "warranted" rate of growth (which in our notation will be y_W) therefore emerges as:

$$y_W = s/O. \tag{7.18}$$

This warranted rate of growth, however, is a rather peculiar concept. It is "warranted" in the sense that is a sort of benchmark for balanced growth, given the state of technology and the average propensity to save. However, Harrod *also* thought that it would be extremely difficult to actually achieve balanced growth in practice. This was because of his additional argument that the system is highly unstable. This is the famous "knife-edge" as described by Sen (1970, 15). The argument is that if the actual rate of growth turns out to be greater than the warranted rate of growth, the entrepreneurs will interpret this as requiring more capital investment, thus pushing the growth rate higher still. On the other hand, if the actual growth rate is less than the warranted rate, the entrepreneurs will mistakenly see this as requiring less capital investment, and the growth rate will fall still further. Note that the only way that this could be conceivably regarded as a contribution to the corpus of Keynesian economics per se would be on the assumption that Keynes himself was somehow asserting the "inherent instability" of the capitalist system, in one sense or another, as discussed in chapter 2. Keynes's actual argument, however, was rather the idea that the system could settle into a state of permanent depression and "underemployment equilibrium." It would be "stable" but at a low level of activity.

Moreover, Harrod's argument does seem to require that the entrepreneurs always form their expectations in a very mechanical and short-sighted sort of way. Never do they seem to attempt to undertake any more sophisticated types of "business analysis." In that sense it is very much an appeal to a special case. The significance of this is that if the knife-edge argument does *not* hold up, that is, if it possible to add some plausible equilibrating mechanism to the discussion, this will explain why the Harrod-Domar formula makes a step back from Keynes into the all too familiar worlds of classical economics and capital theory. Indeed, the stated purpose of Solow's so-called neo-classical growth model which eventually replaced the Harrod-Domar approach in the mainstream literature in the 1950s and 1960s—and remains a staple of the textbooks to this day—was to provide just such an equilibrating mechanism (Sen 1970, 20–24).

Sen (1970, 14), writing about thirty years after Harrod's original contribution, later summed up the issue of "Harrodian instability" (Lavoie 2014, 398) as follows:

> Harrod's model of instability is undoubtedly incomplete,[8] but . . . there are many . . . ways in which . . . [it] . . . can be completed. Some confirm instability while others either eliminate it or make it conditional on certain actual circumstances. In general it will be fair to say that Harrod's instability analysis overstresses a local problem near the equilibrium without carrying the story far enough, and extensions of his model with realistic assumptions about the other factors involved tend to soften the blow.

In the literature of the late 1940s and early 1950s, one popular modification of the Harrod-Domar framework was to add an explicit investment function that eventually came to be known as the "accelerator" (Hicks 1949, 173–74). A first step toward deriving this concept is to re-write equation (7.15) above by simply switching the left-hand-side (LHS) and right-hand-side (RHS) of the original expression as follows:

$$I = K_{+1} - K \tag{7.19}$$

Then, given the capital-output ratio O from equation (7.13), the implication is that there must be an investment function in the model of the form:

$$I = O(Y_{+1} - Y) \tag{7.20}$$

This is the accelerator. It suggest that if GDP is expected to increase from Y now to Y_{+1} next period, and given the existing capital-output ratio, this will determine precisely how much investment the entrepreneurs will decide to make. This is a very different type of economic decision-making process than making investment on a whim, or because of increased business confidence, and then seeing what happens. Using the familiar notation of lowercase y to stand for the growth rate, equation (7.20) therefore becomes:

$$I = Oy_{+1}Y \tag{7.21}$$

The implication is that, in this case, if the expectations of the one-period-ahead growth rate are indeed reasonably accurate the Harrod-Domar formula will yield the following *steady-state* growth equation:

$$y = s/O \tag{7.22}$$

It is certainly worth noting that such a treatment of short-term expectations for the next period would not be at all inconsistent with Keynes own approach. Keynes (1936, 4650) had actually made a sharp distinction between what he called short-term expectation and long-term expectation. The later was supposed to be by far the most important of the two, and as Keynes later stated in a famous expository article in the *Quarterly Journal of Economics* (Keynes 1937, 113–14) involved genuine uncertainty, about such things as

> the prospect of a European war . . . the price of copper or the rate of interest twenty years hence . . . the obsolescence of a new invention, or the position of private wealth-holders in the social system of 1970. About these matters there is no scientific basis to form any calculable probability whatever. We simply do not know.

A change in long-term expectation would show up primarily as shift in intercept of an investment function as, for example, in the discussion of animal spirits in the context of the AMM of chapter 2. On the other hand, in Keynes's exposition of the theory of effective demand in chapter 3 of the *General Theory*, in the discussion of expectations in chapter 5 on "Expectation and Employment," and in chapter 12 on "Long-Term Expectation" Keynes (1936, 50), he evidently took the view that although

> express reference to long-term expectation can seldom be avoided . . . it will often be safe to omit express reference to *short-term* expectation (original emphasis) in view of the fact that in practice the process of revision of short-term expectation is a gradual and continuous one.

To sum up, therefore, if the issue about stability can be resolved (e.g., in the way suggested by Keynes himself in the above passage—by taking the accuracy of short-term expectations for granted), then on the face of it what equation (12) seems to say (what it *does* say) is that when the propensity to save increases the rate of growth increases. This chain of logic is therefore why it can reasonably be argued that, from the point of view taken in this book, the ultimate effect of the contributions of Harrod, Domar, et al. was merely to rehabilitate the pre-Keynesian classical approach. This was a process that was then completed by the whole subsequent development of the mainstream theory of economic growth through the neoclassical growth model of Solow (1956) and Swan (1956) to the "new" growth theory of Romer (1986), Lucas (1988), and Rebelo (1991).[9] In the end, it led directly to the reinstatement of views which were the complete opposite to those of Keynes about the paradox of thrift.[10]

A "Classics-type" Theory of Economic Growth

It follows from the above arguments that even though this was not the intention of the original authors we can use the Harrod-Domar formula to derive a generic growth equation that illustrates the basic results of a "classics-type" theory of growth—in all its permutations. To see this combine equation (7.9), stating that total injections to the circular flow are equal to total withdrawals, with the expression for growth from equation (7.22) above. This gives:

$$O\left(Y_{+1} - Y\right) = \left(T - G\right) + s\left(Y - T\right) + \left(IM - EX\right) \tag{7.23}$$

Next divide through by Y:

$$O\left[\left(Y_{+1} - Y\right)/Y\right] = \left[\left(T - G\right)/Y\right] + s\left[1 - \left(T/Y\right)\right] + \left[\left(IM - EX\right)/Y\right] \tag{7.24}$$

In our lowercase notation, the above expression may then be rewritten as:

$$y = \left[s\left(1 - t\right) + \left(t - g\right) + \left(im - ex\right)\right]/O \tag{7.25}$$

This is the "classics-type" growth equation, and *pace* Harrod, Domar and many others, it gives very strange results. As well as bringing back the old idea that an increase in the average propensity to save should increase the growth rate rather than reduce it, equation (7.25) also seems to say that both a budget *surplus* and a trade *deficit* lead to growth. On one level, I suppose that it may perhaps seem logical enough that a classics-type analysis should lead to the opposite results to a Keynes-type approach. However, we should also take careful note that these are not results that are usually asserted with any confidence in the public policy debate. The supporters of the classics-type approach, strangely, do not actually seem to have the courage of the convictions in the public sphere.

There seems to be no way out of or escape from these paradoxical conclusions, at least as far as the basic algebra is concerned. For example, another way of writing equation (7.22) above would be $yK = S$ and, as $S = I + (G - T) + (EX - IM)$, it might be thought that after all we could perhaps write something which looks more conventional,[11] such as:

$$y = I/K + (G - T)/K + (EX - IM)/K. \qquad (7.26)$$

However, this by no means restores common-sense to the classical model. The reason is, as we have already seen from equations (7.15) and (7.19), that by definition in this framework $I = K_{+1} - K$. Thus the growth rate cancels out on both sides of the expression in (7.26). It will reduce simply to:

$$G - T = EX - IM \qquad (7.27)$$

which adds no further useful information.

What could possibly be the rationale for the seemingly counterintuitive results in equation (7.25)? Undoubtedly there are some pseudo-rational arguments that can be made. For example, on the question of the budget surplus it might be taken as a quite consistent argument that if saving is a "good thing" for the private sector then this should also be the case for the public sector. If this proposition were to be true, however, if increased saving is always a good thing, why not have 100 percent saving and no spending at all (and therefore no economy)? This is a reductio ad absurdum which is indeed the very essence of equation (7.25).

It might similarly be argued about a trade deficit that if foreign economies were indeed always willing to supply the domestic economy with goods and services without asking anything in return, then that would be an excellent thing (for the domestic economy). This is what Friedman and Friedman (1980) actually said on this topic in their bestselling book *Free to Choose: A Personal Statement*. At that time trade relations between Japan and the United States were a matter of intense public debate and according to Friedman and Friedman (1980, 42):

> If Japanese . . . exporters were prepared to burn or bury the dollar bills that would be wonderful for us [the USA]. We would get all kinds of goods for green pieces of paper that we can produce in great abundance and very cheaply. We would have the most remarkable export industry available.

However, who is going to agree to that sort of deal? In fact, Friedman and Friedman immediately have to concede that no one will do so. In the very next paragraph they admit:

Of course, the Japanese would not, in fact, sell us useful goods in order to get useless pieces of paper to bury or burn.

Therefore, they ultimately have to rest their case on the typical classical/neoclassical argument for so-called free trade, depending entirely on certain assumptions about how the real economy operates regardless of money. Specifically, the argument depends upon the idea that there is a unique non-monetary equilibrium for the real exchange rate. This is suspiciously like the analogous argument for a unique non-monetary "natural rate" of interest, and also has little genuine foundation. All in all the various arguments that might be made about budget deficits, saving, and trade, in order to provide some sort of rational basis for the underlying worldview, simply do not convince. This is why an expression like (7.25) never does see the light of day in economic textbooks even though it follows quite logically and inexorably from the classics-type approach set out above.

Real World Political Economy

In the real world, of course, the conventional wisdom on economic policy does not usually call for an actual budget surplus much more frequently the desiderata is simply a balanced budget. It is still less likely that anyone would actively canvas for a trade deficit. Rather, it is taken for granted that budget balance ($g = t$) is a desirable thing in and of itself and it also assumed, but never demonstrated, that external balance ($ex = im$) is also a good thing, and somehow represents the natural state of affairs. In fact, this last argument ties in very neatly with the traditional argument of classical free traders that both sides are supposed to benefit from the so-called gains from trade even when exports are balanced by imports. Indeed, the parties are not supposed to even try to actively to seek advantage for themselves either by gaining a trade surplus., or alternatively (as suggested tongue-in-cheek by the Friedmans in the passage above) "living beyond their means" by running a trade deficit.

To better understand how textbook writers and policy analysts have tried to finesse these difficult issues, notice that if we do arbitrarily set both $g = t$ and $ex = im$ in equation (7.25) the result turns out to be:

$$y = s(1-t)/O \qquad (7.28)$$

This is identical to the supposed "natural rate of growth" of mainstream economics, another concept that is very familiar from the textbooks. It is significant that in this version the natural rate of growth is seen to depend negatively on the average tax rate. This, clearly, is the source of the argument that often crops up in political debates, usually coming from those to the "right-of-center" along the political spectrum, namely the suggestion that tax cuts are really the *only* public policy initiative that will ever increase growth.[12] This goes all the way back to the so-called supply side argument that was prominent in the public policy debates of the 1970s and 1980s.

However, in this sort of discourse no real argument is ever offered as to why it is possible to just assume away the effects of the trade imbalances and the state of the public finances. Nor is there any explanation of why, given the acceptance of the supply side argument about the effects of taxes, the seemingly backwards logic of aiming for budget surpluses and trade deficits should not also apply. What happens is simply that if we arbitrarily set $g = t$ and $ex = im$ these points will drop out of view, and can be conveniently forgotten in the political debate. This is why the textbooks have always argued that budget balance and trade balance are desirable things to aspire to and, either that they can be achieved without significant economic cost, or are simply the natural order of things to which the "market" is tending.

Growth and Profit

Returning now to the Keynes-type growth equation, note that in the closed economy the expression in (7.8) above will reduce to:

$$y = (x - s_1) + (g - t), \tag{7.29}$$

where $x = X/Y = [(I/Y) + (C_0/Y)]$.

How does this equation relate to the expression defining aggregate demand growth previously used in the exposition of the AMM in chapter 2 above? In chapter 2 this growth equation was written as $y = e_0 + e_1 k + (g - t)$. It should now be obvious that this specification actually contained within itself an explicit "investment function" whereby the ratio of investment spending to GDP depends on an intercept term $(I/Y)_0$ and also on profitability. For example:

$$I/Y = (I/Y)_0 + e_1 k, \qquad 0 < e_1 < 1 \tag{7.30}$$

Therefore the remaining components of the e_0 term in the original AMM must be given by:

$$e_0 = (I/Y)_0 + C_0/Y - s_1 \tag{7.31}$$

We can now define the e_0 variable as something like the "*net* autonomous expenditure of the private sector as a percentage of GDP" (note emphasis). This magnitude will rise either if the autonomous component of investment spending increases or if the autonomous component of consumption spending similarly increases. It will fall if the marginal propensity to save increases. The full growth equation for a closed economy in the AMM is therefore:

$$y = e_0 + e_1 k + (g - t). \qquad 0 < e_1 < 1 \tag{7.32}$$

More generally, the full specification for the growth equation in an open economy (one that does trade with the rest of the world, as in our discussion above) will be something like:

$$y = e_0 + e_1 k - e_2 q + (g - t), \qquad 0 < e_1 < 1, e_2 > 0 \tag{7.33}$$

This formula has added a term suggesting that a real *appreciation* of the exchange rate will lead to a *slowdown* in economic growth. This will occur because the depressing effect on the trade balance will be more than offset any possible benefits to be gained via cheaper production costs. Note that in a number of jurisdictions with either flexible exchange rates or fixed-but-adjustable exchange rates the empirical evidence does tend to support this specification (see, e.g., Collis 2016, 2018).

CONCLUSION

On several occasions in recent years I have tried to explain my position on the various issues discussed in this chapter in correspondence by e-mail to colleagues and friends all over the world. I usually fall back on saying that there are ultimately only two alternative (and mutually exclusive) ways of characterizing the theory of production in macroeconomics, either $Y = AN$ or $Y = AK$. These are contemporaneous relationships, but in both cases the individual analyst/theorist can put in as many lags as is thought necessary or desirable. I hope that it has already been made sufficiently clear that the basic premise of this book is the *former* specification, albeit with a one-period lag as in $Y = AN_{-1}$. This one-period production lag is chosen because it is the simplest possible theoretical specification that allows for an interest charge on variable capital,[13] but over the years some of my graduate students have gone further than this and have been able to provide an empirical distributional framework with multiple production lags, allowing for a comprehensive estimate of the average/aggregate interest charge on production in the presence of debt instruments of varying terms to maturity.[14] Regardless, the analysis in this chapter, or so it seems to me, forces us to recognize that the two different approaches to production theory are mutually exclusive. They cannot be reconciled either by the standard neoclassical production function $Y = F(K, N)$ or by a two-sector approach. The competing approaches lead to quite different conclusions about the sources of economic growth and cannot successfully be mixed. Put simply, the $Y = AN$ approach is correct and $Y = AK$ is not.

Keynes used the former approach as did, for example, the original American Post Keynesians such as Davidson (2011), Davidson and Smolensky (1964), and Weintraub (1958, 1961). In this, they were faithful to the original Keynesian model. Weintraub's (1958, 9) famous pricing equation, for example, was explicitly written as:

$$P = KWN/Y = KW/A, \tag{7.34}$$

where P is the price level, K is the mark-up $(K = 1 + k)$, W is the money wage, N is labor input, Y is output, and A is the average product of labor.[15] Another writer who used the $Y = AN$ approach was, of course, Karl Marx (of all people). For example, in a recent book on the transformation problem Moseley (2016, 32) has shown that Marx's explanation of aggregate surplus value, in *Capital* Vol. 1, may be finally be written as:

$$s = AN - v \tag{7.35}$$

where (as in chapter 6 above) s is surplus value, v is variable capital, N is labor input, measured as socially necessary labor time, and A is the proportionality factor.

On the other side of the economic fence, the neoclassicals, the Austrians, Harrod and Domar, the modern "new" growth theorists, and mainstream economists in general, have all used some variant of the $Y = AK$ approach. However, as we already have seen, this classics-type approach leads to some very strange results. This is more than enough to explain why the views of most economists on the causes and consequences of economic growth have been, and are, so unreliable. A later generation even of Post Keynesian economists have also (unfortunately in my opinion) tried to use a production function involving "capital" in an attempt to deal with issues of accumulation, growth, and physical measures of capacity utilization. This was true, for example, of most of the literature surveyed by Lavoie (2014, 347–455), in a chapter explicitly entitled "Accumulation and Capacity." As Lavoie (2014, 347) puts it, the objective of these later Post Keynesians was to:

> combine the classical concerns for growth and distribution with the Keynesian principle of effective demand . . . the focus . . . move(s) to rates of growth of output, rates of profit and rates of capacity utilization.

The problem with this objective, however, is that a return to classical concerns *must* imply a baseline theory of growth similar to that in equation (7.25) above. As we have seen in the present chapter this is not compatible with Keynesian ideas and is not really defensible as a viable macroeconomic theory. The only way to effect a reconciliation (of sorts) would be to try to counteract the classical inertia by proposing some much more complicated specifications for the investment function, savings/consumption function, and/or net exports function, than those used in equation (7.23). In that case, then at least for certain parameters values, growth can be restored and we can arrive at taxonomy of different growth regimes, such as "profit-led growth," "wage-led growth," "export-led growth," and so on (Lavoie 2014, 384). But this still begs the question of *why* it is even necessary (after Keynes) to engage with the classical model at all? As we have seen, the Keynes-type growth theory of equation (7.8) above already provides a comprehensive theory of growth without resort to any notion of a physical measurement of capital, and also is able to identify at least three of the different growth regimes.[16]

In much of the analysis in the present book we have been content to work with a simplified specification even of the production function $Y = AN_{-1}$ with a one-period production lag in which the average product of labor was assumed constant.[17] The reason for this, however, was simply mathematical convenience. These specifications did not prevent the development of a comprehensive growth theory, and put no restrictions at all on the scope of future empirical work. In fact, an empirical production function which works well in several different jurisdictions is as follows:

$$a = a_0 + a_1 y_{-1} + a_2 \left(y - y_{-1} \right) + \text{error}, \qquad a_1 > 0, \quad a_2 > 0 \tag{7.36}$$

where a is the natural logarithm of A, measured as real GDP/employment, and y is the growth rate of real GDP. Using the techniques of time-series econometrics (first differencing, etc.) it is then possible to extract a time-series for the exogenous variable a_0 which, in effect, is a measure of Schumpeterian innovation.[18] This turns out to be a good predictor of both the business cycle and fluctuations in the stock market, as also are the similar series for liquidity preference, animal spirits, perceived currency risk, the budget deficit as a percentage of GDP, the real policy rate of interest, the socio-political power of labor, and so on (Collis 2016, 2018).[19]

As shown in this and previous chapters the key to growth is actually the pursuit of expansionary polices (of various kinds—not necessarily only the conventional ones)[20] which can generate enough credit and money creation for the realization of monetary profit. This is an absolute prerequisite. Without sufficient credit creation occurring, there can never be any monetary profit, hence no "real" profit, and never any incentive for growth.

At this stage it now remains only to remind the reader of the point originally made in chapter 2 that in order for the sorts of growth-friendly policies suggested in this chapter to be put in place another requirement is that each individual polity possesses a measure of what we have been calling "monetary sovereignty." A growth-oriented economic policy is viable only in the cases of regimes with a floating exchange rate, or with a fixed-but-adjustable exchange rate. They will not work in the case of a hard peg for the exchange rate, nor in the worse-case scenario of a currency union. These regimes are conducive only to economic stagnation and instability. We will return to a more detailed discussion of these important open economy issues in chapters 9 and 10 to follow.

NOTES

1. "Mercantilism" as such (with no qualifier) was traditionally thought of as simply the opposite of classical free trade, but it is important to stress that the argument to follow really has very little to do with the advocacy of tariff or nontariff "barriers to trade," that is, with *protectionism* as it is usually defined. The main focus in this chapter is on measures to increase the trade surplus via other types of policy, such as monetary and fiscal policy. It is interesting to note that Humphrey (1998, 2) has also used the expression mercantilism in a similar way to that chosen here (albeit without the qualifier "monetary"). Humphrey casts the whole history of economic thought as a contest between mercantilism in the monetary sense and "classical economics." Figures like Law, Stueart, Tooke, Keynes, and Kaldor were on the "mercantilist" side and Hume, Smith, Thornton, Ricardo, and Friedman were on the other.

2. Keynes (1936, 16) said it best: "The classical theorists resemble Euclidean geometers in a non-Euclidean world who discovering that in experience straight lines apparently parallel often meet rebuke the lines for not keeping straight—as the only remedy for the unfortunate collisions that keep occurring. Yet, in truth, there is no remedy but to throw over the axiom of parallels and to work out a non-Euclidean geometry. Something similar is required today in economics." It still needs to be done eighty plus years later. Keynes did not ultimately succeed and the mainstream of the profession has spent all this time attempting to rehabilitate "Euclid." Heterodox economists have done the same with respect to Ricardo and Marx.

3. As for household spending versus firm spending surely, for example, the purchase of an automobile by a line worker to commute to work is more likely to add to the total productive capacity of the economy than (for example) redecorating the boardroom with oak paneling and expensive artwork.

4. The expression autonomous expenditure was widely used in the pseudo-Keynesian textbooks of the 1950s and 1960s. More recently it seems to have has fallen out of favor in mainstream economics. It just means expenditures that are undertaken spontaneously, by either

households or firms, rather than in response to actual changes in economic incentives such as changes in interest rates or income. Autonomous spending by the firm corresponds to some extent to Keynes's "animal spirits." Autonomous spending by the household can be taken either to represent consumer confidence, or more prosaically a sociologically determined minimum acceptable level of consumption spending.

5. According to Keynes (1936, 131): "Ancient Egypt was doubly fortunate, and doubtless owed to this its fabulous wealth, in that it possessed two activities, namely, pyramid building and the search for precious metals, the fruits of which . . . did not stale with abundance. The Middle Ages built cathedrals and sang dirges. Two pyramids, two masses for the dead are quite as good as one; but not so two railways from London to York. Thus we are so sensible, have schooled ourselves to so close a semblance of prudent financiers, taking careful thought before we add to the 'financial' burdens of posterity by building them houses to live in, that we have no such easy escape from the sufferings of unemployment."

6. As there is no intercept in the consumption function this means that the average propensities to consume and save are equal to the marginal propensities.

7. Recall that in chapters 2 and 6 above, the symbol A was used alternatively to stand for the average product of labor. As a matter of fact, this discrepancy well illustrates the basic difference in the theory of production as between the two different approaches to the theory of growth.

8. This first statement actually appears immediately after the rest of the quote in the original text. However, in context it appears to be more in place in its present position.

9. The book by Jones (1998) entitled *Introduction to Economic Growth* provides a survey/overview of these developments through the end of the twentieth century.

10. The other conclusion that can be drawn from equation (7.22) is that technological innovation increases growth, but this is uncontroversial. This was a standard argument in both the classical and neoclassical literature, and it is also true in the AMM.

11. I am grateful to an anonymous referee of one of my earlier published journal articles on this subject (Smithin 2013c), who had originally drawn my attention to the possibility, at least, of making this argument.

12. It should be stressed at this point that in the AMM of chapter 2 it was also true that a tax cut not offset by any decrease in government spending will lead to growth. There is no disagreement with the supply siders on this specific point. Recall, however, that in the AMM this result was a combination of *both* supply side and demand side effects. Many other public policy initiatives, beside tax changes, will also have an effect. It is not the intention in this passage to argue against a policy of tax cuts. The point is rather that the supply siders' analysis of the issue was inadequate. It was partial and one-dimensional.

13. Recall the discussion in chapter 2 above.

14. On this topic again consult Collis (2015, 2017).

15. For the sake of clarity equation (7.25) uses the same notation already used in the current book rather than that used by Weintraub himself.

16. The exception being "wage-led" growth. Recall from chapter 2 above that the AMM also predicts a positive relation between real wages and economic growth. In that case, however, the causation goes from economic growth to real wages via the increased bargaining power of labor, and not the other way around.

17. At this point the reader can refer back to the discussions in chapters 2, 5, and 6 above.

18. It replaces the previous (constant) a used in the theoretical work with an empirically based indicator of technological innovation.

19. In chapter 1 above it was explained how this procedure can be rendered compatible with the undoubted presence of fundamental uncertainty in the social world.

20. Recall the discussion of the negative balanced budget multiplier in chapter 2 above.

Chapter 8

Alternative Views on Inflation

INTRODUCTION

The theory of inflation adopted in this book has already been explained in some detail in chapters 2 and 5 above. That theory is consistent with the facts of endogenous money and bank credit creation, and is therefore well able to accommodate the various cost-push influences and productivity changes that affect inflation. However, unlike many other endogenous money theories, it also takes into account changes in the parameters of the explicit money supply and demand functions (liquidity preference, etc.).

This purpose of the present chapter is to compare this set of ideas to some of the other views about inflation that have been influential within the economics profession and in the wider world over many years. None of these, however, are anything like as comprehensive as the approach to inflation already elaborated in previous chapters.

The Traditional Theory of Inflation based on the Quantity Theory of Money and Monetarism

The backbone of the orthodox or mainstream theory of inflation has usually been the so-called equation of exchange from the quantity theory of money. In the "income version of the quantity theory of money" (Friedman 1989, 1–15), as opposed to the transactions versions ($MV = PT$) discussed in chapter 4, this is written as:

$$MV = PY \tag{8.1}$$

where M is supposed to be one of the so-called monetary aggregates, V is the income velocity of circulation, P is the aggregate price index and Y stands for real GDP.

In principle this expression is an identity—even a tautology (Smithin 1994, 31). However, if it can be assumed that the money supply M is exogenous (i.e., tightly controlled by the central bank), that the velocity of circulation V is more-or-less a constant, at least over the relevant time horizon of the analysis, and that money is both neutral and superneutral,[1] it also produces a simple theory of the aggregate price level, P, in the form:

$$P = MV/Y \tag{8.2}$$

Therefore, when the money supply M increases the price level P will increase in the same proportion, and vice versa. For example, a doubling of the money supply will cause a doubling of the price level. In terms of the rates of change of the variables (including the rate of inflation $\Delta P/P$) by definition we must have:

$$\Delta P/P = \Delta M/M + \Delta V/V - \Delta Y/Y \tag{8.3}$$

However if, as already mentioned, the velocity of circulation V is taken to be a constant, then $\Delta V/V = 0$. Thus the expression for inflation reduces to:

$$\Delta P/P = \Delta M/M - \Delta Y/Y. \tag{8.4}$$

In the lower case notation used in previous chapters let $p = \Delta P/P$, $m = \Delta M/M$, and $y = \Delta Y/Y$. Note that the economic growth rate itself does not have to be zero. It is whatever it is. The only assumption made above is that this growth rate (whatever it is) is not affected by *monetary* changes. Thus equation (8.4) can be rewritten as:

$$p = m - y \tag{8.5}$$

This formulation states that the inflation rate is determined by the rate of growth of the money supply minus the rate of growth of real GDP. This is essentially a mono-causal theory of inflation in the sense that almost all of the changes in inflation that occur in practice are attributed to variations in the rate of monetary growth.

Further if it can be asserted, or assumed, that the economic growth rate over the long-term is likely on average to be at or around the supposed "natural rate" of growth, y^N, we might also write:[2]

$$p = m - y^N \tag{8.6}$$

The underlying theory of inflation is therefore that the inflation rate is believed to be, on average and roughly speaking, equal to the rate growth of the money supply minus the "natural" rate of growth of the real economy. To be sure, in detailed empirical applications some adjustments would have to be made to this formula simply for the sake of realism. However, these would not affect the economist's underlying beliefs about the causal mechanism. For example, if velocity was allowed to change somewhat, but always in a fairly predictable manner, there might be a coefficient different from unity on the growth term (Smithin 1994, 31–35). Nonetheless, the core idea would remain that if the rate of monetary growth is consistently higher than the economic growth rate there will be inflation.

This is the theory of inflation illustrated in Figure 8.1. Moreover, in studying the diagram it should be borne in mind that these same notions about the underlying causes of inflation were held by the majority of mainstream economists for more than 250 years, from the mid-eighteenth century to the late-twentieth century. It is true that the grip of these ideas on the minds of professional economists and of policy-makers was somewhat shaken during the Keynesian *hiatus* of the mid-twentieth century. After that time, however, they underwent a strong revival in the guise of the doctrine of monetarism. This was the approach championed by the famous Nobel prize-winning economist Milton Friedman, even though he personally claimed to dislike the popular expression "monetarist" (Friedman 1983, 4). In Figure 8.1 which illustrates the basic monetarist theory economic growth is assumed always to be at its natural rate shown by the vertical line y^N. The demand side of the economy is supposed to be fully represented by the downward-sloping schedule which graphs the dynamic version of the equation of exchange. It can be seen that if the rate of monetary growth increases the downward-sloping schedule, $p = m - y$, will shift upward and the inflation rate will increase—and vice versa.

The typical policy proposals associated with Friedman and his monetarist colleagues are very well-known. The main such proposition was that the rate of growth of the money supply should be kept low on average, steady, and predictable. A specific policy proposal made by Friedman himself was that the rate of growth of the money supply (somehow defined) should actually be a constant set to deliver roughly stable prices. Friedman (1960, 90–93, 1968, 16, 1983, 5–6) was certainly well aware that much more sophisticated rules might well be devised. Nonetheless, he opted for constancy on the political grounds that it would be easier to obtain public support and understanding for a simple rule.[3]

In the model depicted in Figure 8.1, it is clear that in order to get zero inflation (i.e., absolutely stable prices) we would have to apply a rule such that the rate of growth of the money supply is exactly equal to the natural rate of growth of the economy. That is:

$$m = y^N. \tag{8.7}$$

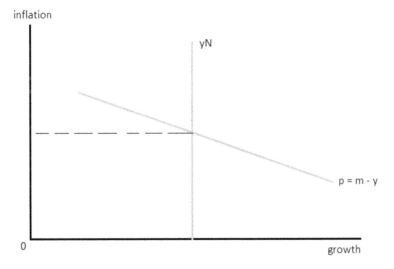

Figure 8.1   Inflation and the Quantity Theory of Money. *Source*: Author.

In the real world, of course, there is a very large problem with this approach as nobody knows what the natural rate of economic growth actually is. In reality there is no such thing, as has been pointed out several times in previous chapters. It does not exist, even though mainstream economists to this day still try to pretend that it does.[4] In fact, the inability to come up with a specific number for the natural rate of growth to plug into equations (7.6) or (7.7) is exactly why pragmatic short-cuts, such as Friedman's suggestion of a constant rate of growth of the money supply, would have their appeal.

But, even within the very limited intellectual framework of mainstream neoclassical economics which does rely on natural rates of growth, interest, unemployment, and so on, there are several other fairly obvious problems with this approach to inflation. Some of these have already been touched on in the various discussions of monetary economics in previous chapters. For example, how could it be possible to define the money supply precisely in an era of rapid financial innovation? Also, how can the money supply sensibly be regarded as "exogenous" as soon as there is any type of banking system in place with the capacity for credit creation? And, practically speaking, even if we were somehow able to know what the definition of the money supply actually is, how could the growth rate of "the" money supply ever be controlled without an appeal to the entirely discredited notion of the money multiplier?

One such glaring problem is that, in practice, the monetary policy instrument has usually been a short-term interest rate of some kind, such as the overnight rate in Canada or the federal funds rate in the United States, rather than any quantitative measure of either the monetary base or the money supply. By the end of the twentieth century (the high-tide of monetarism having been reached in the 1980s) this discrepancy had become very obvious in the public policy debates. As everyone who reads the business and financial press already knows, by that time the whole debate in the media had been actively reframed in the terms of whether the central bank would, or would not, change the policy rate. Before each meeting, the urgent question would be whether the central bank would "hike" (increase) interest rates, "cut" interest rates, or "stand pat"?

Recent Neo-Wicksellian Theories of Inflation

As a result of the various problems with monetarism, apparent by the end of the twentieth century and around the turn of the twenty-first, modern central bankers seem to have reverted a practical theory of inflation owing much more to the nineteenth-century Swedish economist Knut Wicksell (1898) than to quantity theorists such as Irving Fisher (1911) or Milton Friedman (1960). This was the type of theory which, at least before the global financial crisis (GFC) of 2008, came to be known as the "new consensus" (Lavoie and Seccareccia 2004). One significant feature of the new consensus was that it was forced to pay far more attention than monetarism had ever done to the theory of banking, and therefore to the obvious relation between credit creation and money creation.

About a hundred years after Wicksell was writing, towards the end of twentieth century, there had been for some considerable time a relative lack of attention to the interest rate instrument of monetary policy on the part of academic theorists. From the time of publication of the first modern textbooks in the late 1940s, and up to about the early 1970s, the pseudo-Keynesian models of the "neoclassical synthesis" had been the order of the day. These models did stress the importance of aggregate demand, but crucially had assumed a fixed money supply. Next, from roughly the late 1970s to the early 1990s the standard textbook fare was based on monetarism, the twentieth-century version of the quantity theory of money. As we have seen, the policy advice coming from this body of work was to try to directly control and limit the growth of the money supply, and therefore not to worry very much about interest rates. The neglect of interest rates, however, turned out to be a major embarrassment after the collapse of the "monetary targeting" experiments of the early 1980s, and that episode eventually did force the central banks to revert to a pragmatic interest rate and/or exchange rate focus (Smithin 1990, 1994, 2003a). Thus from the roughly the mid-1990s onward up until the GFC of 2008, a new textbook orthodoxy developed in the form of the simple three-equation neo-Wicksellian model of the new consensus.

The most salient features of the new approach were (a) that it was now belatedly recognized that the main monetary policy instrument is a nominal interest rate (the policy rate) and (b) that the supply of credit and money is endogenous. It became impossible for textbooks to go on making statements to the effect that the central bank "cannot control interest rates," and so forth, at a time when the central banks themselves were saying and doing exactly the opposite. Moreover, by now interest rate policy had become a favorite topic for discussion in the financial press. By the beginning of the twenty-first century the new situation was widely acknowledged. According to Benjamin Friedman of Harvard University (B. Friedman 2000):

> (in the late 1960s) . . . the Federal Reserve, like most central banks at that time, made monetary policy by setting interest rates. The same is once again true today. In retrospect, much of the intervening experience proved to be a historical detour.

It was the Wicksellian element *itself* in the new orthodoxy that was meant to be the "face saver." To save the day, there was still supposed to be a natural rate of interest in existence in the economy (somewhere, somehow) that eludes the control of the central bank, and secretly exerts a decisive influence behind the scenes. Thus, as Wicksell had done a century earlier, economic outcomes were made to hinge on any discrepancy between the policy rate and the so-called natural rate.

Wicksell-type theory does accept the argument that ultimately the rate of growth of money supply growth, $m = \Delta M/M$, is determined by credit creation (bank lending). To illustrate, let the symbol L stands for the nominal value of bank loans. A Wicksell-type theory might then, for example, suggest that bank lending can be explained by something along the lines of:

$$\Delta L/L = \alpha\left(r^N - i_0\right), \qquad \alpha > 0 \tag{8.8}$$

This formulation says the rate of change of bank lending will increase, the higher is the interest differential between the natural rate and the policy rate, and vice versa. The greater the difference between what the bank's customers think that they can earn (by acquiring assets with borrowed money) and what they have to pay when doing the borrowing,[5] the faster they will be scrambling to take on debt. From the commercial bank balance sheet, as discussed in chapter 4 above, the money supply itself on the other side of the balance sheet will also be growing at the same rate:

$$\Delta L/L = \Delta M/M \tag{8.9}$$

Thus using equations (8.8) and (8.9) and reverting to the notation that lower case $m = \Delta M/M$, the rate of growth of the money supply will be:

$$m = \alpha\left(r^N - i_0\right). \qquad \alpha > 0 \tag{8.10}$$

For the sake of simplicity in the exposition we will continue to assume that the so-called velocity of circulation does not change very much. If so, then recall that most economists who, as well as accepting the idea of a natural rate of interest, also believe there is a natural rate of economic growth, will therefore assume that the inflation rate will be roughly equal to:

$$p = m - y^N. \tag{8.11}$$

Finally, substituting equation (8.10) in to (8.11) we obtain:

$$p = a\left(r^N - i_0\right) - y^N \tag{8.12}$$

The expression in equation (8.12) thus reflects the basic set of ideas in a Wicksellian/neo-Wicksellian framework. The inflation rate depends on an interest rate differential, in this case on the differential between the natural rate of interest and the policy rate of the central bank, and also negatively on the natural rate of economic growth. Thus, if the policy rate of interest is less than the natural rate of interest, inflation will rise; but if the policy rate is set higher than the natural rate, it is believed that inflation will fall. If there is an increase in the natural rate of growth, the inflation rate will also fall.

I think that the above is a fair enough representation of the basics of Wicksell's own approach from well over a hundred years ago.[6] We should also note, however, that there are still quite a few problems remaining if we wish to bring it up to date.

One such problem is that in Wicksell's time very few writers were able to make the distinction between the real rate of interest and the nominal rate of interest that is considered essential today. Presumably, the natural rate of interest is supposed to be a real rate of interest. It certainly would be thought to be so in any modern interpretation. On the other hand, the symbol i_0 definitely does stand for the nominal policy rate only. How might this particular inconsistency be resolved? Recall from chapter 3 that the ex-post or inflation-adjusted real policy rate is defined as simply the nominal policy rate minus the currently observed rate of inflation:

$$r_0 = i_0 - p \tag{8.13}$$

Moreover, and as we have already seen, in some circumstances the ex-post real policy rate can be taken as proxy for the real policy rate itself. Therefore, substituting equation (8.13) into (8.12), we might reasonably modify the theory of inflation set out above to:

$$p = \alpha(r^N - (r_0 + p)] - y^N \qquad (8.14)$$

Solving for the inflation rate, this becomes:

$$p = \left[\alpha/(1+\alpha)\right]\left(r^N - r_0\right) - \left[(1/(1+\alpha))\right]y^N \qquad (8.15)$$

In orthodox economics, and as discussed in chapters 5 and 6 above, the natural rate of interest in equation (8.15) is assumed to be determined in the market for "real capital" and is independent of any monetary influence. Thus, equation (8.15) now makes borrowing from the commercial banks, and hence the rate of monetary growth and inflation, dependent on the gap between the natural rate of interest and the real policy rate. Inflation is now thought to depend on the real interest rate differential.[7] If the real policy-determined interest rate is set too low this will provide an incentive for continued borrowing from the banks as long as the discrepancy exists. There will therefore be an endogenous increase in the money supply and ultimately in inflation. If, on the other hand, the real policy rate is set too high there will be a deflation. In fact, this set of ideas is probably closer to the way that contemporary central bankers tend to see policy issues than to the original Wicksellian framework per se. Nonetheless, it is still very much in the spirit of Wicksell. And, also as in Wicksell, it remains the case that increases in the supposed natural rate of growth that happen on their own initiative (for example, because of spontaneous improvements in productivity) are thought to reduce the inflation rate and vice versa.

This generic neo-Wicksellian approach to inflation can therefore be illustrated graphically as in Figure 8.2 below:

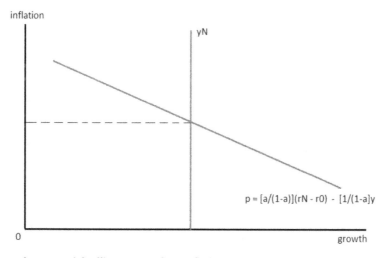

Figure 8.2 The Neo-Wicksellian Approach to Inflation. *Source:* Author.

In this sort of world "wisdom" in monetary policy now seems to entail searching for the correct setting of the real policy rate to precisely match the natural rate of interest adjusted for economic growth. At least in the minds of neoclassical/mainstream economists were such a situation to be achieved there would be no inflation. Moreover, the real rate of interest, the unemployment rate, and the real GDP growth rate would also all be at their "natural" levels. The extensive discussions of "interest rate rules," such as the "Taylor rule" (Taylor 1993) and the related "Taylor principle" (Davig and Leeper 2007, Mankiw 2001, 2003, Woodford 2010), that took place in the late twentieth and early twenty-first century, can usefully be interpreted in precisely these terms.

The neo-Wicksellian approach to inflation is not exactly a mono-causal theory of inflation but there are still only a limited number of possible sources of inflationary pressure. Inflation or deflation is caused by a gap between the natural and policy-determined real interest rates. This can be created either by deliberate monetary policy or by a change in the natural rate of economic growth not matched by the monetary authority. In either case, the monetary authorities are perceived to be at fault whether the observed inflation rate is deemed to be "too high" or "too low." If the authorities wish to achieve zero inflation in these specific circumstances, clearly they must apply a (real) interest rate rule, as follows:

$$r_0 = r^N - (1/\alpha) y^N. \tag{8.16}$$

The basic problem, however, with this sort of framework for monetary policy will readily be apparent to the reader of this book, as it relies heavily on the dubious concepts of the natural rate of interest and the natural rate of economic growth. We have insisted throughout that these things do not actually exist. Logically, therefore, they are quite unable to help in providing any sort of credible explanation for the real phenomenon of price inflation (or of deflation).[8]

Cost-Push and Conflict Inflation

Contrary to the above, according to Joan Robinson (1979) (emphasis added):

> one of the important insights of the Keynesian revolution was . . . that the general level of prices in an industrial economy is determined by the general level of *costs*, and . . . the main influence upon costs is to be found in the relation between money-wage rates and output per unit of employment.

This can be illustrated by a formula such as $P = KW/A$ which is a rival or antidote to the orthodox equation of exchange and is associated, in particular, with the work of the Post Keynesian economist Sidney Weintraub (see Davidson 1991, 149–50) in his book *A General Theory of the Price Level, Output, Income Distribution, and Economic Growth* (Weintraub 1958).The notation in this version of the pricing equation is the same as that used earlier in this book where P is the price level, W is the average nominal wage rate, A is average labor productivity, and K is the mark-up factor. The term K is equal to $(1 + k)$, where lower case k is the profit share. According to the formula prices will rise if money wages rise, or if the mark-up rises, or if productivity falls. If it can further be assumed that the profit share stays more-or-less constant this gives precisely the theory of inflation suggested by Robinson—to the effect that inflation is caused mainly by a rate of increase of money wages faster than productivity growth. Letting lower case p stands for inflation as before this can be written as:

$$p = \Delta W/W - \Delta A/A \qquad (8.17)$$

where $\Delta W/W$ stands for the rate of wage inflation, and $\Delta A/A$ is the rate of productivity growth.

Meanwhile the money supply itself must be adjusting endogenously. If we combine the markup pricing equation $P = KW/A$ with the equation of exchange $MV = PY$ while setting $\Delta K/K = \Delta V/V = 0$, then, given the definition of average labor productivity, $A = Y/N$, this yields:

$$\Delta M/M = \Delta W/W - \Delta N/N. \qquad (8.18)$$

Therefore, the rate of growth of the money supply is equal to the rate of growth of the nominal wage bill. To visual how this works in practice, one can imagine the employers, having just conceded a large wage increase to the labor unions, then having to go to the banks to ask for a loan to pay for all this. As seen in previous chapters the very lending activity itself increases the money supply, and thus validates the new higher levels of nominal wages and of prices.

The remedy for inflation would then be neither deliberate changes in rate of money supply growth as suggested in monetarism (this is not actually possible in the endogenous money environment), nor changes in interest rates as suggested by the neo-Wicksellians, but rather an "incomes policy" of some kind. What is meant by this is either regulation or agreements restricting the growth of nominal incomes including, very prominently, wages (Davidson 2009, 73–82). It has always seemed to me that this is very much a weak point in the Post Keynesian approach to inflation. Such types of polices, it goes without saying, have very serious problems of design and implementation, including most obviously the need to gain public support for the restrictions on their own incomes. A particular concern of labor whenever incomes policies are suggested is that the so-called wage and price controls should not turn out to be wage controls only.[9]

Although the quote from Robinson identifies the main influence on costs (in practice at her time of writing) as being changes in money wages, it should also be mentioned that the general approach clearly leaves open the possibility that other cost increases would have similar effects. It would therefore not be correct to suggest that this approach to inflation is a mono-causal theory. As a general principle, as soon as it is admitted that the money supply is endogenous, this always opens up the analysis to possible multiple causes of inflation. As already discussed, this point seems not to have been grasped at all by neo-Wicksellian writers in the modern era around the turn of twenty-first century.

Another large loose end in the argument for the generic wage-push/cost-push model evidently concerns the motivation for the ongoing nominal wage-push (or other cost-push). Just to assume, for example, an exogenously given rate of increase in nominal wages is not really very convincing. Surely workers and their agents in the unions are interested primarily in real wages? The motivation in asking for a raise in nominal wages must be the hope that this will be a lasting increase relative to prices. There would be no point if the wage increase is always going to be completely offset by an increase in the inflation rate as soon as it has occurred. This insight thus leads on to another version of the cost-push argument that has sometimes been called "conflict inflation" (Lavoie 2007, Rowthorn 1977, Smithin 2012b). In this type of argument, inflation is caused by, or rather is a spillover from, the conflict over real income shares. To illustrate, let us suppose that wage-bargainers (e.g., labor unions) do have a target real wage in mind, and that they always ask for a nominal wage increase sufficient to compensate for any price level increase in the previous period. The target real wage target, $(W/P)_0$, might therefore be written as:

$$\left(W/P\right)_0 = W/P_{-1} \tag{8.19}$$

This implies that if the bargainers want to improve their relative position, they must actually try to increase the value of the target real wage $(W/P)_0$ itself. To achieve any give value of $(W/P)_0$ the nominal wage rate in negotiation will then be given by:

$$W = \left(W/P\right)_0 P_{-1} \tag{8.20}$$

Next, using (8.20) in the expression $P = KW/A$, taking natural logarithms, and reverting to the earlier lower case notation, we may write:

$$p = k + w_0 - a \tag{8.21}$$

where a is the natural logarithm of average labor productivity ($a = lnA$), w_0 is the natural logarithm of the target real wage [$w_0 = ln(W/P)_0$], and k is the natural logarithm of the mark-up factor [$lnK = ln(1+k) = k$ (approx.)]. Therefore, the inflation rate p will increase if either the markup or the target real wage increases. It will fall if productivity increases. The money supply itself always continues to adjust endogenously. The reader will have noticed that expression for the inflation rate in (8.21) resembles in some respects the equation for inflation studied in the course of the exposition of the AMM in earlier chapters. One difference is that the formulation in (8.21) makes no allowance for what we earlier called "speculative" changes in either money demand or money supply. Another important difference is that in the AMM the entrepreneurial markup was ultimately treated as the residual component of income (see chapter 6 above). That is, the markup is decided after the real interest rate has been established in the financial markets—with the active participation of the central bank—and the real wage rate has been determined by wage bargaining. The AMM certainly allows for individual firms to take steps to try to enhance their own mark-ups. In the end, however, the aggregate markup turns out to an endogenous variable. In equation (8.21), on the other hand, the conflict seems only to be a two-way Marxian-type struggle between the "workers" and "capitalists." If both groups are adamant about defending their own position the result can only be an ongoing inflation but without either any lasting impact on the economic growth rate itself, or on profit and wages.

In inflation and growth space the model of inflation set out in equation (8.21) can be graphed as a horizontal straight line. Recall also from chapter 7 that in a "Keynes-type" model the rate of growth of output is determined by the rate of growth of effective demand. This will show up as a vertical line in the diagram. The graphical representation of the causes of inflation is therefore as depicted in Figure 8.3. It is important to notice about conflict inflation that if firms would like to increase the markup k, or if workers want to increase the target real wage rate w_0, and both groups would also like to maintain the new situation into the indefinite future, this will lead to a permanent increase in inflation as shown by an upward shift of the horizontal line. Even if the players do not aim for *continuous* increases in their real shares but only seek to maintain what they see as the new relative level, the inflation will continue for period after period for ever. In essence, essentially the same conflict over real incomes will be repeated every period. Therefore any increases in the profit share or in the real wage that is maintained in the future causes both an immediate increase in the inflation rate which then continues. Conversely, an increase in average labor productivity (the a term) will allow the inflation rate to fall permanently—given the existing profit share and real wage rate. In this case there is more real income available for all, and therefore less reason for there to be any conflict.

As already mentioned in order to reduce inflation an incomes policy of some would have to be introduced. To get zero inflation, for example, such that the inflation schedule coincides with the horizontal axis, we must set:

$$a = k + w_0 \tag{8.22}$$

This will ensure that the total of real incomes shares does not exceed what is feasible given the level of productivity.

These types of policy intervention to directly influence people's incomes were widely discussed in several jurisdictions in the 1960s and 1970s. In some places, such

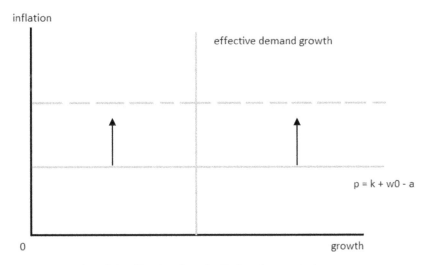

Figure 8.3   Cost-Push and Conflict Theories of Inflation. *Source*: Author.

as Canada, these discussions continued even into the early 1980s.[10] The basic idea is not to let real incomes increase unless there is also an increase in productivity. Obviously, if these sorts of rules are to be implemented without violating the public's sense of fairness they would have to apply across the board and with equal effect. However, such a delicate balancing act has always proved to be impossible to achieve in actual political practice.

Demand-Pull versus Cost-Push Inflation

One way to make a brief shorthand statement or summary of the differences between the various orthodox or mainstream approaches to inflation—including that of the "neoclassical Keynesians" whose views are described by De Vroey (2016, 27–49)[11]— and the Post Keynesian or other heterodox approaches, is to invoke the old distinction between demand-pull and cost-push inflation. Back in the third quarter of the twentieth century this used to be a staple even of fairly orthodox textbooks. However, it is now frequently neglected. If we look at the question from this point of view we might say that the various orthodox theories have inflation determined on the demand side of the economy, with output growth determined on the supply side. The simplest version of Post Keynesian theory on the other hand (and as we have just seen) reverses this causality. This theory has inflation determined on the supply side via cost-push, and output, employment and growth determined via effective demand. Meanwhile the "Phillips curve" explanation of inflation, postulating a trade-off between inflation and unemployment to be exploited by policy which was embraced for a time by the mainstream "neoclassical Keynesian" school, has always had an ambiguous status among Post Keynesians (Davidson 2011, 173–74).

It would be going too far, however, to say that Post Keynesian economists (and others who recognize the endogeneity of money) have altogether neglected the concept of demand-pull inflation. The key underlying assumption of endogenous money allows for an eclectic view in this respect. Suppose, for example, that there is some positive slope to the inflation and growth relationship as shown in Figure 8.4 below.[12]

This, by the way, need have nothing to do with the logic of the Phillips curve argument. It does *not* imply a causal relationship between inflation and output, as is explained in detail by Smithin (2012b), and also in chapter 2 above. The causality is actually the other way around. The point is simply that costs tend to increase with the level of output and the rate of growth for the obvious sorts of reasons. In particular, the fact that the bargaining power of labor will itself be increasing as the economy grows. Note that even with an upward-sloping relationship between inflation and growth the cost-push or conflict explanation of inflation goes through exactly as before. If the inflation/output relationship itself were once again to shift upward in the diagram the inflation rate will increase. But now, however, and as shown in figure 8.4, an increase in effective demand growth will cause an increase in inflation, as well as in output and employment growth.

Most certainly the situation depicted in Figure 8.4 could reasonably be called a demand-pull inflation. The AMM approach to inflation, as discussed in chapters 2 and 5 above, provides another example of a model that is well able to accommodate elements of both cost-push and demand-pull inflation.

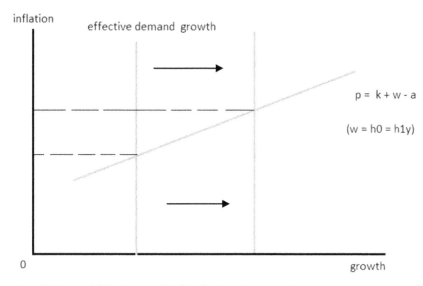

Figure 8.4 The Potential for Demand-Pull Inflation. *Source*: Author.

CONCLUSION

Inflation is a complex social process, and it seems unlikely on the face of it that there is any one explanation of the phenomenon that is valid for all times and places. Empirically, all possible combinations of growth and inflation have actually been observed in reality. There have been periods of high growth with high inflation (an inflationary boom), low growth with low inflation (a depression), low growth with high inflation (stagflation) and, more benignly, non-inflationary growth (Smithin 2002, 584). Therefore, the approach to inflation embodied in the AMM ultimately has the advantage over all of the other explanations of inflation discussed in the present chapter, precisely because of its open-ended and eclectic nature. The key features in the AMM approach are money supply endogeneity and the rejection of any and all natural rate concepts, whether of the interest rate, the GDP growth rate, or the unemployment rate. This ultimately allows for coherent explanations of all of the empirical possibilities.

NOTES

1. Such monetary changes will affect neither the level nor the growth rate of real GDP.

2. This has indeed typically been the assumption of most economic theory produced by the mainstream of the economics profession.

3. When I have advocated an alternative "real interest rule" as in Smithin (1994, 1996, 2003, 2009a, 2013a) and also in chapter 2 above, I have also usually suggested a relatively simple objective, for example that the target for the real policy rate should be set at a "low but still positive level" (Smithin 1994). This was for exactly the same sort of reasons as Friedman.

4. Even to the extent of periodically coming up with empirical estimates of what the natural rate of growth is at any point in time. Invariably, however, these estimates always seem to converge to the actually observed rate of growth. Thus, if the economy ever experiences an actual

period of low growth the explanation will always be that the natural rate of growth has fallen, and vice versa.

5. In the case where the policy rate is *higher* than the natural rate, the suggestion is that the larger the discrepancy the faster will the debtors be paying off the loans. "Power-paying" as this is sometimes called.

6. One difference is that Wicksell himself usually argued that an interest rate differential would lead simply to an increase in the aggregate price level rather than directly to an increase in the inflation rate (the rate of change of the price level). The specification in (8.12) seems to be more consistent with typical behavior in actual financial markets.

7. In a detailed macroeconomic model, such as that in chapter 2 above, it would also be useful to append an explicit pass-through equation from the monetary policy transmissions mechanism in order to show how changes in the real policy rate affect the actual real lending rates of the commercial banks.

8. In the Alternative Monetary Model (AMM) of chapter 2, the only thing that remained of Wicksell-type ideas was the suggestion that a lower setting of the real policy rate of interest will indeed tend to increase the inflation rate, and vice versa.

9. The practical experience of the implementation of incomes policies, in several jurisdictions during the 1960s and 1970s, more than justified labor's concerns in this regard.

10. In the early 1980s, for example, the Canadian federal government instituted a so-called 6 and 5 program designed to restrict the growth rates of the salaries of public sector employees to 6 percent and 5 percent in successive years. That these were supposed to be *low* figures shows the great change in inflation expectations that has occurred over the past thirty-five years.

11. Also recall the discussion in chapter 1 above.

12. For illustrative purposes the wage function from in chapter 6 above is used here to provide the positive slope. This is $w = h_0 + h_1 y$ where $h_0 > 0$ and $0 < h_1 < 1$.

Chapter 9

The Balance of Payments and Exchange Rates

INTRODUCTION

In previous chapters there has been a fair amount of discussion of the importance of the balance of international payments and of the foreign exchange rate. So far, however, no really detailed technical exposition has been provided. This is therefore the task of the present chapter.

The balance of payments is essentially the record of a domestic economy's dealings with the rest of the world during a specific accounting period such as a quarter or a year. The foreign exchange rate, as we will define it here, is the foreign currency price of one unit of the domestic currency.[1] For example, if Switzerland is the domestic economy and at the time of writing it takes 0.66 euros to buy a Swiss franc, then we will say that the exchange rate of the Swiss franc with the euro is 0.66. Similarly, if Australia is the domestic economy and it currently takes 73 US cents to buy an Australian dollar, the exchange rate of the Australian dollar with the US dollar is 0.73.

The Balance of Payments and the International Flow of Funds

The overall balance of payments of the domestic economy is defined as the balance across the current account and the capital account. The capital account reflects new international borrowing and lending and the results of international equity investment. The current account comprises the balance of trade in goods and services, plus the net interest and dividend payments on past capital transactions (i.e., foreign investment income which can be positive or negative). In symbols, the overall balance of payments can thus be written as:

$$BP = CA + KA \tag{9.1}$$

where BP stands for the overall balance of payments, CA for the current account, and KA for the capital account.

In a fixed exchange rate system it is always possible for an overall surplus or deficit on the balance of payments to occur. This will be reflected in changes in the level of foreign exchange reserves (*FE*) held by the domestic central bank. Using the symbol Δ to stand for "change" this can be written as Δ*FE*. If there is balance of payments surplus, official holdings of *FE* will increase. Official holdings will decrease if there is a balance of payments deficit. Hence:

$$\Delta FE = BP = CA + KA \qquad (9.2)$$

Table 9.1 gives some illustrative numbers for the current account, capital account, and changes in foreign exchange reserves, for the domestic economy in a particular year.[2] In each case the figures supplied are net figures. A positive number therefore implies a net flow of funds into the domestic economy, and vice versa. In the particular year illustrated the current account for the domestic economy was positive. This means either that exports were greater than imports, or that foreign investment income was high (or both). The capital account, meanwhile, was negative which means roughly speaking that the citizens of the domestic economy were lending more to foreigners than the other way around. In short, the current account turned out to be greater than the capital account and the overall balance of payments was in surplus. This is reflected in an increase in central bank or "official" holdings of foreign exchange reserves of the same amount. The reason that official holdings of foreign exchange reserves increased must have been in order to keep the exchange rate fixed as the central bank was intervening in the foreign exchange markets at various times during the accounting period to prevent the domestic currency from appreciating. In other words, they must have been selling their own currency and buying foreign exchange.

On the other hand in a pure floating exchange rate system (otherwise known as a flexible exchange rate system) the domestic authorities should not, in principle, be intervening in the foreign exchange markets. Indeed, if they kept strictly to this rule overall deficits or surpluses in the balance of payments would not emerge. They would always be eliminated by exchange rate changes. In this case there will be no change in official holdings of *FE*. That is:

$$\Delta FE = BP = 0 \qquad (9.3)$$

Admittedly such a situation probably never occurs in practice. Even in systems where the exchange rate is supposed to be flexible there will usually be some small changes in *FE* that show up during the accounting period. There is almost never a pure float. Even when the exchange rate is supposed to be completely flexible the domestic authorities sometimes get nervous about what is actually happening in the foreign exchange (*FE*) markets. Therefore they may indulge in at least some invention. These sporadic episodes probably make, very little difference to the operation of

Table 9.1 Annual Balance of Payments for the Domestic Economy (billions of dollars)

CURRENT ACCOUNT:	+31,864
CAPITAL ACCOUNT:	−27,435
OVERALL BALANCE OF PAYMENTS:	+4,429
CHANGE IN FX RESERVES:	+4,429

the flexible exchange system in the long run as eventually market forces will prevail. Nonetheless, they give rise to at least some changes in *FE* during each accounting period. These changes, however small, will thus inevitably show up in the published balance of payment statistics.

In spite of these circumstances, the theoretical case of the pure float—in which equation (9.3) always holds—is still a very informative one to consider. This is because the assumption of a pure float does establish (quite unambiguously so) the very important general principle embodied in the following expression, obtained from equations (9.2) and (9.3):

$$CA = -KA \qquad (9.4)$$

The general principle is simply that the current account usually moves in the opposite direction to the capital account. This will also be true even outside the case of the pure float, up to a correction for changes in the volume of official financing. Moreover, although there have been some historical exceptions in extreme circumstances, the latter will generally/typically not be large enough to upset the basic relationship.

A very important reason for noting the typically inverse relationship between the current account and the capital account is that in the past, and even in many quarters still today, economists have visualized the direction of causality in the balance of payments as flowing from the former to the latter. The theory was that an improvement in "competitiveness" would lead to a current account surplus. Exports would be greater than imports and the nation as a whole would be earning more than it was spending. It would then be natural for the domestic capitalists to try to find outlets to invest these surplus funds abroad—causing capital outflow. On the other hand a nation "living beyond its means," with a negative current account, would (on this view) be forced to borrow abroad to make up the difference—thus causing capital inflow. For very many years this was the standard way of looking at the causes of international capital flows. However, as already shown in chapter 7 above, for example in the discussion about monetary mercantilism and economic nationalism (and as will be further explored in the next chapter), it is much more likely that under capitalism the chain of causality is the other way around. If so capital account developments dominate the current account and the trade performance of the nation emerges as a mere side effect of, or reaction to, what is happening on the capital account. The implications of this reversal are extremely far-reaching. They have the potential for transforming our understanding of how the global economy actually functions.

The balance of payments numbers illustrated in Table 9.1 can be linked up with the standard macroeconomic national income and product accounts framework by recalling the following definition of gross domestic product (*GDP*) , as used in previous chapters. This is:

$$GDP = Y = C + I + G + (EX - IM) \qquad (9.5)$$

where *C* stands for consumption spending, *I* for investment spending, *G* for government spending, and (*X* − *IM*) for net exports. At this stage, we should be thinking of the nominal or dollar magnitudes, rather than the real magnitudes, in order to directly link up with the figures in Table 9.1. That is:

$$\$GDP = \$Y = \$C + \$I + \$G + \$(EX - IM) \tag{9.6}$$

But now we must be careful to note that *GDP* or gross domestic product, as the name implies, is only the value-added produced within the domestic economy's borders. For an open economy there is clearly another potential source of income, namely foreign investment income as already discussed. It is therefore important to distinguish between the so-called gross national product (*GNP*) and *GDP* as follows:[3]

$$GNP = Y + FII \tag{9.7}$$

where *FII* stands for foreign investment income. Note that *FII* can be either positive or negative depending on whether the domestic economy is a net creditor or a net debtor nation. Therefore, in an open economy the total of national income (*GNP*) can clearly be either greater or lesser than what is produced domestically, depending on the foreign credit/debt position.

Next, we can also note that any measure of income, including *GNP*, must by definition be equal to the sum of consumption spending *C*, savings *S*, and taxes *T*. This follows automatically. In principle therefore, whatever the source of income, there are only three things that can ultimately happen to it. Firstly, the government can always take away a big chunk of it in taxes. The unfortunate recipient of the income then only has basically two choices left, to either spend or save whatever is left over. This is as true in the aggregate as it is for each individual. By definition, therefore:

$$GNP = C + S + T \tag{9.8}$$

Using equations (9.5), (9.7), and (9.8), cancelling the *C*s, and rearranging, we can thus arrive at the following algebraic expression:

$$(G - T) + (I - S) = (IM - EX) - FII \tag{9.9}$$

which can also usefully be restated as:

$$(G - T) + (I - S) = -CA \tag{9.10}$$

where (*G* – *T*) is the primary government budget deficit, (*I* – *S*) is the domestic investment/savings balance, and *CA* is once again the current account.

The identity in equation (9.10) became quite well-known at the end of the twentieth century. It was, in fact, the basis for the so-called "twin deficits" argument in the public policy debate in the United States, for example. The basic idea of the twin deficits was the suggestion that a government budget deficit must inevitably lead to a deficit on the current account of the balance of payments. To explain, if (*G* – *T*) stands for the primary government budget deficit, and it turns out to be positive number (if government expenditures are greater than taxation), and if we can also assume that investment is equal to saving ($I = S$) or very close to it, then mathematically there must also be a positive number on the left-hand side (LHS) of equation (9.9). But the term on the LHS is actually the negative of the current account. Therefore the current account itself must also be in deficit-as two negatives make a positive. Hence, it might seem, or could be argued, that a government budget deficit literally causes a current account deficit.

This would obviously be a "hot button topic" for a conservative (small "c") economist. From the conservative point of view, of course, a budget deficit is supposed to be a bad thing. Moreover, a lack of competiveness, leading to a current account deficit, is thought to be equally bad.[4] There is an obvious flaw in the argument but, perhaps needless to say, this did not stop it from being highly influential at times particularly in the last decade of the twentieth century. The flaw is simply that there is no warrant for the $I = S$ assumption on which it depends. In reality, a government budget deficit can be associated with a current account deficit, a current account surplus, or a neutral position on current account—depending only on the sign and magnitude of the term $(I - S)$. Therefore perhaps a more meaningful way of expressing equation (9.10) above would actually be:

$$\left[(G - T) + I \right] - S = KA - \Delta FE \tag{9.11}$$

This now says, reasonably enough (at least as far as the basic algebra is concerned) that if domestic saving is not enough to "finance" both the budget deficit and domestic investment,[5] the funds must either be borrowed from abroad (there must be positive capital inflow) or obtained from sales of FE, with the latter again necessarily relatively small in magnitude. These relationships are sometimes expressed by saying that net national dissaving must be financed either by capital inflow or sales of foreign exchange reserves. Interestingly enough note that this way of describing things again puts the emphasis on the capital account as the active element in balance of payments developments. The net national dissaving leads to capital inflow which in turn leads to a current account deficit. The actual economic mechanism which would bring this about is via changes in the real exchange rate.

Exchange Rates

In what follows we will use the symbol E, as in chapter 3 above, to stand for the nominal spot exchange rate. This is defined as the foreign currency price of one unit of domestic currency. In the Swiss franc to euro example, mentioned in the introduction, and with Switzerland as the domestic economy, the nominal exchange rate would be expressed as $E = 0.66$. When E goes up the domestic currency is said to be appreciating or getting stronger, and when E goes down the domestic currency is depreciating or getting weaker.

A far more useful concept than the nominal exchange rate, however, certainly from the point of view of those making economic decisions on the ground, is actually the real exchange rate. This is given by:

$$Q = EP/Pf \qquad (9.12)$$

Here the symbol Q stands for the real exchange rate, E is the nominal exchange rate, Pf is the foreign price level, and P is the domestic price level. If we want to work out the aggregate or overall real exchange rate for the domestic economy then clearly the P terms would have to involve aggregate price indices of some kind. Notice also, however, that a similar concept can be worked out at the microeconomic level for any individual good or service that is traded.

For example, suppose that an identical automobile is manufactured in plants on both sides of the Canadian/US border in (say) Windsor, ON and Detroit, MI. The price of the foreign (American) vehicle is US\$25,000, and the price of the domestic (Canadian) equivalent is C\$29,000. But which is actually cheaper? Suppose that the Canadian/US dollar exchange rate is $E = 0.73$ (the Canadian dollar is worth 73 US cents).The price of the Canadian vehicle in US dollars is then 0.73 x 29,000, or US\$21,170. The Canadian-made car is actually the more competitively priced and we can work out the real exchange rate for this item as $Q = 21,170/25,000$ or $Q = 0.85$. The Canadian firms (in practice, the Canadian subsidiaries of the US parent firms) will obviously be likely to sell relatively more units in these circumstances. In general then when Q falls, implying a real depreciation, foreign goods will be more expensive and domestic goods more competitive. On the other hand, if Q rises that is a real appreciation. In that case foreign goods become relatively cheaper and domestic goods are less competitive.

Alternative Exchange Rate Regimes

Although the real exchange rate is (by far) the most important concept of the two, the policy debate about the relationship between different currencies has nonetheless often revolved around the issue of whether the nominal rate of exchange between alternative standards of value should be "floating" or "fixed." In the case of floating or flexible nominal exchange rates the exchange rate between any two national currencies is determined proximately by relative supply and demand in the international financial markets. In the fixed exchange rate case the relationship between national currencies is kept within narrow limits according to some international agreement or convention. In this case domestic central banks must stand ready to take whatever action is needed to try to force the nominal value of their currency to remain within the preset bounds. This will include interventions in the foreign exchange markets to buy or to sell as large a volume of the currency as seems to be required.

As well as the extremes of an irrevocably fixed exchange rate and a pure floating rate regime there are also advocates of some compromise between the two. *Cf.*, for example the case of a "fixed-but-adjustable" exchange rate discussed in chapter 2. A "spin doctor" working for the domestic government might well try to frame this the other way round, and call it a "managed float," or a "crawling peg," or some such. Another point of view would be to push the concept of fixed exchange rates to its logical conclusion, and thereby to question whether there is any merit in different political jurisdictions having a separate currency at all. This, for example, is the situation in

Table 9.2   Alternative Configurations for International Economic Relations

A FLEXIBLE (FLOATING) EXCHANGE RATE
A "FIXED-BUT-ADJUSTABLE" EXCHANGE RATE (or similar)
A FIXED EXCHANGE RATE (hard peg)
A CURRENCY UNION (or similar)

the case of a currency union between several states, as also discussed in chapter 2. The different options are therefore once again summarized for the reader in Table 9.2. Presumably, one of the main motivations for fixing the exchange rate, or a fortiori moving toward a single currency, would be to create a more stable environment for business decision-making, and thereby to reduce transactions costs, uncertainty, and so on. If the currency to which the domestic currency is pegged also happens to have a low inflation regime, this may be seen as a way of importing similar "discipline" to the domestic economy. As already argued in chapter 2, however, these arguments are quite simply nonsense.[6] In fact both hard-pegs and currency unions are unstable regimes which are likely eventually to break up. A floating exchange rate regime, or failing that a fixed-but-adjustable regime, turn out to be more sustainable, precisely because they do allow for more policy options on the part of the domestic fiscal and monetary authorities.

The basic problem in choosing between the different exchange rate regimes is that the more firmly fixed is the nominal exchange rate the more limited are the policy options available to the domestic monetary and fiscal authorities. When there is an overwhelming emphasis on fixity, the only policy that can legitimately be pursued is the very act of fixing of the nominal exchange rate itself. Everything else—including the results for output and employment—must be subordinated to this goal. Effectively the domestic country loses all of its economic sovereignty. This is even more obviously so in the case of a currency union in which, by design, the individual member states are supposed to have no policy options. The reason that there is instability in these cases is because, no matter how firmly fixed is the nominal exchange rate in equation (9.2), it is actually the real exchange rate that matters for economic decision-making. If all the policy options are taken off the table, there is no way to influence the behavior of the real exchange rate. This will simply go its own sweet way whether this is good for the domestic economy or not. (In chapter 10 below we will go on to provide formal mathematical proofs of this proposition).

In any event Table 9.3 provides a broad overview of the different exchange rate regimes that have existed in the world economy for the past century and a half, and more. The fifty years or so before World War I were the heyday of the international gold standard. This was a de facto fixed exchange rate regime as each national currency was convertible to a given quantity of gold, thus implying a fixed ratio between the currencies themselves. In a manner of speaking there was effectively already a single world currency, and to a large extent a globalized economy, more than one hundred years ago, albeit at a lower level of technology than today.[7] However, predictably the gold standard broke down with the advent of World War I, and the interwar period was one of the monetary disorder. The various attempts to restore the gold standard at this time all failed, and currencies began to float against one another, but

Table 9.3   The Evolution of the International Monetary System

1873–1914:	THE INTERNATIONAL GOLD STANDARD
1914–1944:	WW1, WW2, AND MONETARY "DISORDER" IN THE INTERWAR PERIOD
1944–1973:	THE BRETTON WOODS SYSTEM
1973–?:	THE MODERN ERA (with the major currencies floating but with several different types of regime being explored, or experimented with, both bilaterally and regionally)

in circumstances that hardly conspired to give the idea of flexible exchange rates a good name. Although in principle floating exchange rates should help the domestic authorities to further their individual policy initiatives, these would (obviously) have to be the correct policies. This was not all the case in the interwar period of the twentieth century. In particular, this was the era of the so-called "beggar-thy-neighbor" policies and the world economic trading system essentially broke down. Perhaps for this very reason, after World War II there was therefore a conscious to restore some order to the international monetary system, and the result was a new regime of fixed exchange rates. This was known as the Bretton Woods system named after a resort in New Hampshire, USA, at which the decisive conference took place in 1944. The Bretton Woods system was dubbed a "gold exchange standard." Only one currency, the US dollar, was theoretically convertible to gold. All the rest were defined in terms of the US dollar itself. Exchange rates were "fixed-but-adjustable" which, as we have argued, does allow more scope for the pursuit of domestic policy initiatives than a hard peg. In practice, however, the necessary adjustments were often delayed far too long, and made in circumstances leading to a number of very high-profile exchange crises during the Bretton Woods years. The system did provide a framework, of sorts, for the international monetary system for around thirty-five years or so down to the international financial crisis of 1971. At that point, however, the United States announced it would no longer redeem US dollars in gold and the system collapsed, in spite of all efforts to repair, it in the two-year period 1971–1973. The only remnant of the Bretton Woods system visible today is the continued existence of some of the controversial international financial institutions that were set up at that time, including the International Monetary Fund (IMF) and the World Bank.

Since the early 1970s down to the present time (and I would imagine for the foreseeable future) there has no longer been any question of money being convertible to precious metals. The major currencies have usually been floating against one another. It is probably fair to say that this has been the main characteristic of the international monetary system for all these years. There have been other initiatives, though, in either a bilateral or regional context that have tended to point in the opposite direction. At different times several countries have tried to fix or "peg" their own national currency against that of one of the major players, often the US dollar. Very many of these attempts, however, have ended in financial crisis when the peg proved unsustainable. There was also a regional regime of fixed exchange rates in place in Europe from 1979–1999 which was known as the European Monetary System (EMS). This had its own periods of crisis most notably in 1992. The EMS morphed into a full currency union after 1999. This new structure was the so-called Euro-zone which has had a very checkered history in the part twenty years, to say the least. Currency unions have also been set up elsewhere in the world between smaller groups of states, for example, in the Eastern Caribbean, and also in West Africa. Another option that seemed to be very much on the table at the end of twentieth century, and was promoted in South America in particular, was the alternative of so-called dollarization. Dollarization can proceed either directly, by simply adopting the US dollar for use in the domestic economy, or via currency board arrangements. But once again, the high-profile currency board arrangement in Argentina, for example, eventually collapsed with disastrous consequences in 2001. Dollarization turned out to be very far indeed from a panacea for the economic difficulties experienced in South America.

The only real conclusions that can be drawn from this brief history of the international monetary system is that international currency arrangements have been in state of flux for as long as anyone can remember. Moreover, the debate over what is likely to be the best or "optimal" exchange rate regime is likely to continue and that professional economists seem rarely to have understood the adverse consequences of the several schemes that have been suggested. We can sum up the main issues in the evolution of the international monetary system as follows:

1. For many decades there has been an ongoing search for an appropriate currency/exchange rate regime at both regional and global levels. This still continues.
2. The downside of a solution involving a fixed exchange rate regime or a currency union, and so on, is that the more firmly exchange rates are fixed the greater is the loss in monetary sovereignty for the domestic economy.

In the following sections of this chapter we move on to discuss some of the more technical aspects of the modus operandi of flexible and fixed exchange rate systems.

Exchange Rate Determination I: Flexible Exchange Rates

In a floating exchange rate system, the foreign currency price of a unit of domestic currency is proximately determined by market forces. Heuristically we can think of a typical demand and supply diagram as illustrated in Figure 9.1. The quantity shown on the horizontal axis of this diagram is that part of the outstanding domestic money supply being offered for sale in the FX market. The supply of domestic currency for this purpose arises from literally anything that is a negative item in the balance of payments. For example, if a domestic resident wants to purchase foreign goods (import foreign goods) they must first acquire the foreign currency needed to pay for them. To acquire foreign currency the relevant amount of domestic currency must therefore be offered for sale on the FX market. Similarly, if a domestic resident wants to make an investment in another country (thus causing capital outflow) they will also need to acquire foreign currency to make these investments and hence offer domestic currency for sale. Similarly, the demand for domestic currency in the FX market arises from anything that is a positive entry in the balance of payments. If a foreigner wishes to buy domestic exports that person must also have a demand for the domestic currency to pay for these items. And if foreigners wish to purchase domestic securities, they also must first acquire domestic currency. Next, putting the demand curves and supply curves together, the argument is, as usual, that the exchange

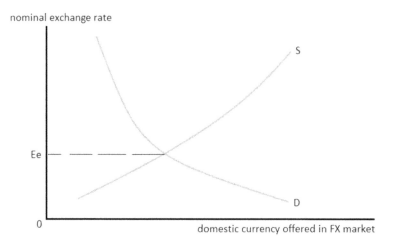

Figure 9.1   The Market for Domestic Currency as Foreign Exchange. *Source*: Author.

rate will be determined by market forces at the intersection of the demand and supply schedules.

We can explore this idea a bit further by considering some examples of how changes in certain economic variables are likely to affect the daily market equilibrium of nominal exchange rates. Suppose, for example, the domestic central bank raises the nominal interest rate in its own country in pursuit of some monetary policy goal, while interest rates in the rest of the world remain unchanged. The results of this action are illustrated in Figure 9.2. There will be an effect on both sides of the FX market. For example, higher interest rates in the domestic economy will encourage some foreign residents to invest in domestic securities, thereby increasing the demand for the domestic currency. At the same time, some domestic residents will now decide not to invest in foreign securities, precisely because domestic interest rates have increased. Thus the supply of domestic currency to the FX market will also be reduced. Putting

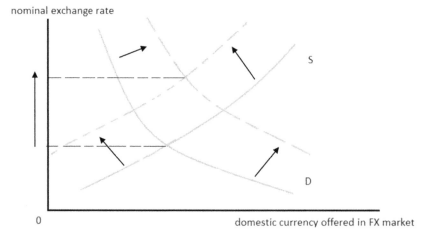

Figure 9.2   An Increase in Domestic Nominal Interest Rates. *Source*: Author.

these two effects together the result will be an increase in the price of the domestic currency—that is, there will be an appreciation of the exchange rate.

In another example of a change in domestic economic conditions Figure 9.3 shows what will be the impact of an increase in the domestic price level on the exchange rate. If prices in the domestic economy rise with no change elsewhere then, clearly, domestic goods will lose competitiveness on world markets. Fewer foreigners will buy domestic goods, and thus inevitably the demand for the domestic currency in FX markets will be reduced. The demand curve for domestic currency in the FX market will shift back and to the left. At the same time, some domestic consumers will switch to buying foreign goods, and therefore the supply of domestic currency to the FX market will be increased. The supply curve of foreign exchange to the FX market will shift down and to the right. The net effect of the increase in prices in the domestic economy is to cause the nominal exchange rate to depreciate. One way of trying to understand this phenomenon might be to say the exchange rate must depreciate in order to offset the effects of the higher nominal prices in the domestic economy.

Finally, in Figure 9.4, we consider an example of an economic change that affects only one side of the FX market. For example, suppose that there is an economic boom in the economy of one of the major trading partners of the domestic economy. Meanwhile, however, economic growth remains sluggish at home. The prosperity of the foreign country will have the effect of increasing everybody's incomes there, and at least some of that increase will surely be spent on what are imports from their point of view. The exports of the domestic economy therefore increase, and the demand for the domestic currency in FX markets by foreigners—in order to pay for the domestic export goods—will increase. But this is actually the only effect going on in the FX market. There will be no similar effect on the supply curve of domestic currency offered on the exchanges. The exchange rate will nonetheless tend to increase. The shift of the demand curve is all that it takes. The ultimate impact of an improvement of economic prosperity abroad is thus that it will tend to lead to an appreciation of the domestic currency.

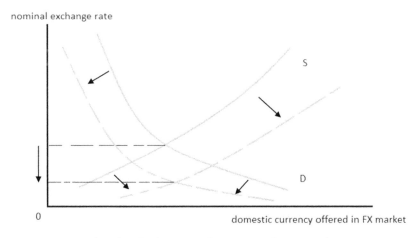

Figure 9.3 An Increase in Prices in the Domestic Economy. *Source*: Author.

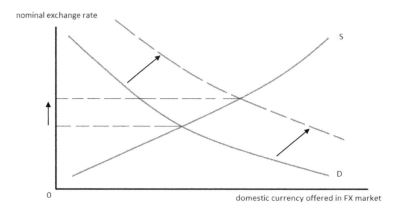

Figure 9.4   An Increase in Income in a Foreign Economy. *Source*: Author.

At this point we will leave it to the reader to work out any further examples of economic changes that are likely to affect the exchange rate in one direction or another.[8]

Exchange Rate Determination II: Fixed Exchange Rates

In the case of fixed exchange rates and contrary to the above discussion the idea is to prevent the various economic changes from having any effect on the exchange rate. How can this be achieved? It obviously will not happen just because the different countries involved come to some kind of agreement or understanding, or sign a treaty. Specific actions will have to be taken, usually by the central bank of the domestic economy, to ensure that the exchange rate peg remains in place.

In the nature of things in a floating exchange rate system the equilibrium nominal exchange rate will be changing every day. Inevitably therefore, when it comes to a fixed rate regime, the domestic authorities will always be trying to fix the exchange rate at some level other than that which market forces dictate. Obviously there are two possible scenarios. In some cases, the desired value of the exchange rate will be overvalued as compared with market outcomes. In other cases it will be undervalued. Figure 9.5 looks first at the case of an overvaluation. In Figure 9.5, the central bank is trying to keep the exchange rate overvalued. According to the "market" the equilibrium should be at a lower level. Actually no one will be willing to sell foreign exchange (i.e., buy the domestic currency) at the overvalued level. Therefore, if the overvaluation is to be maintained, what must happen is that (in effect) the domestic central bank itself must be willing to offer that deal. Typically they will have some foreign exchange reserves on hand that have been accumulated in previous foreign exchange dealings. In order to keep the exchange rate at an artificially high level they must now be willing to sell these reserves (which means to buy their own currency) at the higher level. The hope is that they can keep the exchange rate at the higher level for at least as long as they have any FE left. In the diagram this is shown by a temporary shift of the demand curve for domestic currency over to the right (to a position shown by the broken line.) The central bank is artificially adding its own "demand"—for its own currency—to the demand originally existing in the FX market.

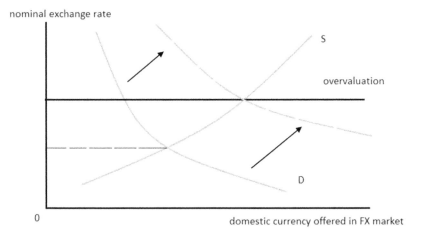

nominal exchange rate

S

overvaluation

D

0

domestic currency offered in FX market

Figure 9.5 The Central Bank Sells Foreign Exchange to Preserve an Overvaluation. *Source:* Author.

Two observations are in order about this process. First, we can now see explicitly why it is that an overall deficit in the balance of payments leads to an outflow of *FE*. By definition when the currency is overvalued the balance of payments will be in overall deficit. This is what it means for a currency to be overvalued. The most obvious way of handling this problem would have been simply to let the currency depreciate. However, if the exchange rate is supposed to be fixed this avenue is ruled out. This is why the central bank must be willing to sell *FE*, to keep the currency at the higher level. Thus a balance of payment deficit leads directly to a fall in official holdings of *FE*. On the other hand, a surplus would cause an increase in official holdings. Second, it should now be quite clear of what a so-called foreign exchange crisis consists. The attempt to maintain an overvalued foreign exchange rate leads directly to an outflow of *FE*. However, this can only go on for as long as the *FE* holds out. When all the reserves have been used up there is nothing left but to let the currency fall, and finally find a lower (usually much lower) level in the marketplace. This is precisely the crisis. The problem may be postponed for a while by borrowing foreign exchange from other central banks, or from the IMF or from some other international financial institutions (IIFs). Clearly, however, there is also a limit to this even if only for political reasons. Eventually the crisis is still going to happen. It cannot be put off for ever. It is also interesting to note that even if the domestic central bank had not been intervening in the FX market all this time, the exchange rate would still have eventually declined to the same level. But, it would not have happened so suddenly, and nobody would have been calling it a crisis.

What possible reason could there be for the central bank to engage in this sort of behavior which seems so contrary to common-sense? That is actually a hard question to answer. The reasons for maintaining an overvalued currency most likely have to do with questions of national prestige, or attempts to maintain "confidence" in the currency, and so forth. Most often, however, these actions end up doing just the opposite.

The alternative possibility for central banks and governments is to try to deliberately undervalue their own currency. The motive here is a little more transparent. Now the idea is to improve price competitiveness in international markets and to increase exports. This case is illustrated in Figure 9.6.

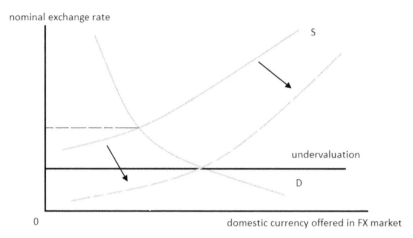

nominal exchange rate

S

undervaluation

D

0   domestic currency offered in FX market

Figure 9.6 The Central Bank Buys Foreign Exchange to Maintain an Undervaluation of the Exchange Rate. *Source*: Author.

Now the domestic authorities want to keep the exchange rate at a lower level than the market equilibrium, in order to gain some advantage in the global marketplace. The other players in the FX market, however, are not likely to be willing to sell any of the domestic currency they hold at the low rate. Therefore, once again the domestic central bank must step in and, this time, offer to sell domestic currency at the undervalued rate, that is, buy foreign exchange at too high a price. This is actually relatively easy for them (unlike the opposite situation of buying domestic currency at a high rate) for they can always create ("print") as much domestic currency as they like. From their point of view it does not matter how many domestic currency units are offered in exchange for a unit of foreign currency. They have an unlimited supply.

In the diagram in Figure 9.6 the supply schedule for domestic currency in the FX market is artificially pushed down and to the right. This occurs because the central bank is continually creating domestic currency and then buying up foreign exchange with it. An undervalued currency will evidently be associated with a surplus on the overall balance of payments. Once again, it is easily seen therefore why a persistent balance of payments surplus under fixed exchange rates leads to an increase in central bank holdings of foreign exchange reserves.

On the face of it, a deliberate undervaluation is a situation that might be sustainable for a longer time period than the opposite case of an overvalued exchange rate. In the overvalued case the problem was that the central bank would soon run out of *FE* and would have had no means of acquiring any more. In the case of an undervaluation, however, there is no difficulty for the central bank in continuing to create as much domestic currency as they would like. There may eventually be a downside nonetheless. If domestic economy starts to do well as a result of the undervaluation it is possible that the domestic prices themselves will start to rise. In the long run therefore, thinking in terms of the real exchange rate ($Q = EP/Pf$), whatever advantage is gained by having a low "E" to start with may well eventually be offset by a higher "P." Moreover, in the real world of political economy at some point the trading partners of the country with an undervalued exchange rate are likely to lose patience with the system.

The complaint will be that an undervalued currency allows the country involved to obtain the full benefits of a trade relationship while at the same time using or manipulating the system to create greater economic activity and jobs for themselves. For example, this was the basis of a long running dispute between the United States and Japan in the last decades of the twentieth century. In more recent years, the United States has had similar difficulties with their trading relationship with China.

To sum up the discussion so far we might say that under a flexible exchange rate regime it is the exchange rate itself that does the adjusting. Under a fixed exchange rate regime, however, it is the various government policy initiatives that must be continually adjusted or modified when necessary to try to make sure that the exchange rate peg is maintained. This last circumstance is the very reason why fixed exchange rate regimes tend to commend themselves to at least some political "conservatives." They can be seen as a method of tying the hands of the domestic government and thereby preventing them from pursuing an aggressive fiscal or monetary policy. This is obviously so in the extreme case of a common currency. In that case, by design, there are literally no policy levers for the national government to be able to manipulate. And needless to say, this causes severe political problems in the context of a supposedly "democratic" system, as has frequently been observed in practice in recent decades, particularly in the context of the Euro-zone within the European Union (EU). As against this there are also other groups of so-called conservatives—really classical liberals—who believe in the rule of the market at all costs.[9] This would tend to militate in favor of flexible exchange rates. Generally speaking, however, this seems to be a case of picking the right sort of policy stance for the wrong sorts of reasons.

CONCLUSION

This chapter has discussed the relationship between the balance of payment numbers for the open economy and the familiar framework of the national income and expenditure accounts, while continuing to recognize the theoretical shortcomings of the latter set of statistics. The importance of the different exchange rate regimes, and of the "international financial architecture," has also been extensively discussed.

The next chapter will show how these relationships work out in practice in the context of the Alternative Monetary Model (AMM) first introduced in chapter 2.

NOTES

1. The reasons for defining the exchange rate this way round were already explained in chapter 3. The reader should be aware, however, that this is not always the practice followed consistently in economics textbooks or in the financial press. Caution is therefore advised when comparing the arguments made in this book to some other treatments that can be found in the literature. The usage in this chapter, and throughout the whole volume, is internally consistent and has the great advantage of conforming with the common-sense meanings of the various terms. Common-sense is a commodity that is often in short-supply in the academic economics and finance literature.

2. The reader should note that in the actually published figures the data is likely to be presented in considerably more detail than in the stylized version of Table 9.1. For example, the total capital account may be subdivided into the capital and financial accounts to reflect the distinction between foreign direct investment and purely financial transactions. Similarly the current account may include separate entries for the merchandise trade balance, the balance in so-called "invisibles," or the separate amount of foreign investment income itself. The purpose of the ultra-streamlined presentation here is to focus on first principles. Another point to notice about the figures in Table 9.1 is that in published statistics the ΔFE term may (seem to) appear with the "wrong" sign in order to conform to the principles of double-entry book-keeping—and make the "bottom line" come out to zero. For example, it may be written −4,429 rather than +4,229. In Table 9.1, however, the idea is to show what is actually happening to *FE*. In the case of a surplus they are increasing.

3. In what follows we will drop the $ prefixes of equation (9.6) to again simplify the notation.

4. We saw in chapter 7 that it usually simply assumed that it is desirable for the economy that there should be both internal balance and external balance. We also saw, however, if regarded as objectives rather than outcomes, there is no solid economic reason for either assumption.

5. I put the term "finance" in quotes here to remind the reader of the several discussions of endogenous money in previous chapters.

6. The reader will have noticed that this is a word which seems to appear very frequently in discussions of the "conventional economic wisdom."

7. Indeed, it is the monetary arrangements (which are social) that seem to matter the most not the technology per se.

8. One factor that must surely be relevant is changes in exchange rate *expectation*s. If, for example, the exchange rate of the domestic currency is expected to appreciate in the future that will probably cause an increase in the demand for the domestic currency in the here and now to take advantage. Hence there will also be a *current* nominal exchange rate appreciation. The issue of exchange rate expectations will be dealt with in much more detail in chapter 10 to follow.

9. The reader will certainly be be aware that terms like conservative, liberal, and so on are very imprecise when it comes to economic discussion. This is due to the complete corruption of these terms in the political discourse in the United States (in that country—in particular) over the past several decades. For example, groups that are now routinely called conservative are usually not conservative at all, but are really classical liberals in disguise (i.e., they are in favor of free markets, free trade, open borders, etc.). Even the present chapter succumbed to this sort of usage, for the sake of convenience, for example in the discussion of the controversy about the twin deficits. On the other hand, the term "liberal" itself has become more or less synonymous with "socialist." In a classic example of "gaslighting" the media even switched the traditional colors of the political parties some years ago. Now red stands for the political party to the right of center and blue for the left. This is mind-boggling to someone of my generation. In chapter 11 below some attempt will be made to sort out these blatant contradictions.

Chapter 10

A Realist Approach to International Currency and Finance

INTRODUCTION

A realist approach to international currency and finance takes seriously questions of the ontology of money and of the importance of the exchange rate regime. These issues have taken on increasing importance in recent decades as debates about globalization, the liberalization of capital flows, the 'international financial architecture," and the push toward regional currency union, have emerged as leading areas for the attention of macroeconomic theorists. One prominent view, based on a fundamentally materialist ontology, and which has had proponents from all sides of the political spectrum, is that not only do these trends inevitably lead to a serious loss of policy leverage for small or medium-sized open economies, but also that there is not much that can be done about it.

However, based on an alternative realist social ontology,[1] this chapter argues to the contrary that it is essential for the government of each domestic economy (of whatever size) to retain as much control as possible over the levers of macroeconomic policy. Moreover, that this is an entirely feasible objective even in the contemporary global economic environment with highly mobile "capital."[2] In adjudicating this debate, there are basically two important theoretical questions that have first to be settled before it is possible to come to any conclusion. The first is the extent to which, in principle, the real rate of interest can be affected by monetary and fiscal policy. That is, even in a theoretical closed-economy context before considering the open-economy implications. This question has been answered squarely in the affirmative in previous chapters. The theory of interest determination developed in this book has indeed shown that the central bank does play a decisive role, that the real rate of interest is in itself an entirely "monetary" phenomenon, and that there is no such thing as a natural rate of interest. The domain of the interest rate of is that of the money and financial markets rather than that of capital theory. The second question, having thus taken up a position on the crucial theoretical issue, is to what extent or degree do the contemporary trends in globalization themselves affect the ability of the local economy to exercise autonomy over both monetary and fiscal policy? In effect, we are here discussing the fundamental question of globalism versus economic nationalism. At the time of writing this is an issue which has become very prominent in political debates globally.

As already discussed in detail in this book (in chapter 5 above, for example) the neoclassical or mainstream position on these matters is based on the contrary idea that the real interest rate is ultimately a "natural rate" determined strictly by supply and demand in barter capital markets. In this sort of discourse, it is simply assumed that the real rate of interest rate can never be permanently affected by the activities of the central bank—regardless of many centuries of practical experience to the contrary. Thus a "policy irrelevance" argument (Scarth 2014, 53–58) is built directly into the model from the start. On this view, the process of globalization serves merely to reinforce the notion that economic decision-making in the individual domestic economy is not viable. There is an underlying fatalistic argument that in all cases, both in the domestic economy and globally, the ubiquitous and inscrutable "market forces" must prevail. Therefore, there would be little or no economic cost to the accession to a currency union, for example, or indeed to any other measures designed to further political aspirations toward ever-increasing economic integration. If monetary policy is believed to be wholly irrelevant in any case, there is nothing to be lost by renouncing it.

A counter argument to the fatalistic position was anticipated, for example, by Paschakis (1993) in an important PhD thesis written around twenty-five years ago entitled *Real Interest Rate Control and the Choice of an Exchange Rate System*. It has since been further developed in a number of papers by such writers as Kam and Smithin (2004, 2008, 2011), Marterbauer and Smithin (2000, 2007), Paraskevopolous and Smithin (1998, 2002), Paschakis, Paraskevopolous and Smithin (1999), Paschakis and Smithin (1998), Smithin (1995, 1999, 2003b, 2012c), Smithin and Smithin (1998), and Smithin and Wolf (1993, 1994, 1999).

Exchange Rate Regimes and International Economic Relations

In chapter 2 above it was suggested that (painting with a broad brush) it is useful to identify four possible alternative configurations for international economic relations. These are (1) a floating exchange rate, (2) a "fixed-but-adjustable" exchange rate, (3) an irrevocably fixed exchange rate or "hard peg," and (4) a currency union.

As argued in chapter 2, and demonstrated in earlier formal models by Smithin (2013a, 2016a), in an economy with a floating exchange rate the results will be qualitatively the same as those in the equivalent closed-economy model. This is a case of full "monetary sovereignty" for the government of the domestic economy (Tymoigne and Wray 2015, Smithin 1999, 2016a). All that would then be needed for a complete analysis of all the economic policy options would be to add results for the real exchange rate and the foreign debt position to those already worked out for the other variables. In an economy with a fixed-but-adjustable exchange rate the results also resemble qualitatively those of the closed economy which again allows for some domestic control over monetary and fiscal policy. In both cases, therefore, the domestic authorities are able to exercise some sort of influence over *both* monetary and fiscal policy. Note that this overturns the old idea, derived from the Mundell-Fleming model of the 1960s (Fleming 1963, Mundell 1963a), that monetary policy can be assigned to floating exchange rates and fiscal policy to fixed exchange rates. In the light of both theoretical considerations and much of the actual experience over the past fifty years this notion has turned out to be seriously misleading.

In spite of the name, a putative hard peg for the exchange rate (such as a metallic standard, a "credible" fixed exchange rate regime, or a currency board with no loopholes) is actually an unstable system, and will eventually break down. There are numerous historical examples as already outlined in chapter 2. There is no effective sovereignty in this case, and it is not, therefore, a viable policy choice for the long run. The idea of a currency union, which in its late twentieth and early twenty-first-century versions owes much to the notion of an "optimal currency area" (OCA)—another ultimately misleading concept also originally due to Mundell (1961)—is to do away with exchange rates altogether. It is a total abandonment of sovereignty. Ironically, even though the intent is to eliminate exchange rate problems, experience shows that when initially applied the currency union has more or less the same (in)stability characteristics as a hard peg (cf. the actual case of the Euro-zone). Unless the domestic economy is willing to give up control over economic policy entirely there are only two possible long-run outcomes, either (a) a break-up of the system which would be the equivalent of an exchange rate crisis in this context, or (b) eventual evolution into a true federal state with a developed system of fiscal federalism. In the latter case, the different countries literally turn into "Provinces" in the specifically Canadian sense of this term.

The Relevance of Interest Parity and Purchasing Power Parity Conditions

These results indicated above may perhaps be better understood by referring to the familiar interest parity conditions from international finance. In a notation that has been used elsewhere (e.g., in Smithin 2013a, 274–77, 2016a), the covered interest parity (CIP) condition may be written as:

$$i - if = (E - F)/E. \tag{10.1}$$

Here i stands for the domestic nominal interest rate, if for the foreign nominal interest rate, E for the current spot exchange rate (defined as the domestic currency price of one unit of foreign exchange), and F for the forward exchange rate. The CIP condition states that financial rates of return in the different international centers will be equalized by arbitrage when covered by a forward contract. If the stronger uncovered interest parity (UIP) condition also holds then we would have:

$$i - if = (E - E_{+1})/E \tag{10.2}$$

which implies that

$$F = E_{+1}, \tag{10.3}$$

and also:

$$lnF = lnE_{+1}. \tag{10.4}$$

In fact, equations (10.3) and (10.4) state the traditional conclusions of a "rational expectations" or "efficient markets" analysis in textbooks on finance. They are expressed here in terms of both the levels and also natural logarithms of the variables. In these sorts of treatment it tends to taken for granted as a theoretical proposition that the forward rate is equal to (and, therefore, for practical purposes is essentially the same thing as) the expected future spot rate. From a realist perspective, however, looking at actual financial markets, this is quite wrong. The UIP condition is a far more onerous condition than CIP and therefore very much less likely to hold in practice. The implication of UIP would be that rates of return in the different international financial centers will be equalized even when not covered by a forward contract. This never seems to bother economic theorists. However, as soon we step outside the theoretical bubble even for a moment, it must be realized that this would mean a quite implausible degree of asset substitutability between financial instruments denominated in different currencies.

To illustrate consider the North American context for example. If we find that CIP holds we might then say that this means it should be easy from the purely technical point of view to be able to transfer funds between Canada, Mexico, and the United States. It could be done simply with a touch on the computer keyboard. So far, so good, this is the meaning of perfect capital mobility.[3] In the real world, however, the actual exchange rates between the Canadian dollar, the Mexican peso, and the US dollar would still be floating. It would be naïve in the extreme for economic agents to pay no attention whatsoever to the proportions of assets denominated in each currency in their individual portfolios. Yet this is precisely what the assumptions of UIP, and of perfect asset substitutability, must be taken to imply. In reality, whenever there are floating exchange rates, and regardless of how expectations are formed, perfect asset substitutability is unlikely to obtain. Therefore, UIP will not hold. The forward rate usually will differ from the expected future spot rate, E_{+1}, due to the existence of the so-called risk premium which we will call Z.[4] Therefore, again expressing the result in terms of natural logarithms:

$$lnE_{+1} = lnF + Z \tag{10.5}$$

The upshot can only be that, in general under flexible exchange rates, domestic nominal interest rates can and do deviate from foreign interest rates according to:[5]

$$i - if = \left[(E - E_{+1})/E \right] + Z. \tag{10.6}$$

In these circumstances the domestic authorities therefore do have a certain amount of leeway to set the rate of interest as they see fit, based on domestic economic conditions.

Even in the case of a fixed-but-adjustable exchange rate regime the domestic authorities do still retain some control over the domestic interest rate. In these circumstances, although the exchange rate is not actually expected to change (that is, $E_{+1} = E$), nonetheless, whenever the domestic authorities decide to make an "adjustment," it could possibly do so. This possibility will certainly be taken into account by participants in the financial markets, and thus priced into all relevant contracts. Therefore, even when it is true that $E_{+1} = E$, domestic nominal interest rates still differ from foreign rates according to:

$$i - if = Z \tag{10.7}$$

Note that this last result does not rely on capital controls, or on any other political impediments to the free flow of funds from one jurisdiction to another. Ironically it is simply the *lack* of firmness about exchange rates that provides the policy space.

The other two regimes listed above, that is, a hard peg or a currency union, provide no such policy space which is exactly why they are unstable. To see why this is so, first note that in such a regime the CIP condition will presumably continue to hold as usual. Also, as the regime is supposed to be irrevocable, it would be logical to assume that $Z = 0$.[6] Therefore, the UIP condition actually does hold in these cases, and as far as nominal interest rates are concerned, domestic nominal interest rates should be equal to foreign interest rates, $i = if$. It is astonishing to realize, however, that in recent real-world political economy this purely theoretical result about nominal rates seems actually to have been thought of as a method of *enforcing* the (real) concept of the natural rate of interest globally. It is almost as if the underlying objective had been solely to make neoclassical economics "come true," as it were, in spite of all the obvious objections that can reasonably be made against it. Rather than applying a realist social ontology to the world of international finance, the supposed experts actually seem to have been "idealists" in the philosophical sense, thinking that reality itself can somehow be remodeled to suit the theory that exists only in their minds. Indeed it is very difficult to explain the initial enthusiasm for such disastrous arrangements as the Euro-zone, for example, in any other way.

In the real world there is a basic problem for the globalists in that the equalization of nominal interest rates does nothing to ensure that *real* interest rates are equalized. There is, in fact, no more sense to the idea of a natural rate of interest for the global economy (i.e., a "world" interest rate of some kind) than there was in the theoretical case of the closed economy taken in isolation. The argument derived from interest rate parity conditions falls apart if the other parity condition discussed in chapter 9 above, namely the so-called purchasing power parity (PPP) condition, itself does not hold. In that case, both the real exchange rate and real interest rates in the different countries are liable to be changing all the time. In the actual political conditions of the late twentieth and early twenty-first centuries, this problem seems essentially to have been ignored by very many academics and also, unfortunately, by the vast majority of economic policy-makers and their advisers.

To explain this point in more detail note that having first defined the nominal exchange rate as in equation (10.1) above, then the real exchange rate Q is given by a formula originally introduced in chapter 3, namely:

$$Q = EP/Pf \tag{10.8}$$

where Pf is the foreign or "world" price level. Further, in the context of equation (10.8) the notion of PPP can conveniently be simulated by the so-called law of one price,[7] or:

$$Q = 1 \tag{10.9}$$

The underlying idea, as already discussed in previous chapters, is that the real exchange rate is determined not by monetary or financial factors but by the barter terms of trade. By assumption in this particular case the terms of trade are fixed at one-for-one.

The standard argument which we are here criticizing would then go to state that *if* CIP, UIP, and PPP *all* hold there will also be real interest parity (RIP). That is:

$$r = rf \tag{10.10}$$

The implication of this expression would therefore be that what we are here calling the foreign real interest rate is actually a sort of natural rate of interest at the global level, the so-called world interest rate. Unfortunately, in reality this "world rate of interest" simply does not exist, any more than does a purely domestic natural rate of interest. It is also definitely incorrect to claim, for example, that a hard peg for the exchange rate, or any other social arrangement, can somehow conjure a world real interest rate into existence. Much less that there is any mechanism to make the domestic real interest rate conform to this *chimera*.

The key point is that even if $Z = 0$ and $i = if$ equation (10.10) cannot be true because PPP will not, in fact, be holding. There will still always exist a real version of equation (10.16) such that the domestic and foreign real interest rates will differ by the expected real appreciation or depreciation of the exchange rate plus the currency risk premium. That is:

$$r - rf = \left[(Q - Q_{+1})/Q \right] + Z. \tag{10.11}$$

It follows from this expression that simply setting $Z = 0$ and $i = if$ is insufficient to eliminate the difference between the domestic and foreign real rates of interest. This can easily be seen with some simple algebraic manipulations. Using the basic definitions of the real rate of interest, both at home and abroad (i.e., $r = i - p_{+1}$, and $rf = if - pf_{+1}$), and then putting these expressions together, given the underlying assumptions of $Z = 0$ and $i = if$, will yield equation (10.12).

$$\left[(Q_{+1} - Q)/Q \right] = p_{+1} - pf_{+1} \tag{10.12}$$

Lagging one period and re-arranging gives the actual rate of change of the real exchange rate as:

$$\left[(Q - Q_{-1})/Q_{-1} \right] = p - pf \tag{10.13}$$

It is this clear that the dynamic processes for the real exchange rate, and for the real interest rate differential itself, are unstable unless inflation rates happen to be exactly the same across the different jurisdictions. A similar equation would also apply in the case of a currency union. In that case the equivalent of the real exchange rate would simply be the ratio of the domestic price level to the foreign price level. Neither in the case of a hard peg, nor that of a currency union, therefore, will the real exchange rate ever reach the supposed PPP equilibrium. For example, if inflation is lower in the rest of the world (ROW), or in the partner nations, than it is in the domestic economy, there is no way of enforcing $p = pf$ except with draconian austerity policies. The latter in no way constitutes a reliable transversality condition for the international economy because of the inevitable social instability (Smithin 2013a, 284–92) that will result. This problem should really have been very much to the forefront in the various discussions of international political economy taking place in the early twenty-first century. It was not, however, ever taken sufficiently seriously either by academics or politicians.

The Complete Open-Economy Version of the Alternative Monetary Model (AMM)

Having now dealt with the different behavioral patterns that emerge in the various potential configurations for international economic relations, we can now set out the complete open-economy version of the AMM of Smithin (2013a, 221–33) in equations (10.14) through (10.20) below. The results derived below are applicable only to the first two configurations discussed above, namely, floating exchange rates and fixed-but-adjustable exchange rates. The other two configurations are unstable.

$$y = e_0 + e_1 k - e_2 q + (g - t), \quad 0 < e_1 < 1, \ e_2 > 0, \tag{10.14}$$

$$k = a - r_{-1} - w_{-1}, \tag{10.15}$$

$$p = p_0 + w_{-1} - a, \tag{10.16}$$

$$w = h_0 + h_1 y - h_2 q, \qquad 0 < h_1 < 1, \ h_2 > 0, \tag{10.17}$$

$$r = m_0 + m_1 r'_0 + (1 - m_1) p_{+1}, \quad 0 < m_1 < 1, \tag{10.18}$$

$$b = b_{-1} + e_2 q + (r - y) b_{-1}, \tag{10.19}$$

$$q = q_{-1} + r_{-1} - r_f + z_0 + z_1 b_{-1}, \quad z_0 > 0, \quad z_1 > 0. \tag{10.20}$$

The endogenous variables in the system, seven in all, are listed in Table 10.1. The exogenous variables may be conveniently grouped into three broad categories, involving policy changes, changes in real costs and productivity, and changes in

Table 10.1   List of Endogenous Variables

y = the real GDP growth rate,
k = the natural logarithm of the aggregate profit markup,
w = the natural logarithm of the average real wage rate,
p = the inflation rate,
r = the real prime interest rate,
b = the foreign debt position as a percentage of GDP,
q = the natural logarithm of the real exchange rate.

market psychology, respectively. The variables representing policy changes are listed in Table 10.2.

As was the case in the closed-economy version of the AMM in chapter 2, there are also a number of exogenous variables that must be taken into account associated with spontaneous changes in real costs and productivity. These are listed in Table 10.3.

An important innovation of the AMM in chapter 2 was its ability to quantify variables indexing the various degrees of confidence prevailing among firms, consumers, and participants in the financial markets. Moreover, Collis (2016, 2018) has now shown how it is possible to derive a literal time series to indicate the current state of such collective states of mind as "animal spirits" and "liquidity preference." Some time ago, in the original thesis by Paschakis (1993), a similar exercise was undertaken with respect to the currency risk premium in international financial markets. For present purposes, the exogenous variable measuring psychological states in both domestic and international markets are listed in Table 10.4.

Finally, the given parameters of the system are shown in Table 10.5. The signs and magnitudes of these parameters are based on the logical requirements of the model, and on empirical plausibility (Collis 2016, 2017).

Equation (10.13) illustrates what, in chapter 7 above, we called a "Keynes-type"[8] theory of economic growth. It suggests that the economy will grow if firms are more profitable (undoubtedly the essential principle of capitalism), if there is an up-turn in "animal spirits" (an increase in the autonomous spending of the private sector as of percentage of GDP), if the government is running a primary budget deficit as a percentage of GDP, and if there is a trade surplus as a percentage of GDP.[9] Equation (10.14) is a log-linear adding-up theory of income distribution such as that described in chapter 6. The (natural logarithm of) average labor productivity resolves into three components, the (natural logarithm of) the average/aggregate mark-up of business firms, the real rate of interest, and the natural logarithm of the average real wage rate. Next, equation (10.15) explains inflation in a formulation that has already been used in chapters 5 and 8. Given the existence of endogenous money there must be a significant cost-push component to inflation. However, inflation is also influenced such by things liquidity preference and "speculative demand" on both sides of the money market.

Table 10.2   Exogenous Variables: Policy

g = government spending as a percentage of GDP,
t = the average tax rate,
r'_0 = the target for the real policy rate (this is the real overnight rate in Canada) – as set by the central bank.

Table 10.3 Exogenous Variables: Real Costs and Productivity

m_0 = the commercial bank markup,
r_f = the foreign real interest rate,
w_0 = the natural logarithm of the base real wage rate,
a = the natural logarithm of average labor productivity.

The term p_0 is actually a composite variable that reflects the net effect of these money demand and supply parameters. Equation (10.16) exhibits a wage function which suggests that the (natural logarithm of) real wages will increase when the socio-political power of labor increases (e.g., because of such things as legislation favorable to labor, or an increase in the rate of unionization, etc.). Real wages will also tend to increase in a growing economy, in this case because of the increased bargaining power of labor in such circumstances. The real wage rate will fall if the real exchange rate depreciates. Equation (10.17) shows that real interest rates in the market-place will increase if the central bank increases its target for the real policy rate in pursuit of a tight money policy, but on the other hand it will fall if the inflation rate increases. This last phenomenon is nothing other than the historical "forced savings" effect (Hayek 1939)[10] as discussed in chapter 5 above which, in the twentieth century, came to be called the "Mundell-Tobin effect" after Mundell (1963b) and Tobin (1965).[11]

The final two equations, (10.18) and (10.19), illustrate the dynamics of the balance of payments and the real exchange rate, respectively. Equation (10.19) describes the balance of payments situation and, therefore, the consequent changes in the foreign debt position as a percentage of GDP, under a situation of flexible exchange rates. The debt position will worsen if a real appreciation causes the current account to deteriorate, and also if the real interest rate exceeds the rate of GDP growth, thereby exacerbating the interest burden on the foreign debt. Equation (10.19) describes how international capital flows affect real exchange rates. The real exchange rate will appreciate if the domestic real interest rate is greater than the foreign real interest rate minus the currency risk premium, and vice versa.

Table 10.4 Exogenous Variables: Market Psychology

e_0 = a measure of animal spirits, that is, net autonomous spending by the private sector of the domestic economy, as a percentage of GDP,
p_0 = a measure of the state of liquidity preference in domestic financial markets,
z_0 = the intercept in the expression that explains the "currency risk" premium in international financial markets, this is essentially a measure of international liquidity preference.

Table 10.5 Parameters

e_1 = the sensitivity of firm spending to profitability,
e_2 = the sensitivity of the trade balance as a percentage of GDP to the natural logarithm of the real exchange rate,
h_1 = the sensitivity of the natural logarithm of the average after-tax real wage rate to lagged GDP growth,
h_2 = the sensitivity of the natural logarithm of the domestic real product wage to the natural logarithm of the real exchange rate,
m_1 = the pass-through coefficient in the monetary policy transmissions mechanism,
z_1 = the sensitivity of the currency risk premium to the real foreign debt position as a percentage of GDP.

A "Complicated" Policy Rule Simplifies the Model

As I have argued on many previous occasions (e.g., Smithin 1994, 2003, 2009a, 2010, 2016a, 2016c), and also as shown in chapter 2 above, the central bank must be pursuing a "real interest rate rule" of some kind if they wish to promote macroeconomic stability. If they focus only on the level of the nominal rate of interest (as is unfortunately very often the case in practice) the system will be unstable, and it will be impossible to have any coherent discussion of economic policy. In the system under discussion here, recalling that there is no natural rate of interest in the system either domestically or internationally we can use this condition to greatly simplify what would otherwise be quite a complicated mathematical model. At least in principle, for example, the central bank could actually try to fix the real prime rate of the *commercial* banks themselves at a level $r = r'$ by following the rule:

$$r_0 = (1/m_1)(r' - m_0) + \left[(1-m_1)/m_1)\right]p_{+1} \qquad (10.21)$$

This rule is clearly quite complicated in and of itself. In the theoretical context, however, if the central bank can be assumed to somehow be able to achieve the desired effect this will greatly simplify a theoretical model that would otherwise be difficult to solve analytically.[12] In what follows, therefore, and simply to better understand how the model works, we will indeed make the assumption that the central bank is following the rule in (10.20). In practice the rule that the central bank will follow is obviously going to have to be much more straightforward that this, such as the formula $r_0(t) = r'_0 + [1/(1-m_1)]p_{+1}$, as suggested in chapter 2. In the real-world situation it is doubtful that the central bankers will be able to cover every contingency in the manner implied by equation (10.20). The main objective for a real-world central bank should be to resolve not to add to the instability of the system and hence pursue a "park-it" policy with respect to the real policy rate of interest (Palley 2015, Rochon and Setterfield 2007, 2012, Smithin 2016a, 2016c).[13] Nonetheless, the results derived below will be useful for our objective of illustrating some of the main principles of economic policy formation in an open economy with flexible exchange rates and, in that sense, will therefore still have many important practical policy applications.

The Dynamic System (Continuous Time Approximation)

The dynamics of the system may be inferred from equations (18) and (19). These are in discrete time. However, setting $dr_f = dr' = dz_0 = 0$, and given inflation stability via the real interest rate, it can also be seen that a continuous time approximation to the original dynamic system will be given by:

$$\begin{vmatrix} db/dt \\ dq/dt \end{vmatrix} = \begin{vmatrix} r'-y & e_2 \\ z_1 & 0 \end{vmatrix} \begin{vmatrix} db \\ dy \end{vmatrix} \qquad (10.22)$$

For global stability in the exchange rate and foreign debt system (i.e., "global stability" in the mathematical rather than the geopolitical sense) the trace of the right-hand side (RHS) matrix, A, should be negative and its determinant should be positive. However, we find that in the context of the system in (10.21) the trace could well be positive. If $r' - y > 0$, for example, we would have:

$$Tr\, A = r' - y + 0 \quad > 0. \tag{10.23}$$

On the other hand, the determinant is definitely negative, as:

$$Det\, A = -e_2 z_1 \quad < 0. \tag{10.24}$$

Therefore the dynamic system has a saddle-point solution. Global stability per se can be ruled out but, nonetheless, there exists a "stable arm" in the phase diagram which could always be reached in the presence of an appropriate transversality condition. When this situation occurs in the standard economics literature it is then usual for the author or authors immediately to argue that it is legitimate to move right on to the analysis of the equilibrium or steady-state solution. Paschakis and Smithin (1998, 711, fn.) explained the reasoning typically employed by orthodox economic theorists in the following way:

> The basic argument is that for "rational"[14] agents a saddle-point solution is a desirable [system] property. Agents will [supposedly] be aware of the two potential alternatives [stability or instabililty]. . . . Therefore, for any individual, to act as if the stable solution will emerge is the best alternative.

This argument may not seem all that plausible to many heterodox economists (or most others!) as a general proposition and there are indeed good reasons for this skepticism. As shown by Smithin (2013a, 288–92 even if the solution is a saddle-point there is not necessarily a plausible transversality condition, inherent in the market mechanism, to activate the so-called jump variable (or variables) needed to push the system on to the stable path. In this particular case however, specifically involving international financial markets with flexible exchange rates, we probably can think of exchange rate changes themselves as providing such a mechanism. Suppose, for example, that the exchange rate has recently been depreciating. Should agents always bet on the depreciation to continue? If they do so and thereby also continue a rapid accumulation of foreign denominated assets, they will risk serious capital losses if the behavior of others does not conform. But, everybody will be making a similar calculation, and will also realize that others are doing exactly the same thing at the same time. The safest bet for everybody, therefore, may very well be to assume that the depreciation will not continue indefinitely. In these circumstances it would be relevant to go on to work out the characteristics of the equilibrium solution. This, therefore, is the exercise that will be carried out in the next section of this chapter.

An Equilibrium Model of the Modified Open Economy AMM

Given the arguments about stability and real interest rates set out above we now proceed to work out the equilibrium or steady-state solution. Because of our interest rate assumptions the model conveniently reduces to the following four equations:

$$y = e_0 + e_1(a - r') - e_1(h_0 + h_1 y - h_2 q + t) - e_2 q + (g - t), \quad 0 < e_1 < 1, e_2 > 0 \quad (10.25)$$

$$p = p_0 + h_0 + h_1 y - h_2 q + t - a, \quad 0 < h_1 < 1, h_2 > 0 \quad (10.26)$$

$$0 = e_2 q + (r' - y)b \quad (10.27)$$

$$0 = r' - rf + z_0 + z_1 b. \quad z_1 > 0 \quad (10.28)$$

This is a relatively simply four-equation system with four unknowns. The unknowns are y, the real GDP growth rate, p, the inflation rate, q, the natural logarithm of the real exchange rate, and b, the foreign debt position as a percentage of GDP. The reduced system is fortunately far more tractable than the full seven-equation system defined by equations (10.14) to (10.20).

Total Differentiation

Next, totally differentiate each of equations (10.25) through (10.28) holding the exogenous variables (e_0, h_0, p_0, rf, and z_0) constant. We thus have $de_0 = dh_0 = dp_0 = drf = dz_0 = 0$. This results in the following totally differentiated system:

$$(1 + e_1 h_1)dy - (e_1 h_1 - e_2)dq = dg + e_1 da - e_1 dr - (1 + e_1)dt \quad (10.29)$$

$$-h_1 dy + dp + h_2 dq = -da + dt \quad (10.30)$$

$$-bdy + e_2 dq + (r' - y)db = -bdr' \quad (10.31)$$

$$-z_1 db = dr' \quad (10.32)$$

This is a 4 x 4 system, involving changes in just four key exogenous variables. These are the domestic real interest rate, determined by the central bank real interest rate rule in (10.20) the two fiscal policy instruments, and the average productivity of labor (assumed to be determined by the existing state of technological progress). In matrix form the system can be written as:

$$\begin{vmatrix} (1+e_1h_1) & 0 & -(e_1h_1 - e) & 0 \\ h_1 & -1 & h_2 & 0 \\ b & 0 & -e_2 & -(r'-y) \\ 0 & 0 & 0 & z_1 \end{vmatrix} \begin{vmatrix} dy \\ dp \\ dq \\ db \end{vmatrix} = \begin{vmatrix} -e_1 & 1 & -(1+e_1) & e_1 \\ 0 & 0 & -1 & 1 \\ b & 0 & 0 & 0 \\ -1 & 0 & 0 & 0 \end{vmatrix} \begin{vmatrix} dr' \\ dg \\ dt \\ da \end{vmatrix} \qquad (10.33)$$

The reason that so many zeros appear in the two matrices in (10.32) is because of the "clever" monetary policy rule specified in equation (10.21). In effect this eliminates or neutralizes any economic changes that might have worked through the interest rate channel. This would not be a realistic assumption in and of itself (i.e., as applied to an actual economy). However, this move is still very much in the spirit of realism. It is a theoretical simplification but, nonetheless, is one which does help to explain more clearly the basic principles by which a real economy actually works.

The determinant, B, of the left-hand side (LHS) matrix is as follows:

$$Det\ B = e_2 z_1 (1 + e_1 h_1), \qquad > 0. \qquad (10.33)$$

Given the sign of $Det\ B$ it is then possible to work out the final results of the model, in the form of long-run multipliers, by the application of "Cramer's rule" (Chiang and Wainwright 2005, 103–7).

Long-Run Multipliers

The final results for the long-run multipliers of the system are shown in Table 10.6. At this point we should once again recall that, formally speaking, the various propositions apply to a single jurisdiction with a floating exchange rate holding economic conditions in the rest of the world (ROW) constant. The results would be more-or-less identical, at least qualitatively, also in the case of a fixed-but-adjustable exchange rate regime (Smithin 2013a, 296–97). The signs of the long-run multipliers are next summarized in Table 10.7.

Looking at the results in the first row of Table 10.7 we see, for example, that a permanently lower real rates of interest on money will tend to permanently increase economic growth, albeit at the cost of a somewhat higher inflation rate. Although the

Table 10.6 Long-Run Multipliers in the Open Economy with Flexible Exchange Rates

dy	dp	dq	db	
$-[e_1/(1+e_1h_1)]$	$-[e/(1+e_1h_1)]$	$[(bz_1+r'-y)/e_2z_1]$	$1/z_1$	dr'
$[1/(1+e_1h_1)]$	$[h_1/(1+e_1h_1)]$	0	0	dg
$-[(1+e_1)/(1+e_1h_1)]$	$[(1+e_1)/(1+e_1h_1)]$	0	0	dt
$[1/(1+e_1h_1)]$	$-[1/(1+e_1h_1)]$	0	0	da

Table 10.7   **Signs of the Long-Run Multipliers**

dy	dp	dq	db	
−	−	?	+	dr′
+	+	0	0	dg
−	−	0	0	dt
+	−	0	0	da

inflation rate does increase it does not continue to "accelerate" after the new equilibrium is reached. (It does not get totally out of control.) At the same time the foreign debt position will be reduced (or the foreign credit position will be strengthened). This occurs because if lower real interest rates can be achieved then in addition to its direct effects on growth this will also cause capital outflow. In turn, this means that the current account of the balance of payments will improve. Interestingly enough, the effect on the real exchange rate of a lower target real rate of interest is ambiguous. It depends on the initial conditions. It is quite possible that a cheap money policy will actually improve the economy so much that in the end the real exchange rate appreciates. Therefore, fears that a cheap money policy will always lead to real exchange rate depreciation are unfounded. In general, in an open economy with flexible exchange rates the real exchange rate simply adjusts to whatever the new situation is. It may either appreciate or depreciate without there being any major consequences for the growth rate itself.

In the next two rows of Table 10.7, row 2 shows the effect of a change in the level of government spending as a percentage of GDP, and row 3 documents the effect of a change in the average tax rate. They both describe the results of fiscal policy in one sense or another. An expansionary fiscal policy by means of an increase in government spending ratio will increase the growth rate—just as Keynesian advocates of fiscal stimulus have always argued. As a result of the stimulus there will indeed be a somewhat higher inflation rate. However, as already mentioned, this will not be an "ever-accelerating" increase. (There is no "natural rate" of unemployment in the economy to make this happen.) A reduction in the average tax rate is also an expansionary policy and such a tax cut also definitely has the effect of increasing the rate of growth of real GDP. In the case of a lower tax burden, however, this is not simply a question of increasing aggregate demand. As already discussed in chapter 2, tax cuts actually work via a combination of demand side and incentive (or supply side) effects. It is important to notice that when taxes are reduced the inflation rate does not rise (the assumption that was always made in the era of *faux* Keynesianism in the thirty years or so after World War II) but actually *falls*. This is due to the impact of the lower taxes on production. This is the main difference between the alternative types of fiscal expansion brought about via either spending increases or tax cuts (Smithin 2013a, 259–60).

As we are here focusing on the open economy issues it is striking to see that changes in the fiscal policy variables (unlike changes in real interest rates brought about by monetary policy) ultimately have no effect on either the real exchange rate or the foreign debt position. There are zeros everywhere in the last two columns of rows 2 and 3 of Table 10.7. These seem to be very strong theoretical results, but we should be clear that they only come about because of the underlying assumption that the monetary authorities are always pursuing a strict real interest rate rule. Central bankers never allow either inflationary or deflationary tendencies to affect the real lending rates of the commercial banks. Indeed, the only circumstances in which the real interest rates charged by commercial banks are allowed to rise or fall are when there is a deliberate monetary policy choice to do so. For this reason there will never be a change in the foreign debt position or the real exchange rate, unless the central bank is prepared to let this happen,

Although it is doubtful that this sort of monetary policy regime could be maintained in practice, the strong results do at least have the advantage of reinforcing the point that *both* the real interest rate and the real exchange rate are above all monetary variables. Moreover, once this point is understood, it is also fairly easy to work out what would be likely to happen if the monetary authorities are not able to pursue such a well-defined monetary policy. Suppose, for example, that instead of following the rule in (10.21) we think of the authorities as simply set a target for the inflation-adjusted real policy rate, r'_0, at some arbitrary level (as assumed in previous chapters). What will now happen when there is, for example, an increase in government spending as a percentage of GDP? We can safely conjecture that, as before, the growth rate will again increase at the cost of a somewhat higher inflation rate. In short, fiscal stimulus will continue to work. The difference now, however, is that the real lending rate of the commercial banks, r, will also be allowed to fall as a result of the increase in inflation. This occurs via the negative relation between real interest rates and inflation in equation (10.18). And, the fall in interest rates will actually give yet another further boost to economic growth. More to the present point, the foreign credit position and the current account will also both improve. The expansionary fiscal policy itself now appears directly in the guise of a "monetary mercantilist" policy which lowers interest rates and improves the current account.[15] These are the precisely the opposite results to those assumed in much of the conventional wisdom on the effects of fiscal policy as, for example, those based on the old Mundell-Fleming model. In the present interpretation the likely international effects are that the credit position will improve, whereas the real exchange rate could go either way. This is a drastic reversal of orthodox thinking about the international economy.

In the case of a tax cut rather than a spending increase, also assuming that this is now allowed to have an impact on the real rate of interest, the actual results will be slightly different. Tax cuts still represent an expansionary fiscal policy, and the rate of economic growth will still increase. However, there is now a *lower* rather than a higher rate of inflation. This therefore causes an increase in the real lending rates charged by the commercial banks. In this case, we would therefore get a worsening of the current account of the balance of payments and an increase in foreign indebtedness. Again the effect on the real exchange rate will be ambiguous.

We turn finally to row 4 of Table 10.7, showing the effect of an increase in productivity occurring in the domestic economy (say) as a result of technological innovation. As might be expected this increases the growth rate, and also reduces the inflation rate because of lower production costs. If the central bank is again pursuing the strict real interest rate rule from equation (10.21), there will be no impact on either the real exchange rate or on the foreign debt position. When monetary policy is not so strict it may again be inferred what is likely to happen to these variables because of the effect of inflation on the real rate of interest. In this case the real interest rate is likely to increase. Note, however, that this has nothing whatever to do with ideas about how productivity changes affect the supposed "rate of return to capital." It is the real rate of interest on *money* that is affected via the impact on international financial markets. It does not occur if there is no such impact. The real exchange rate, of course, will depreciate.

CAPITALISM IN ONE COUNTRY?

The title of this section is a pun on Stalin's notion of "socialism in one country," an idea which he first floated in the second edition of *Foundations of Leninism* in 1924 (Stalin 1924). "Capitalism in one country," to the contrary, is meant to refer to the prospects for a non-socialist domestic economy having the ability to control its own economic destiny by putting in place the appropriate macroeconomic policies.

How best to characterize the type of policy stance that would be most conducive to this sort of outcome? Kam and Smithin (2008, 2011) and Smithin (2013a) have used the term "*monetary* mercantilism" (emphasis added), also briefly mentioned in the first section of this chapter. This does not refer to protectionism as such but, rather, in the specific context of the open or international economy, to a general policy of stimulating effective demand, and thereby trying to bring about full employment, economic growth, and general prosperity by various *financial* and *monetary* techniques. This terminology is not ideal, mainly because of the negative connotations of the expression "mercantilist" to almost all professional economists on both the left and right of the political spectrum. Nonetheless, some such convenient expression is clearly needed to denote the space between international socialism, on the one hand, and "free trade," "globalism," "the power of market forces," and so on, on the other.

Smithin (2009, 193–94) suggested a four-quadrant diagram to illustrate the different policy choices that are available. A slightly different version of this diagram is therefore also presented in Table 10.8 below. This distinguishes between socialism and enterprise (which does seem to be a much better term for a commercial society than the amorphous "capitalism")[16] as alternative economic systems, and also globalism versus nationalism in politics. The terms in the NW, NE, and SW quadrants of the diagram are self-explanatory. Each of them, for different reasons, clearly carries a lot of intellectual and historical baggage. There is a question mark for the label in the SE quadrant which, as I say, is unfortunate as this seems to be the only option left for the promotion of an "open society" in the domestic economy, to use Popper's (1945) term for it. What to call this type of policy stance? It will surely have to be *something* along the lines of "economic nationalism," "capitalism in one country," "monetary

Table 10.8   Different Orientations in Political Economy

	Globalist	*Nationalist*
Socialism	International socialism	National socialism
Enterprise	Globalization	?

mercantilism," or similar, as already essayed in this chapter. I do not want to suggest that any of these expressions would be ideal. As Keynes says, in the quote about mercantilism versus free trade below, all such expressions seem always to have had a variety of diverse, and even contradictory, connotations to different people. It would be an extremely useful contribution to the debate if someone could come up with a concise and unambiguous term for what is required.

On this general question of terminology it is interesting to note that Humphrey (1998, 2) has also used the expression mercantilism, albeit without the qualifier monetary, in a very similar way to the usage here. However, he (Humphrey) makes it clear that he does not approve of the idea of conducting policy according to its tenets. Humphrey does concede that the majority of economists usually think of the notion of mercantilism in the narrow sense, as having to do with putting up "barriers to trade" and with the sole objective of achieving a trade surplus. Nonetheless, he also insists that there are some much subtler issues in monetary theory that are involved in the debate, and is surely correct in having done so. As mentioned previously (in a footnote to chapter 2 above) Humphrey actually went on to cast the entire history of economic thought as a contest between "mercantilism" in this monetary/macroeconomic sense and the "classical economics" of which he is himself an advocate. Figures like Law, Stueart, Tooke, Keynes and Kaldor were placed on the mercantilist side, and Hume, Smith, Thornton, Ricardo, and Friedman, on the other. According to Humphrey:

> This policy prescription . . . [protectionism] . . . was, of course, the mercantilists' main claim to fame. But the hallmark that secured them a permanent niche in the history of monetary doctrines was their contra- or anti-quantity theory of money.

Keynes, interestingly, seemed entirely to concur with this (although coming down firmly on the opposite side of the issue). Chapter 23 of the *General Theory* is entitled "Notes on Mercantilism, the Usury Laws, Stamped Money, and Theories of Under-Consumption." According to Keynes (1936, 333):

> For 200 years both economic theorists and practical men did not doubt that there is a peculiar advantage to a country in a favourable balance of trade and grave danger in an unfavourable balance, particularly *if it results in an efflux of the precious metals* (emphasis added). But for the past one hundred years[17] there has been a remarkable divergence of opinion. . . . The majority of statesmen and practical men in most countries . . . have remained faithful to the ancient doctrine; whereas almost all economic theorists have held that anxiety concerning such matters is groundless . . . since the mechanism of foreign trade is self-adjusting . . . attempts to interfere with it are not only futile but . . . impoverish those who practice them because they forfeit the advantages of the international division of labor.[18] It will be convenient, following tradition to designate the older opinion as *Mercantilism* and the newer as *Free Trade* (original emphasis), though . . . each has both a narrower and broader signification . . . [and must be interpreted] . . . with reference to the context.[19]

Later, Keynes (1936, 335) goes on to say:

> Let me . . . state . . . what now seems to me be the element of scientific truth in mercantilist doctrine. . . . Given the social and political environment and . . . national characteristics which determine the propensity to consume, the well-being of a progressive state . . .

depends on . . . the sufficiency of . . . inducements . . . [to invest]. . . . They may be found either in home investment or foreign investment . . . the opportunities for home invest-ment will be governed by . . . the domestic rate of interest; whilst . . . foreign investment is necessarily determined by the size of the favourable balance of trade. Thus, in a society where there is no question of direct investment . . . [by . . . public authority] . . . the . . . objects, with which it is reasonable . . . to be preoccupied, are the domestic rate of interest and the balance of foreign trade.

It seems significant as Keynes does not claim that any of the historical contributors to larger mercantilist literature themselves ever correctly articulated, or understood, this particular "scientific truth." Nonetheless, as far as the specifically international repercussions of their policy preferences are concerned, presumably the expectations of those pursuing the various strategies that historically might be described as versions of "monetary mercantilism" would indeed have been that, along with higher domestic growth, such policies would also lead to a strong current account and the building up of a foreign credit position, rather than becoming indebted either to other nations or to international financial institutions.

These effects would occur most easily and obviously under a system of flexible exchange rates, but the above analysis has shown how this might also occur under a fixed-but-adjustable exchange rate regime. Kam and Smithin (2008, 2011) have also pointed out that, historically, whether under flexible exchange rates or not, and regardless of whether or not the issues were fully understood/articulated by the rel-evant decision-makers at the time, strategies that might be characterized as monetary mercantilism were indeed employed by many of the nations that did eventually suc-ceed in achieving stronger economic growth, and thus ultimately a prominent global geopolitical position in the capitalisms of their day.

It has always seemed to me that this is a quite different argument from protection-ism, as such, meaning by this the active advocacy of tariff or nontariff barriers to trade. As for the latter it does seem reasonable to argue, as economists have done for centuries, that conventional protectionist measures are unlikely to achieve the results claimed for them. Most likely they would have the negative sorts of macroeconomic impact similar to those of higher taxes, as already discussed in detail in this chapter and in chapter 2 above.

CONCLUSION

The framework set out in this chapter has been able to illustrate several of the growth scenarios for an open economy, and also to predict the impact of "monetary mercan-tilist" or "economic nationalist" policies on such things as the real exchange rate and the foreign debt position. The key to "capitalism in one country," returning to our original expression from the penultimate section heading, is the existence of a sepa-rate monetary and financial system with either a floating exchange rate regime or, at least, a fixed-but-adjustable exchange rate regime in which adjustments can be made as required without excessive political or other difficulties. The framework is also capable of explaining the problems that have often been experienced by jurisdictions that are not in a comparable state of affairs. For example, those jurisdictions that are trapped in the hopeless situations of either an irrevocably fixed exchange rate regime or a currency union with no adequate system of fiscal federalism.

It seem important to restate here the point (already made in chapter 7 above) that it is not necessarily correct to describe the monetary mercantilist type of approach as similar to the "beggar-thy-neighbor" policies of the 1930s. It is certainly true that if one country alone pursues the type of policy suggested here, and others do not, this will be to the first mover's sole advantage. They may thus eventually gain a hegemonic position and build up a commercial and/or political empire. This has frequently been the case historically, with the British Empire itself (of which Canada was an integral part) in the period 1694 to 1944 as the outstanding example.[20] However, our analysis also very strongly suggests that the principles of monetary economics, if correctly understood, and hopefully as explained in this book, show that the world economy is not in principle a zero-sum game. Given the necessary socio-political preconditions in all of them, if each nation were to pursue the same types of policies simultaneously the result would simply be higher overall world growth and eventually actual balance across both the current and capital accounts of the balance of payments - in each case (Kam and Smithin 2008, 2011, Smithin 2013a). There seems to be nothing, therefore, to preclude the economic analyst from offering the same, or similar, policy advice to each jurisdiction separately. It is up to the decision-makers in each individual polity to decide whether or not to accept the advice and, thereby, whether they end up as either creditors, debtors, or in balance. As the saying goes (which I have had cause to repeat on several occasions in recent years) "on their own heads be it" (Smithin 2011, 2013a).

NOTES

1. On what this might entail see, for example, Mendoza (2012) and Smithin (2009a, 2–4, 2013b).

2. As usual I have put the word "capital" in quotes because of the multiple levels of ambiguity associated with the term—and as discussed throughout this book.

3. In actual practice, as everyone knows, it is much easier to transfer funds from Canada to the United States than from Mexico to Canada. This is primarily for political reasons.

4. A true Keynesian, as we have previously observed, would no doubt prefer to say "uncertainty premium." The point is that, in reality, statistical probability theory in invalid in the social world (including the realm of international finance). Recall the discussion of this topic in chapter 1 above.

5. The first term on the RHS of equation (10.6) could alternatively be written as $lnE - lnE_{+1}$.

6. But *why* do the supposedly rational agents get fooled about this, time after time? The answer is that these "rational agents" will most likely have "studied" (or rather imbibed) the efficient markets hypothesis in business school and, almost certainly, will never have been exposed to the types of issues discussed in this book.

7. In the general case of "relative purchasing power parity" Q need not be equal to one (as in the case of the numerical examples in chapter 9 above) but is nonetheless taken to be a constant—again determined by the barter terms of trade. The key point to notice, once again, is that a materialist ontology is taken for granted.

8. Recall that this terminology is due to Sir John Hicks in *Methods of Economic Dynamics* (Hicks 1985, 108).

9. Therefore, the domestic economy will tend to shrink if the real exchange rate appreciates (making domestic goods less competitive). If $e_2 > 0$ the implications is that this effect is greater than any possible offsetting impact on domestic costs.

10. This terminology has always been extremely unfortunate. Smithin (2013a, 185–86) explains that a better term would really have been "forced *investment*." Indeed, the so-called Austrian economists of the 1930s actually used the term "overinvestment." However, they were never able to conclusively demonstrate that the additional investment brought about by lower real interest rates was, in fact, superfluous. In the AMM, it certainly is not.

11. For further discussion of this topic see Kam (2000, 2005), Kam and Smithin (2012), Kam, Smithin and Tabassum (2016) and Smithin (2013a).

12. This is a case in which computer simulation methods, such as those discussed in chapter 1, would need to be employed in order to obtain more precise results.

13. "Park it" as applied to the rate of interest is a term originally coined by Rochon and Setterfield (2007, 22–27) in their article "Interest Rates, Income Distribution and Monetary Policy" published in *The Journal of Post Keynesian Economics*.

14. In the original article, it was necessary to make use of this very awkward term from the mainstream economics of the time in order to be intelligible to the target audience.

15. As discussed in chapter 7.

16. As mentioned in chapter 3, above, this expression is originally due to Weber (1927).

17. That is, the past one hundred years or so at Keynes's time of writing. It is more like the past 200 years today. Moreover, it is now a full 250 years since the publication of Adam Smith's disastrously misguided *Wealth of Nations*. That book seems to me to have studiously ignored almost all of the practically relevant factors that might explain economic growth and prosperity in favor of an abstract and naively materialist theory, albeit marked by the addition of very many long historical digressions and asides in the typical eighteenth-century fashion. As we have already seen in chapter 6, Ricardo later took this process of abstract theorizing to a whole different level.

18. The fallacy of this last argument (based as it is on an entirely materialist ontology) has already been demonstrated in chapter 7 above.

19. This is evidently the same point as that being made by Humphrey in the earlier quote.

20. The Bank of England was founded in 1694, providing the necessary financial superstructure, and twenty years later, by the end of the War of the Spanish Succession in 1714, Great Britain was already a world power. The British state itself had actually only come into being seven years earlier via the Act of Union between England and Scotland of 1707, an event arguably motivated, at least in part, by the desire of the Edinburgh merchants to "get in on the action." In spite of the setback caused by the loss of the American colonies in the American War of Independence, 1775–83, the British Empire continued to expand down to the beginning of World War I in 1914 (and even afterward, counting the territories conquered in that conflict). At that point it was the largest, wealthiest, and most powerful empire that the world has ever seen. What I want to suggest is that this hegemony seems, ultimately, to have come into being by a process exactly similar to that just described theoretically in the present chapter. We should immediately anticipate the point, to made in more detail later in the text, that although, historically, Great Britain was very clearly the main "winner" and some other nations were "losers" for a period of 200 years, the analysis of this chapter has shown that the process of "capitalist development" (Sweezy 1942) *need not* have been a zero-sum game had there been floating exchange rates and with similar policies also pursued in other jurisdictions. It is not possible to rewrite history but it certainly is possible, in the light of that history, to make different policy proposals for the future. The last part of our period—the thirty years from 1914–44—was an

era of very rapid financial, economic, and political decline for Great Britain. Churchill actually called it the "second thirty years war." It was exactly this process of decline that Keynes and others were trying to understand and to cope with in the 1930s. As discussed in the previous chapter, the Bretton Woods agreement of 1944 effectively ended British hegemony, and replaced it with that of the United States which turned out to be far less durable by several orders of magnitude, primarily due to the deep, and seemingly irreconcilable, political and ideological divisions within that country itself. It now seems to me that, in a very real sense, the whole subject of political economy, economics, or whatever one cares to call it, as it has developed in the universities, was (and is) really all about the developments in this historical period 1694–1944, why they originally came about, and why the system eventually fell apart. Certainly, nothing worthwhile has been added to the subject in the past seventy years or so—as amply demonstrated in the histories by DeVroey (2016) and Scarth (2014) cited in chapter 1. Hopefully this book will be an exception to the rule. For the modern era, *if* these principles can first be understood, and then applied to modern conditions in the different jurisdictions, then perhaps the mistakes of the past can be avoided.

Chapter 11

Towards a Philosophy of Money and Finance?

INTRODUCTION

A few years ago I contributed a paper with a similar title to the above chapter heading to a *Festschrift* for Geoffrey Ingham, a distinguished economic sociologist and political economist at Cambridge University. Ingham has contributed greatly to the development of a sorely-needed genuine "monetary science," to borrow a term coined by Mendoza (2012), as opposed to the limited scope of monetary economics as this is usually defined. A notable feature of his (Ingham's) work has been:

> a long-standing impatience with the disciplinary boundaries of the social sciences in academia (Ingham 2004a, vii),

and a concerted effort to break them down. In a previous work (e.g., in Smithin 2009a, 2011b, 2013b), I have similarly argued that a full understanding of monetary and financial issues (and thus of economic issues in general) will require far more of an interdisciplinary approach than is currently the norm in academia. The present chapter therefore accepts Ingham's position essentially without reservation.

In what follows, the first section of the chapter identifies each of the academic disciplines which seem to be relevant to our project, and also how they relate to the traditional branches of philosophy itself. This was the origin of the idea of the "Requirements for a Philosophy of Money and Finance" as I put the point in Smithin (2013c, 19–22). Later sections then address in turn a number of the questions which naturally arise from the overall scheme, and make some attempt to answer them. By now, it should be apparent to the reader that much of the material already covered in this book falls into one or another of the various categories. A main objective in this eleventh and last chapter, therefore, is to explain retrospectively what has been going on in the previous ten.

Interdisciplinary Approaches to the Economy, Business, Money, and Finance

According to Smithin (2009a, 2011b, 2013c), a realist approach to monetary and financial issues that is able to effectively cross interdisciplinary boundaries would require study in each of the following fields, in order:

(1) A Realist Social Ontology,
(2) Economic Sociology,
(3) Monetary Macroeconomics,
(4) Political Economy.

Here the term "realism" is used in the same sense as Searle (1995, 1998, 2005, 2010) or Mendoza (2012), and the term "ontology" as in the work of Lawson (1997, 2003, 2016), Kim (2011), Mendoza (2012), and Zelmanovitz (2016). The argument is that there needs to be developed a *realist ontology* of the underlying social institutions that are relevant and necessary to the conduct of economic activity. It must include an examination of all such things as business firms, money itself, banks, governments, and so on. In short, there has to be an investigation of the basic nature of social institutions and social facts (Searle 2010, 90–100).[1] It is particularly important to stress the large difference in kind between the "social facts" and the facts of the physical or biological world, the so-called "brute facts" studied in natural science. Back in 1995, for example, the philosopher John Searle who, more recently, has become a somewhat controversial figure in the fractious academic politics of the contemporary United States,[2] wrote extensively about this in his *Construction of Social Reality*. That was a very clever title. It is important to note that the title of Searle's book was *not* the *Social Construction of Reality*. The latter would have implied the false postmodern notion that somehow objective reality itself can be molded or modified to suit the whims of the various social and political actors. (I do think, however, that mainstream/neoclassical economists have themselves nurtured similar ambitions.) Searle on the contrary, or so it seems to me, is simply asserting the common-sense notion that social relationships are themselves real phenomena, even if they cannot be reduced to any purely material or physical elements. Yet, in turn, these social relationships can and do have definite causal effects in the physical/material world.

The idea of *economic sociology* implies a study of the specific social institutions in a given socioeconomic system. The research problem of the pioneering economic sociologist Max Weber (1927), for example, in the *General Economic History* was to decipher the "meaning and presuppositions of modern capitalism," *aka* the "method of enterprise" (Collins 1986, 122). Meanwhile, Schumpeter (1934) also wrote about *The Theory of Economic Development* set quite explicitly in the context of a specific social institution, that of "capitalist credit-money" (Ingham 2004a, 105–33).

Monetary macroeconomics is (I would say) by far the most important technical field of economics. It has also, not coincidentally, been the main area of interest for a great many heterodox and dissenting economists, including such groups as the Post Keynesians, circuit theorists, contemporary adherents of modern money theory (MMT), and others, as discussed in previous chapters. The main thing to notice about

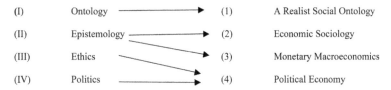

Figure 11.1 Correspondences. *Source*: Author.

this general area of research is the overwhelming emphasis on the qualifier monetary. Macroeconomics *is* monetary economics, nothing more, nothing less. Certainly the titles of Keynes's most important books, such as *A Tract on Monetary Reform* (1923), *A Treatise on Money* (1930), and *The General Theory of Employment Interest and Money* (1936) seem to have been intended to make this very point. The focus on money, itself a social institution, is also the essential reason why social ontology and economic sociology need to be thought about, in depth, before the topic of macroeconomics can even get started.

Political economy, finally, deals with questions of economic policy and governance, comparative economic systems, notions of equity, and the distribution of income and wealth.

The requirements set out in the list in (1) through (4) seem to correspond, with some overlap, to the different branches of philosophy itself. We could therefore set out a second list, again in order, as follows:

(I)   Ontology,
(II) Epistemology,
(III) Ethics,
(IV) Politics.

In this double scheme there is a straightforward correspondence between categories (1) and (I). However, categories (2) and (3) from the list of disciplines both relate to category (II) from the philosophical list. The argument must be, therefore, that economic sociology and monetary macroeconomics together *comprise* the relevant epistemology as opposed (in particular) to neoclassical microeconomics. Similarly, the subject of political economy, in category (4) from the first list, corresponds to ethics and politics in the two categories (III) and (IV), from the second. This is the precise point at which the ethical and political dimensions become relevant. A graphical representation of the correspondence between the two lists appears in Figure 11.1.

In the next section of this chapter it will be necessary to highlight a few of the basic questions that might now be asked about the overall scheme in Figure 11.1, and its interconnections. Naturally, some of these will already have suggested themselves to the mind of the reader.

Epistemological Problems of Economics?

As I have already done in several places throughout this book, I have borrowed the current section heading from the title of a well-known book in monetary theory or philosophy. In this case, it is the title of the work *Epistemological Problems in Economics* by Ludwig von Mises (1960). This is what seems to be the best fit in this particular place. To explain, I should say that, at least to me, Figure 11.1 above irresistibly recalls a quote from Simmel's *Philosophy of Money* (1907, 53) which runs as follows:

> Every area of research has two boundaries at which the process of reflection ceases to be exact and takes on a philosophical character. . . . If the start of the philosophical domain marks, as it were, the lower boundary of the exact domain, then its upper boundary is where the ever fragmentary contents of positive knowledge seek to be augmented by definitive concepts into a world picture and be related to the totality of life.

This was probably a fairly common understanding of the relationship between philosophy and science in the first half of the twentieth century. The lower boundary is presumably the place where ontological and metaphysical reflection stops and scientific research begins. Then, when the results of these "scientific" investigations are in, it will be possible to ruminate on the broader significance of it all. Simmel's rival Knapp, the author of *The State Theory of Money* (Knapp 1924), seems to have referred to this attitude when he stated that:

> he [Simmel] concludes with the style of life, I conclude with the Austrian currency. (as quoted by Frisby 2004, xvii)

Simmel himself would actually have preferred to avoid the supposedly exact domain entirely. He even went so far as to claim that:

> not a single line of these investigations is meant to be a statement about economics. (Simmel 1907, 54)

According to the scheme set out in Figure 11.1, however, this is entirely disingenuous. It is simply not going to work. Figure 11.1, in contrast, has no such boundaries. There is a philosophical character throughout. An important implication is that, although there certainly can be precision of a distinct kind in solving the various research problems in the social sciences, there cannot be the sort of "exactness" that is presumably, or allegedly, found in the natural sciences. Once again, the subject matter is different.

This leads on to the question of the type of knowledge that is sought. There is a Greek word *episteme* which comes from the same root as epistemology and is often translated as "scientific knowledge" (Robinson 2004, 310). Is this the sort of knowledge that we seek? Unfortunately, a problem with this translation, already hinted at in the previous paragraph, is that the use of the modern term science in the financial or monetary context is likely to be misleading. This is for the primarily cultural reasons identified by Lawson (2003, 247–82) and as discussed in chapter 1 above. It would be better to say something like an understanding of the "principles of things." Another type of knowledge might be labeled *technical knowledge*. In the present context, this must be thought of as the type of material learned in functional courses in business school, such as accounting, finance, marketing, and so forth. In these sorts of offerings the student learns about such things as double-entry book-keeping, balance sheets and income statements, and so on. Also, the technical details about how the various financial instruments (e.g., stock and bonds), and their derivatives (e.g., options and futures), are supposed to work. A third type of knowledge is *practical knowledge* which is also much praised, at least in lip service, in business schools and similar arenas. This, however, is really something quite different to technical knowledge. The term suggests "hands-on" experience which, by definition, can never be found in a college course. It is a clear case of "do it yourself" (DIY). In the financial world, the sort of thing I have in mind is something as simple as (e.g.) being physically able to turn on a computer, access one's account, and actually to buy and sell stocks or bonds.

I think it is clear that we are here mainly interested in the first type of knowledge. As I have tried to impress on several generations of my students enrolled in business administration courses, in the university setting we must surely be interested primarily in the financial equivalent of *episteme*. There is not much use in playing the market, for example, or in knowing how some complicated financial derivative work (or even in earning an academic PhD in Finance), without some idea of the basic principles of credit and money. One question that I invariably ask at PhD oral examinations in fields like accounting, banking, finance, and so on (and naturally also in economics) is do "loans make deposits" or do "deposits make loans"? I leave it to the reader to guess the most frequent answer to this question, very often made after maybe seven or eight years of intensive study of the topic on the part of the person answering it.

I think that it is crucially important to note exactly where the disciplines of ethics and politics fit in as part of the overall logical scheme. It is not possible to discuss either of these until *after* the ontological and epistemological issues have been decided. There may well exist an "objective science of ethics" which was the desiderata of libertarian scholars such as Rothbard (1998), for example. The argument is not relativism or pragmatism. However, nor does it lead to the a priori system of ethics for which Rothbard and others have argued. Rather the implication is that the ethical scheme must be coherent in some sense. What I mean to say by this is that it must be consistent with the "way the world works." Smithin (2011, 68) has therefore argued that Weber was quite correct in his insistence to a left-wing group of students that social science, in the first instance, should be *Wertfrei* (value free). The reason for this, according to the sequence set out here, is that the ethical and political questions cannot reasonably be dealt with before the ontological and epistemological issues have been decided. The ethical and political attitudes that are eventually adopted must ultimately be compatible with the underlying nature (ontology) of the social reality (Smithin 2009a, 35–38).

What has Happened to Neoclassical Microeconomics?

There is one omission from the above discussion which will certainly be striking to most economists from the academic mainstream and also, for that matter, to scholars from many heterodox schools of thought. This is the absence, so far, of any reference to the discipline of microeconomics as taught in the universities. Why does this not appear explicitly? The answer is that it does not really need to be there. Once it is recognized that the term "economic sociology" already includes all such things as value theory, pricing theory, the theory of the firm, the study of market behavior, and so on, the omission becomes entirely reasonable. This way of expressing it, however, has the advantage of putting the whole notion of market forces in its place in the broader social order, so to speak, rather than being the only thing discussed. Indeed the ordering of the list (1), (2), (3), and (4) above makes it crystal clear that the market cannot logically even be the *first* thing discussed. In reality, neither the concept of the market, nor the academic discipline of neoclassical microeconomics as this has developed over the years, is "foundational" in the sense implied by the rather recent coinage of the term "microfoundations."

We touch here on issues raised in the recent work by John King (2012) on *The Micro-Foundations Delusion: Metaphor and Dogma in the History of Macroeconomics*. The very title of that work seems emphatic enough. It is worth inquiring further, however, into exactly what it is that King finds delusional. Specifically, these are the ubiquitous dynamic stochastic general equilibrium (DSGE) model of early twenty-first century mainstream macroeconomics, and its underpinning in the concept of the RARE individual (where the acronym stands for the "representative agent with rational expectations"). These sorts of constructs have entirely ignored the requirement to develop a plausible social ontology. However, if King is dismissive of the modern literature on the "micro foundations of macroeconomics," he is equally skeptical of the reverse notion of the "macro foundations of microeconomics" which would presumably start at point (4) in the list (1), (2), (3), and (4) and loop back from there. In Smithin (2004) following Crotty (1980) I had earlier expressed a more favorable view of this concept than does King. I do not withdraw those remarks. Now, however, the suggested ordering in the list of disciplines above does seem to put the various issues into the correct relationship to one another. In the end, therefore, in addition to that of Ingham, the discussion here seems to have mirrored King's position fairly closely.[3]

If we thus abandon, as we must, the entirely misleading notion of the micro foundations of macroeconomics, the question then arises as to how important university courses in microeconomics really should be in the study of the economy, business, money, and finance? I take a rather minimalist position on this. I think that the study of microeconomics per se should be confined to maybe only a half-course, or at most a full-course, dealing with the sort of neo-Marshallian analysis that now typically appears in Economics 101. This includes the basics of demand and supply analysis (but please no indifference curves!), the concept of elasticity, the difference between marginal cost and average cost, the notions of cost curves, and so on. Also, terms like perfection competition, monopoly, imperfect competition, and so on. Moreover, the purpose of the exercise should really only be to introduce the students to the sort of terminology that they will continue to encounter in mainstream discussions of these topics. They will certainly need to be able to recognize them and deal with them in debate as is done, for example, in this book. It is not possible, however, to learn anything very much about the operation of any actual economy or about the methodology of the social sciences in general, by the use of these techniques. Too much has always to be "held constant" whenever they are invoked. By the time we move on to the supposedly more "advanced" courses in the field, microeconomics will definitely have outlived its usefulness. Indeed, in practice I have frequently found that students have to actively unlearn much of their microeconomics education if they are ever to make sense of what is going on in the real world.

What Should be Studied?

In chapter 3 above (entitled the *Role of Money in Capitalism*) I mentioned that if there is much confusion about the concept of money in mainstream economics, this is true to an even greater extent about the very idea of an economy itself. All too frequently the notion of an "economy" is taken simply to refer generically to all of the possible (and even some of the purely hypothetical) methods of obtaining provisions. At least five separate such methods were identified in chapter 3. These were:

(i)   The Crusoe Economy
(ii) A Traditional Economy
(iii) A Command Economy
(iv) A Barter Exchange Economy
(v)   The Method of Enterprise

All of these have their own logic and principles. As explained earlier, however, the two that have been highlighted are essentially fictional or mythical. They can be used only for "thought experiments" about how things would work out in the assumed circumstances. On the other hand, the likes of command economies and traditional economics certainly can exist, have existed, and do exist in some places still today. However, in both these cases it is actually very easy to understand the principles of how they work without any need for the services of a "professional economist" (Heilbroner 1992, 10–16, Heilbroner and Milberg 1992). Our ontological enquiries, therefore, seem to inevitably lead to the conclusion that the object of study of monetary theory, and of economic theory in general, is simply the modus operandi of Weber's "modern capitalism" (Collins 1986, 122) represented by category (V) in the list above. Recall that the definition of this system, previously quoted in chapter 3, was as follows:

> The provision of human needs by the *Method of Enterprise* which is to say by private businesses seeking profit. (emphasis and capitalization added).

This therefore is the system that should, indeed must, be studied, in order to understand the sort of society in which most of us still live almost a century after Weber's death. The key question raised by this definition is, what is this "profit" that is supposed to provide the incentive for economic activity in such a system? Most obviously it is a sum of money. Hence, the vital importance of the ontology of money, of credit creation by the banking system, the availability of both initial and final finance, and so on as discussed throughout this book.

An "Iterative Sequence" as Applied to Economic Sociology

In order to further discuss the role of economic sociology in pursuing our investigations about business and economic conditions, another philosophical concept that needs emphasis is the notion of "iteration" (Searle 1995, 79–87, 1998, 128–30, Smithin 2009a, 1–22, 2013b, 24). This is the idea that one set of social institutions builds on another in a logical sequence. In fact, this point is already implicit in the idea of a correct order. Via a process of iteration it is therefore thought possible to build up a cognitive structure of almost any degree of complexity from what are apparently the simplest of underpinnings.

Barrows and Smithin (2009, 323–27) and Smithin (2011a, 71–73), for example, have argued that for the establishment of something like Weber's method of enterprise to have occurred there must have been a sequential development (again in order) of the following series of social institutions, or social facts:

(A) A political settlement of some kind.
(B) Money (including under this rubric both the concepts of the unit-of-account and means-of-payment, and also the existence of some method of credit creation).
(C) Private property (in the specifically legal sense, not the mere concept of possession).
(D) Markets.
(E) Entrepreneurial business.

It is true, of course, that much of the debate in the mainstream economic literature focuses on the question of so-called government interference in the economy, as if the two concepts, government and the economy, are totally unrelated to one another. The focus is always on how government regulations, and so forth, may hinder economic development. And, to be fair, it is easy to see that some forms of government can indeed be entirely predatory, such as the *ancient regime* in France in the eighteenth century, or Stalinism in the USSR in the twentieth century. Nonetheless, it is also clear from our iterative scheme that the existence of *some* form of state authority or sovereignty, that is, a political settlement, must also be regarded as a *prerequisite* for the establishment of commercial society in the first place. It is certain that no such society has ever existed without some type of governmental structure and such things as laws, contracts, a unit-of-account, a means of settling debt, and so on. Consider, for example, recent arguments of the neo-chartalist school, to the effect that "taxes drive money" (Mosler 2011, Wray 2012). This refers to the view that it is the ability of the state to levy taxes, as a matter of sovereignty rather than of confiscation, and not because of any perceived "need" to "finance" government expenditures, that is actually the foundation of the monetary system.

The term "money," as used here, clearly involves all of the social phenomena that were identified in chapter 3 as constitutive. These include, first, a money of account, second, a well-identified asset, not necessarily a physical asset, serving as the final or ultimate means of settlement, third, a developed financial and banking system that ensures secure credit relations. These are the necessary conditions for all such things as price lists and rational accounting to come into existence. Ultimately, they are necessary for the very feasibility of a system of production that entails taking a long position in goods and services, and functions via the generation of profits calculated in monetary terms. As for the precise place of money itself in the iterative sequence, Ingham (2004a) quotes Weber as definitely asserting that "money is the father of private property," not the other way around.

Property rights are important for such a society because in a system centered on the profit motive (and, for that matter, in one also dependent on the receipt of wages for services rendered), it is important that the recipients of the various income streams be able to control their final disbursement and not be subject to arbitrary confiscation. This statement does not delegitimize taxation in principle particularly, and as mentioned, when thought of as an act of sovereignty rather than as confiscation. However, the concept of private property does imply a definite set of both economic and legal principles that sharply delineate the scope of taxation, that is, *if* the system is actually to function.

The idea that the market appears only in fourth place on the iterative list will no doubt seem strange from the viewpoint of orthodox economic theory. From that perspective, market exchange is usually treated as co-extensive with economic activity. The market is supposed to be the mainspring of the whole system based on a "natural propensity to truck, barter, and exchange" as in the formulation of Adam Smith (1776, 25). On this view, markets *as such* perform all the necessary functions of providing information, coordinating activity, and ensuring productive efficiency. Money, in fact, need not really be involved. In principle, all that is thought to be going on in a "market" is some form of barter exchange. The supposed information content is believed to consist of just these hypothesized barter exchange ratios rather than, as in reality, basic accounting notions of profit. As against the primeval belief in the supremacy of the mere act of exchange, in actual social systems things are far more complicated. Both markets and market exchange, as they function in the real enterprise system, must be built upon the *prior* institutions of money and private property.

Exchange specifically for money finally slots into the picture primarily because if there is to be a system in which the incentive for production is profit, actually quantifiable in monetary terms (not merely vague notions of utility or satisfaction), there must exist a number of actual or virtual locations where the output of production can eventually be sold. This is evidently the main function of markets in the real system. Hence, the crucial functions of marketing and advertising in actual business. If the output cannot be sold there can be no profit. Once having established this as our main point, it could then quite easily be conceded that markets also do serve the regulatory, or validating, function over-emphasized by neoclassical economics, and which, for that matter, also shows up in the old Marxian notion of "socially necessary labor time" discussed in chapters 3 and 6. If someone, somewhere, is eventually prepared to buy the output of the producer, then presumably the effort that went into its production was indeed socially necessary, at least in the opinion of the purchaser at the time of sale.

The role of entrepreneurial business in the system is clearly to organize productive activity in the pursuit of profit. The term "business" is used here in a generic sense, including all types of business organization, the individual entrepreneur, partnerships, and all corporate forms. It might have been adequate to use the term "business operations" following Heinsohn and Steiger (2000, 67). The qualifier "entrepreneurial" is employed, however, to recognize the point, stressed by both Schumpeter and Keynes that given an accommodative framework provided by the other institutions (particularly financial institutions) the essence of the system is then the profit incentive for innovation and dynamic change. Earlier, in chapter 6, we identified a number of difficulties that arise in describing the different practical variations on the method of enterprise, for example, because of the different forms of business organization in different societies and at different time periods. Identifying the true entrepreneurial profit or surplus in accounting terms is much complicated, in practice, by the different regulations in place in different jurisdictions, and by different systems of corporate governance. On the other hand, if we were alternatively discussing the generic types of either the traditional economy or command economy there would also be a great many practical and/or historical variations that would have to be taken into account in any discussions of cases. This would not detract in any way from the value of discussions of the "ideal type" itself (Heilbroner 1999, Ingham 2004a, Smithin 2009a).

Recapitulation of the Key Issues in Monetary Macroeconomics

At the end of chapter 2, during the discussion of the AMM, it was mentioned that there are five key issues which always seem to arise in debates about monetary macroeconomics. These were:

- The nature and functions of money (the ontology of money), and the role of money in capitalism, *aka* the method of enterprise.
- Endogenous money versus exogenous money.
- Interest rate determination (most importantly the determination of real interest rates).
- The choice of monetary policy instrument.
- How do changes in monetary variables affect other economic variables, real and
- nominal? Is money "neutral" or "non-neutral," in both the short and the long run?

The first of these questions has actually already been dealt with in some detail in the discussion just completed. The remaining four are the subject matter of monetary economics proper. As far as the second and third questions are concerned the key arguments made throughout this book were the insistence that in principle the money supply is always endogenous, and that the real rate of interest is a purely monetary phenomenon. There is no such thing as a "natural rate of interest" or, for that matter, natural rates of economic growth, unemployment, or of anything else in the socio-economic sphere.

The essential monetary policy instrument, on the other hand, is a nominal interest rate, namely the nominal policy rate of the central bank. This means that adjustments to the nominal policy rate must always be calibrated to pursue a real interest rate rule of some kind, examples of which have been given in chapters 2 and 10 above. If this is not done the economy will be unstable. The other influences on interest rates (including those of so-called unconventional monetary policy initiatives) were discussed in chapter 5, and may be inferred by considering the effects of changes in the intercept term, p_0, and the other terms of the following inflation equation:

$$p = p_0 + \lambda(r - r_{-1}) + w_{-1} - a, \qquad 0 < \lambda < 1 \qquad (11.1)$$

where the term p_0 is essentially an (inverse) measure of Keynesian liquidity preference, and the other terms are defined as they were initially in chapters 2, 5, and 6 above. There is an inverse relationship between the inflation rate and the real rate of interest in equilibrium (i.e., when $r = r_{-1}$). Hence, the effects on the equilibrium real rate of interest may also be deduced (see chapter 5). At the end of the day, the upshot of the macroeconomic theory first outlined in chapter 2 (and then repeated, in the context of the open economy with flexible exchange rates, in chapter 10) is that conventional macroeconomic economic ideas about the "neutrality of money," "policy irrelevance," and so on, are nonsense. Each of monetary policy changes, fiscal policy changes, and spontaneous changes in the other macroeconomic variables will always have some sort of effect on the economy for good or ill. Such changes are inevitably "non-neutral"—in both the short run and the long run. This much should perhaps have been obvious enough from the actual course of economic history over the last 150 years and more, since "the crime of '73" (1873). However, economic theorists notoriously live in their own "bubble" safely insulated from the real world. They have usually been content to "hide themselves in a thicket of algebra," to borrow Joan Robinson's memorable phrase (Robinson 1962).[4] These observations, in themselves, do not give any guidance as to the sort of policies that should be actually pursued in order to improve economic performance. Hopefully, however, the analysis in chapters 2, 5, 6, 7, and 10 above has at least provided some guidance in that direction.

The Ethics of Income Distribution

With the result of our investigations into monetary macroeconomics in hand, it is now time to return to the question of ethics, specifically the ethics of income distribution. What is thought to be important in this field? There are a number of possibilities, such as:

- The Personal Distribution of Income
- Social Justice
- The Functional Distribution of Income

Ideas about either the *personal (individual) distribution of income*, or sometimes the household distribution of income, usually focus on the notion of equality versus inequality. In the culture of contemporary North America, in fact, there is an overwhelming emphasis on equality as a normative ideal for the reasons famously identified by Allan Bloom (1987, 88–91) in *The Closing of the American Mind.* This attitude tends to be entirely reflexive, even (or perhaps particularly?) in academic discussion. However, to the extent that there are any intellectual underpinnings for this stance, one place in which they may be found is in John Rawls's (1971) influential book *A Theory of Justice.* There is an old saying that you cannot judge a book by its cover (or I suppose its title) and this was most certainly true of Rawls's work. The use of the term "justice" in this context is something which, in particular, requires comment. Traditionally "justice" was interpreted as implying that people should get what they deserve, in some definite sense, and not really that everybody should be equal, or that outcomes should always be equal. Five decades after the publication of Rawls's book, however, the notion that justice somehow requires equal shares for all, regardless of their deserts, has become commonplace. From this point of view a better title for Rawls's book might have been something like *A Theory of Equality.*[5] Rawls's argument was actually that income equality would be *chosen* by rational individuals in a hypothetical situation of a social contract drawn up beforehand, by individuals ignorant both of their eventual standing in society and what their endowments of talent, ability, drive, and so on will turn out to be relative to others. But, obviously, this safety-first argument is not compelling from the logical point of view. It is entirely possible, for example, that even the lowest absolute level income in a competitive society, or in one with some sort of safety net that nevertheless falls short of equality, could well be higher than the average in the egalitarian case. However, this meme about equality has been, and still is, highly influential and even decisive, in debates about political economy in North America. This has been true in the past several decades, and remains so to this day.

Social justice (again with the emphasis on the adjective rather than the "traditional" meaning of the noun) is another concept which has had a great deal of resonance in the contemporary political scene. It is the legacy of the so-called cultural Marxism of the Frankfurt school as opposed to the classical Marxism discussed in earlier chapters. When Hitler came to power in Germany in the 1930s many prominent members of the so-called Frankfurt school, scholars such as Adorno, Fromm, Horkheimer, and Marcuse, were exiled to the United States. There they were well received. They received a sympathetic hearing in New York, for example, at Columbia University, also in Washington, DC in government service, and in Southern California via Hollywood and the universities. As is well known the role of Marcuse, who remained in the United States after World War II after his colleagues returned to Germany, and eventually retired as a professor at the University of California at San Diego, was particularly important in shaping opinion on the left of the political spectrum in America. As the name implies, in discussions of distribution of income the emphasis in this approach is indeed very much on the term "social," that is, on distribution by, for example, (in strict alphabetical order) social groupings such age, class, ethnicity, gender, national origin, physical disability, sexual orientation, religious affiliation, or some other collective attribute. There is much less emphasis on the economic contribution of each individual to the society.

Finally, by contrast, the *functional distribution of income* is simply distribution by economic class. It is therefore, by definition, closely tied to economic function, but nonetheless is always contested. In some societies the functional distribution may entirely cut across the various social distinctions. In other cases, in more highly stratified societies, there could well be a greater correspondence between economic function and social status. For example, in any given polity entrepreneurs may primarily be drawn from a particular ethnic group or gender, and similarly with the workforce. As already discussed in chapter 6 above it is unfortunately the case that the notion of the functional distribution of income has often been drastically oversimplified. Typically it is reduced to a conflict between two classes only, such as "capital versus labor" or some such. This was certainly the case in classical Marxism, for example. In the present book, however, concerned as it is particularly with monetary and financial issues, it has been insisted that the most appropriate division is that between entrepreneurs, rentiers and workers, or between *Profit, Interest, and Wages* as the title of chapter 6 would have it.

The Functional Distribution of Income

A basic equation describing the three-way functional distribution of income was derived in chapter 6. This is as follows:

$$k = a - r - w, \qquad (11.2)$$

Here the symbol k stands for the aggregate profit markup factor across all business firms, a is the natural logarithm of average labor productivity per employed person, r is the average real interest rate, and w is the natural logarithm of the average real wage rate per employed person. By this time, at this stage in the development of our argument, is it now natural to ask how we might add some "actual numbers" from the available statistical data in order to make equation (11.2) operational.

Thus, starting with the term a, note that we have earlier defined upper-case A as real GDP per employed person, or as Y/N. Lowercase a is then the natural logarithm of upper-case A such that $a = lnY - lnA$. Next, the term r is given by $i - p$, where i is the average nominal yield on the relevant set of financial instruments and lower case p stands for the inflation rate, where $p = (P - P_{-1})/P_{-1} = lnP - lnP_{-1}$ and P is the aggregate price level. Finally, if upper-case W stands for the average nominal wage rate, then the term $w = ln(W/P) = lnW - lnP$ is the natural logarithm of the average real wage rate per employed person.

Suppose, therefore, that in the national income and product accounts of a given economy real GDP is equal to one trillion "constant dollars,"[6] and 10 million persons are counted as having been employed during the relevant accounting period. In this case $A (= Y/N)$ will be 10,000 and $a (= ln\ A)$ is 9.2. Similarly, if the labor share in real GDP of the same economy is actually 55 percent, then the average real wage per employed person will be 5,500 and $w (= lnW - lnP)$ is 8.6. The next step is to work out a reasonable measure for the average real rate of interest. However, this is not necessarily such an easy task as it might sound. The various alternative methods making these calculations with real world data have been described in detail by Collis (2016, 2018)—who also attempts an evaluation of the usefulness of the various approaches. To cut a long story short, suppose that, for the sake of argument here, our calculations come out to $r = 0.15$.[7] Given the existing levels of real wages and productivity the implication of this level of real interest is that the average entrepreneurial mark-up is $k = 0.45$. That is:

$$k = a - r - w = 9.2 - 0.15 - 8.6 = 0.45 \qquad (11.3)$$

An alternative way of writing equation (11.2) would be to put the term a on the left-hand side (LHS) of the expression and move the other terms over to the right-hand side (RHS). The resulting expression then explains how the natural logarithm of labor productivity is split between entrepreneurial profit, interest, and wages. That is:

$$a = k + r + w \qquad (11.4)$$

which expression may then be "normalized" by dividing through by a itself. This gives:

$$1 = k/a + r/a + w/a \qquad (11.5)$$

The resulting ratios are the various income shares relative to the natural logarithm of average labor productivity. They therefore represent one measure, among others, of how much output there actually is in existence at any point in time which is then available to be distributed between the recipients. I am afraid that I have not been able to discover any established mathematical terminology for these concepts and these ratios[8]. Therefore, I have ventured to coin the term "logarithmic shares," or (*ln*)shares, to stand for the three ratios. The important point is that together they must always sum to unity. Given the assumed numbers from equation (11.3) the result is:

$$1 = 0.05 + 0.02 + 0.93 \tag{11.6}$$

$$\nearrow \qquad \uparrow \qquad \nwarrow$$

firm (*ln*)share   rentier (*ln*)share   wage (*ln*)share

Perhaps at first sight this concept of (*ln*)shares does not seem to shed much light on the practical "struggle for income distribution" as it will be experienced by the participants themselves. The (*ln*)share of labor in equation (11.6), for example, is 0.93 whereas we know that the actual labor share in GDP is 55 percent.[9] As we will see, however, this way of putting things does turn out to be useful in defining, quite precisely, what is actually meant by the various normative concepts that arise in the discussion of the functional distribution.

For example, if now recall the discussion of the Marxian notion of "exploitation" in chapters 4 and 6 above, we can see that Marxian exploitation will occur whenever:

$$k + r > 0 \tag{11.7}$$

On the other hand if $k + r = 0$ there is no exploitation, and:

$$a = w \tag{11.8}$$

This is therefore a case where the whole value of the output accrues to those who are (supposed by Marx to be) the actual producers.

Similarly, given some initial assumptions about fairness, we are also able to define the concept of "usury." This was a staple of the historical literature on money and banking. The word "use" is actually an archaic synonym for interest and the notion of usury would come into play whenever the rate of interest charged on loans on money was deemed to be excessive, in some particular sense. Historically, for example, *usury laws* were often passed limiting the amount of interest that may be charged for any financial transaction. Evidently, in order for this concept to be operational, there has to be some method of determining what is and what is not excessive. In terms of our current notation, the case can be made that there will be usury whenever the real interest, *r,* is greater than zero. That is, if:

$$r > 0. \tag{11.9}$$

Therefore, there would be *no* usury when:

$$r = 0. \tag{11.10}$$

In this case, we would have:

$$a = k + w, \tag{11.11}$$

where the total income available is divided solely between the entrepreneurs and the workers. In this case, contrary to Marxism, the economic function of entrepreneurship is recognized as well as that of labor. However, the so-called rentiers (the recipients of interest income), although they are able to preserve the real value of previously accumulated financial capital, will not be able to participate in (take any share of) the returns to *current* production.

Is the Optimal Real Rate of Interest Rate Zero?

Given the above discussion, perhaps the answer to this question is yes? Admittedly, starting with a succinct statement in Smithin (1994, 188), and then subsequently in many other places over the next twenty-five years, I have usually argued central banks should pursue a monetary policy that sets a target for the real policy rate of interest at a "low but still positive" level. The basis for this argument is, first, that low real interest rates do promote economic growth and, moreover, as shown in chapter 2 above, a target for the real policy rate would at least stabilize the inflation rate. These sorts of statements, however, were always meant to be only in the spirit of pragmatic policy advice. I have not usually given any precise quantitative target for the real policy rate of interest. Therefore, a central bank that followed my advice might decide, for example, to set a target for the real policy rate at something like one percent. That is:

$$r_0 = 0.01. \tag{11.12}$$

In this case, the actual real rate of interest in the market would be given by:

$$r = m_0 + m_1 0.01 - (1 - m_1) p. \tag{11.13}$$

The hope is that this would also turn out to be quite a low real rate of interest, but obviously we cannot be sure about this. The overall levels of interest rates in the marketplace also depend on each of the parameters m_0, and m_1 and also on the inflation rate, p (and thereby on liquidity preference as explained in chapter 5).

What would happen if the central bank went still further and actually set the real policy rate of interest at zero, that is, $r_0 = 0$? In this case the general level of the real rate of interest, r, would turn out be:

$$r = m_0 - (1 - m_1) p, \tag{11.14}$$

Again the real rate of interest itself would not be zero, except by accident. It could equally well turn out to be either positive or negative, depending on the values of m_0, m_1, and p. This is actually unfortunate because a strong ethical argument can be made that the general level of real interest rates, not merely the policy rate, should ideally be zero.[10] My "real rate rule" for the central bank may perhaps be the best that can be done in a practical situation, but it is not necessarily the optimal solution in the sense in which economists like to use this term.

The ethical argument is based on the idea that the current wealth holdings of the rentiers must have arisen from *past* receipts of either wages or profits. Therefore, whereas their owners are certainly entitled to preserve the real capital value of any past gains due to their own efforts, there is no argument, from the point of view of fairness, for them to share in the proceeds of current income. Current income is being generated by the work effort, entrepreneurial activity, and risk-taking of others. In the sort of language introduced in the previous section of this chapter *usury* should not be allowed. In order to achieve an effective real interest rate of $r = 0$, the target for the real policy rate would have to be:

$$r'_0 = \left[(1 - m_1)/m_1 \right] p - (m_0/m_1) \qquad (11.15)$$

If this can be achieved, and continuing to assume that $a = 9.2$ and $w = 8.6$ as before, the average markup across business firm will thus be increased from the level of 0.45, previously calculated, to now stand at 0.60. That is:

$$k = a - r - w = 9.2 - 0.0 - 8.6 = 0.6. \qquad (11.16)$$

Given the new value of k we can once again rearrange the distributive equation and normalize to obtain the following result for the (ln)shares:

$$1 = 0.07 + 0.00 + 0.93. \qquad (11.17)$$

$$\uparrow \qquad \qquad \uparrow$$

firm (ln)share   wage (ln)share

There is now no rentier share. It is zero. The other (ln)shares have either increased in the case of firms, or remained the same in the case of labor.

It is interesting to note that there is a definite family resemblance of the above argument to the rules of so-called Islamic banking as described, for example, by Arnold (2014, 351–52). This idea of Islamic banking is usually understood to be a code of conduct for bankers who wish to comply with certain religious requirements in their business dealings. In this discourse, there is a basic underlying presumption that the charging of interest for loans of money is somehow unethical as opposed to the receipt of income earned from profits and wages. Certain rules are therefore set down for business and financial dealings which, in one way or another, are able to avoid interest charges entirely. This is actually not so in the current argument, as it is not possible to avoid a nominal interest charge. The difference from the overtly religious argument is whether the nominal or real interest rate is set to zero. If it is the real interest rate that is set to zero the nominal interest rate must always be equal to the inflation rate. Therefore the nominal interest rate will be positive whenever the inflation rate is positive. Nonetheless, as no *real* income is actually being received by the rentiers, regardless of the level of the inflation, the result does seem to be well within the spirit if not the letter of the various religious proscriptions.[11] It also seems important to stress that if there is a zero real rate of interest the rentiers are not actually being "euthanized" as Keynes (1936, 375–77) predicted that they would be. They are still able to preserve full the value of any financial capital acquired from previous work effort or entrepreneurial effort.

Is the Optimal Nominal Policy Rate of Interest Zero?

Earlier in this book, in chapter 2, some of the consequences of setting the nominal policy rate itself at level of zero were discussed in some detail. One problem with this alternative suggestion was the finding that a nominal interest rate peg of any kind (not just zero) will lead to inflationary instability. For example, if the inflation rate is positive to start with it will just become and higher and higher. Another problem is that a zero nominal interest rate will not be distributionally neutral, even as regards those sources regarded as legitimate, that is, wages and entrepreneurial profit.

In the inflationary case suppose that at the current point in time the inflation rate is 14 percent, $p = 0.14$. Treating the currently observed inflation rate as a proxy for expected inflation (see chapters 2 and 3 above); the real interest rate is given by the following expression:

$$r = m_0 + m_1 r_0 - (1 - m_1) p, \tag{11.18}$$

As $i_0 = 0$ by assumption, this reduces to:

$$r = m_0 - p, \tag{11.19}$$

Thus, as $p = 0.14$ and if (say) $m_0 = 0.02$, we have:

$$r = 0.02 - 0.14 = -0.12 \tag{11.20}$$

The real rate of interest is negative at (−) 12 percent. Therefore, if $a = 9.2$ and $w = 8.6$ as before, the entrepreneurial mark-up will now increase to $k = 0.72$.

$$k = a - r - w = 9.2 + 0.12 - 8.6 = 0.72 \tag{11.21}$$

And, the relative (*ln*)shares come out to:

$$1 = 0.08 - 0.01 + 0.93 \tag{11.22}$$

$$\nearrow \qquad \uparrow \qquad \nwarrow$$

firm (*ln*)share   rentier (*ln*)share   wage (*ln*)share

The workers are holding their own but the rentier share is negative. What is going on is that resources are being transferred from the holders of financial capital to business firms. The firms are, in effect, "profiteers" from inflation exactly as was described by Keynes (1923, 18–27) in the relevant passage in the *Tract on Monetary Reform*. What is worse, from the point of view of the rentiers, is to recall that the system is unstable. This is a situation which will continue to worsen as time goes by. The inflationary case really does lead to the "euthanasia of the rentier" (Keynes 1936, 376). *Pace* Keynes, however, this does not represent an ethically defensible position from the point of view of fairness set out above.

To consider the deflationary case, suppose alternatively that the price level is currently falling at a rate of 10 percent per annum. The rate of *deflation* is $p = (-)\,0.16$. In this situation, even though the nominal interest rate remains at zero, the real interest rate will now be strongly positive at $r = 0.18$. Meanwhile, the entrepreneurial mark-up will fall dramatically to $k = 0.42$.

$$k = 9.2 - 0.18 - 8.6 = 0.42 \qquad (11.24)$$

The (*ln*)shares in this case will thus be:

$$1 = 0.05 + 0.02 + 0.93 \qquad (11.25)$$

$$\nearrow \qquad \uparrow \qquad \nwarrow$$

firm (*ln*)share   rentier (*ln*)share   wage (*ln*)share

In this case resources are being transferred to the holders of financial capital from business firms. This is an example of the process that in Smithin (1996, xi) I called "the revenge of the rentiers." Again, the system is unstable and the situation is only going to worsen over time, this time from the point of view of Main Street. The "boot is on the other foot" and now it is business that will eventually be euthanized, and with it the entire economy. For this particular example, if the deflation rate eventually proceeds to an order of magnitude of around 68 percent, the average business "mark-up" will begin to turn negative, and firms will be making losses. With a 68 percent rate of deflation, for example:

$$k = 9.2 - 0.8 - 8.6 = -0.02. \qquad (11.26)$$

I would say that this is the very essence of the process of deflation and depression.

New Directions in Political Economy?

In the first decade of the twenty-first century the political scientist Kenneth R. Hoover published an very interesting book on the relationship between economic and politics entitled *Economics and Ideology* (Hoover 2003). In my own *Money, Enterprise and Income Distribution* (*MEI*), I have already commented on this work in some detail (Smithin 2009a, 28–31). Hoover's strategy was to explore the linkages via a discussion of the lives and works of three famous economists and political scientists of the twentieth century, namely Laski, Keynes, and Hayek. This was an effective way to get into a discussion of the issues—although I think that Hoover would concede that, of the three, Laski (famous enough in his own day) is the least well-known to a contemporary audience, and not in the same league as the other two as a theorist (Smithin 2009a, 29). In the mid-twentieth century, Laski had been the champion of an ideology called *democratic socialism* which is something of a contradiction in terms. For present purposes, therefore, we may as well cut right to the chase and substitute for the name of Laski that of another theorist this time from the nineteenth century. A theorist, moreover, who clearly is very much in the same league as Hayek and Keynes, and whose views have already been discussed in some detail in this book, namely Karl Marx (1818–83).

With this substitution, and also as discussed previously in *MEI*, the picture painted by Hoover of the relationship between economics and politics may then be represented by the simple linear diagram shown in Figure 11.2.

For the purposes of Hoover's thesis, therefore, we will take Marxism to exemplify the left of the political spectrum. Hoover next places Keynes's macroeconomic policy interventionism is in the center. This means that the right wing must be occupied by Hayek's neo-Austrian version of *laissez-faire* (greatly to the annoyance of "free market" economists themselves) as there is nowhere else to put it. The basic principle that supposedly differentiates these political stances is clearly the degree of collectivism versus individualism (Smithin 2009a, 28–31). On the level of practical politics this translates to the degree of so-called government intervention in the economy. (Presumably most people would agree that the idea originally floated by Marx, that the state would "wither and die" under communism, can safely be dismissed as either wishful thinking or as simply disingenuous.)

It is immediately obvious that there are some serious problems with this underlying notion of left wing versus right wing in terms of broad political philosophy, and indeed, these labels are very widely abused in contemporary political commentary. They are very frequently, and in some cases seemingly quite deliberately, used in a contradictory and confusing manner. To take the most obvious examples, both the Italian *fascism* and German *national socialism* of the mid-twentieth century are routinely labeled as "right wing" in spite of their clear collectivist and statist tendencies.[12] (In terms of Figure 11.2, therefore, they should actually be on the left.) Similarly, the various authoritarian, racially based, or even populist, political groupings of the present day are also usually described as right wing and, indeed, if sufficiently beyond the pale of contemporary journalistic opinion as "far right." But the first two such groups, at least (not so much in the case of populism), also typically have little interest in individualism. In their essence they are collectivist. For the same reason, as mentioned, the supporters of free markets, laissez-faire, libertarianism, and so on themselves strongly object to their positioning in the diagram. From their point of view they are classical liberals, a doctrine which would indeed have been considered to be on the left of the

| Marx | Keynes | Hayek |

Figure 11.2   A Middle Way? *Source:* Author.

Figure 11.3   Conventional Opinion about Marx and Keynes and Hayek. *Source*: Author.

political spectrum in the eighteenth and nineteenth centuries, in that case as opposed to the supporters of monarchy.[13]

Evidently this way of looking at politics, in terms of a linear spectrum from left to right, is altogether confusing and misleading. Ideally, it should be replaced, but with what? I would argue, in fact, that the materials discussed in this book already provide the basis for an alternative delineation or categorization of the various approaches. That argument will be illustrated by the new circular diagram that appears in Figure 11.4.

However, before discussing this alternative approach in detail there must be a brief reference back to our original discussion of politics in chapter 1 above. In that chapter it was argued that, in practice, protagonists in the economic arena do not themselves accept the parameters for debate as set down by the political scientists. Keynes himself, had thought that he was "knocking away the Ricardian foundations of Marxism." We also made the point, that neither the Post Keynesian economists, who in chapter 1 represented the left of the economic spectrum, nor the Austrians representing the right seem ever to have taken this seriously. The conventional opinion about Marx, Keynes, and Hayek on all sides, is therefore much more like that depicted in Figure 11.3—with both Marx and Keynes over to the left.

One thing, however, that the present book can definitely claim to have established is that the conventional opinion is quite wrong on this issue. The reason that Keynes felt able to dispense with both Ricardo and Marx was that he was trying to develop an alternative *monetary* analysis in the Schumpeterian sense as defined in chapter 1. On the other hand, all of the classical economists, including Marx, were stuck with a pedestrian real analysis focusing on notional ideas of the market exchange of commodities and which, in spite of both Marx's claims and his genuine sociological contributions, ultimately had little to do with the actual social system of enterprise,

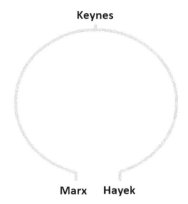

Figure 11.4   Keynes as a Theorist of Monetary Production. *Source*: Author.

resting as heavily as it does on the basic foundations of credit and money. Tellingly, Marx begins both *A Contribution to the Critique of Political Economy* (Marx 1859, 27–52), and Vol. 1 of *Das Kapital* (Marx 1867, 125–38), with a discussion of market exchange and real exchange ratios. Therefore if, on the other hand, we are to think of Keynes as first and foremost a theorist of monetary production the circular diagram in Figure 11.4 does come into focus as the best way of illustrating the truly radical difference between Keynes and both Hayek and Marx, and also of finally ditching the obsolete labels of left and right.

As shown in chapters 1, 3, 4, and 6 above, the main thing that Hayek and the Austrians had in common with the classical economists, Marx, the neoclassicals and modern mainstream economists, was the reliance on Schumpeterian *real* analysis. None of them seems to have arrived at a genuine monetary theory. To the Austrians, for example, money was only a disruptive force. Their ideal was to make the actual economy operate "as if" it was a barter economy which would eliminate the business cycle in their opinion (Hicks 1982, 3–4). To the neoclassicals meanwhile money was simply neutral, and Marx had put forward a commodity theory of money rather than a credit theory. This then is why Marx and Hayek, in particular, whose views most people would assume are diametrically opposed, can finally be grouped together side by side as in Figure 11.4.The connection is their joint inability or unwillingness to attempt a genuine monetary analysis. Marx called his method historical materialism which is strongly indicative. On the other hand, the Austrians liked to call their method subjectivism (Dow 1985, Boettke, Lavoie and Storr 2001, Boettke and Leeson 2002, 2–3) based on the claim that economic value is rooted only in the subjective evaluations, by the various economic actors, of the goods and services on offer. Nonetheless, the end result is still an entirely "real analysis" in the Schumpeterian sense, as explained in chapter 4. In particular, there is no trace of the collective intentionally which is the only possible foundation for a set of social relations or social facts that have deontic power. Therefore if Marxism is *Historical Materialism*, then perhaps both Austrian economics and neoclassical or mainstream economics might be called *Subjective Materialism*.[14] By the same token, the neo-Ricardian or Sraffrian approach, dutifully

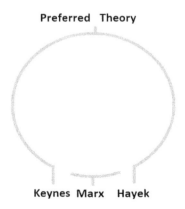

Preferred Theory

Keynes Marx Hayek

Figure 11.5   Keynes as a "Planner." *Source*: Author.

adding up "240 qr, wheat + 12 t. iron + 18 pigs" to get "450 qr. wheat" (Sraffa 1960, 4), could well be called *Quantitative Materialism*.

There is a possible caveat to the above. One does sometimes see a critique of Keynes to the effect that he was also moving toward some sort of planned economy similar to that advocated by the socialists. For example, in 1944 Keynes (1944, as quoted by Smithin 2011b) wrote to Hayek:

> I should . . . conclude your theme rather differently. I should say that what we want is not "no planning," or even less planning . . . we almost certainly want more. But the planning should take place in a community in which as many people as possible, both leaders and followers, share your own moral position.

There is also the apparent evidence of the arguments made in such articles as "The End of Laisser-Faire?" (Keynes 1931, 273–94), first published in 1926. Ten years later there is further evidence, in the shape of the famous passage about the "socialization of investment" in the *General Theory* (Keynes 1936, 378). Moreover, one of the main points made in this book is that Keynes in the end did not actually succeed in providing a complete theory of a credit economy or monetary production economy. Putting all this together, there is therefore an argument to also lump Keynes himself in with Marx and Hayek, at the bottom of the diagram in Figure 11.4. From this point of view they are all "planners," albeit with Hayek having his planning done for him by the all-powerful market. My own view, in fact, is that we really cannot and should not accept this sort of critique of Keynes. His rightful place is at the top of the diagram of Figure 11.4, in direct opposition to both classical liberals *and* to socialists. Nonetheless, if it became necessary to do so in the advocacy of the correct economic policy agenda, we could even throw Keynes himself under the bus as is illustrated in Figure 11.5. Even if Keynes in the 1930s was ultimately not able to arrive at a completely convincing "general theory," I hope that this book, nine decades later, has definitely made the case that it is at least possible to do so. The construct that in chapter 2 above I called the "preferred theory" provides a very different set of principles for the conduct of successful economic policy than Marxian economics, Austrian economics, neoclassical economics, or any of the existing interpretations of Keynes.

For myself, I would like to reiterate that I am not willing to throw Keynes to the academic wolves. It would have been impossible to arrive at the insights presented in this book without Keynes's pioneering efforts. I do not agree, therefore, with the views presented by David Laidler in his influential and scholarly book *Fabricating the Keynesian Revolution* (Laidler 1999), whose very title indicates the nature of the argument. In order to process what Keynes said, or tried to say, there would had to have been, first, a sympathetic and intelligent reception of his ideas on the part of the economics profession of the time, and then very much hard work on the part of the succeeding generations to promote their further development. This never happened. The whole project floundered in a morass of "busy work" on the part of academic economists interested primarily in mathematics. The starting point for this tendency was Samuelson's (supposed) *Foundations of Economic Analysis* (Samuelson 1947), then came the influence of the Cowles Commission (Rima 1988, 18–20, 1995, 218–21) in promoting econometrics as the only acceptable empirical method in economics, closely followed by the disastrous fad for Walrasian general equilibrium analysis in the 1960s and 1970s (Leijonhufvud 1981, Rima 1988). Instead of undertaking a serious study of economic sociology, economists came to rely on differential and stochastic calculus linear algebra, game theory, and so on, culminating in the "dogma" (King 2012) of the "microfoundations of macroeconomics" and of the DSGE model (as discussed in chapter 1 above).

CONCLUSION

Economics is supposed to be a social science, dealing with social relations, social facts, social institutions, and so on. There are few, if any, valid analogies with the natural sciences such as physics or evolutionary biology, in spite of the continuing popularity of such analogies with both mainstream economists, and also very many heterodox economic researchers. In truth, the social institution that economics is supposed to be studying is nothing other than "capitalism," best defined in the Weberian manner as "the provision of human needs by the method of enterprise, which is to say by private businesses seeking profit." There really was no such thing as economics, or political economy, until social life began to be organized along these lines. Although capitalism itself evolves, and there exist all kinds of mixed economies, different national versions of capitalism, and different strands of historical development, it remains true that the fundamental principle which needs to be explained is the profit motive, and all that this implies. Neoclassical economics does not event attempt to perform this task. It restricts attention to the derivation of a theory of rational choice and market exchange which, or so it is thought, can be approached in a manner similar to that of natural science. The logic of market exchange itself is supposed to be a given, as in Adam Smith's "natural propensity to truck, barter and exchange" (Smith 1776, 25). Markets are literally treated as something akin to natural phenomena, rather than being social institutions in their own right. On this view they do not need any further ontological grounding than Smith provided.

The argument in this book however suggests a different logic of economic explanation. In this final chapter we have argued that four steps are required to develop such a narrative and which (unfortunately for the modern scholar) involve a number of different academic disciplines. Because of the way in which social science research is currently organized in academia, and because of the relentless compartmentalization and specialization inherent in modern academic life, it is rarely possible for any one individual to pursue all the themes that require investigation.

First, there needs to be an account of *Social Ontology*. That is, an inquiry into the nature of social facts and social institutions, and how these differ from the reality described by the natural sciences. Second, it is necessary to develop an *Economic Sociology*. This would deal with the specific sets of social institutions and their sequences and interrelations that concretely constitute an economy. Third, there must be a *Monetary Macroeconomics*. This is the arena in which the great economic thinkers have traditionally made their contribution, and it is this field (rather than neoclassical microeconomics) that should be pre-eminently the technical part of economics. It is literally impossible to understand how the whole system hangs together, and how it operates, unless these questions are understood. Microeconomics, the institution-free study of the logic of rational choice, cannot do this. Monetary problems to Keynes (1931a, 57) are those which "not one man [*sic*] in a million can diagnose." Hopefully, however, some of the results presented in this book, particularly those in chapters 2 and 10 above, have been able to point the way toward possible solutions. The fourth and final stage of the argument is *Political Economy*, at which point the ethical and policy issues can legitimately be discussed and their implications for the good of the commonwealth can be debated.

NOTES

1. Indeed, Geoffrey Ingham's most important book was entitled *The Nature of Money* (Ingham 2004).

2. This is because of allegations of sexual harassment by a former student/co-worker in 2017.

3. I am grateful to Geoff Harcourt for a most fruitful correspondence about these issues. Harcourt was the organizer of the session "Post Keynesian Economics a Promise that Bounced?" at the 1979 annual meetings of the American Economic Association where the paper by Crotty was first presented.

4. I have not actually been able to find the precise page reference for this quote. I had always thought that it was in Robinson (1962) but I have not been able to see it there. It must exist somewhere else in Robinson's *ouvre*.

5. I am most grateful to Torrey Byles for having suggested this point to me—and for much else besides.

6. Relative to some arbitrary base year.

7. For example, this might be interpreted to mean that the average real yield on "all property income," in turn determined by the real rate of interest on money, is 15 percent. This is one of the alternatives discussed by Collis (2016, 2018). Torrey Byles warns me that this brief explanation may not be enough to satisfy the discerning empirically minded reader. However, the purpose of this chapter is not so much empirical work per se but, rather, an overall summing-up of the "big picture." The empirical researcher will find much more detail in the works of Collis just cited.

8. I did once raise these issues a year or so ago, at a seminar at the Fields Institute for Mathematical Research in Toronto. I can at least report that none of the mathematicians present raised any specific objection to the suggested terminology. I am grateful to the then Associate Director of the Institute, Mathias Graselli, for the invitation to attend.

9. There is, of course, a precise mathematical relationship between the different notions of "shares," but this is not obvious simply by looking at the raw numbers.

10. If the effective real rate of interest were to be zero this would also continue to ensure inflation stability. This can be seen by inspection of equation (11.1) above, recalling that in equilibrium the real wage w will also be a constant.

11. Needless to say, very similar ideas have been present in many other religious traditions beside that of Islam. The latter is simply a convenient example because it is a tradition (or traditions) which has a very large number of adherents worldwide at the present time, and is therefore much discussed in the contemporary news media, including the financial/business media. Another example, but with far less contemporary relevance, would be that of medieval Catholicism in the scholastic period. See, for example, Hayes (2017).

12. The full name of the Nazi party in Germany from c. 1922 to 1945 was actually "The German National Socialist Worker's Party."

13. The terms "left" and "right" originated in the seating arrangements in the National Assembly during the French revolution of the late eighteenth century. The supporters of monarchy sat on the right of the chamber and those who supported the aims of the revolution on the left.

14. I derive this concept by analogy to the Buddhist concept of "spiritual materialism" (Trungpa 1973, 13–22). In that context there is a sharp dichotomy between spirituality and materialism in the sense of possessiveness. Nonetheless, some individuals who claim to be following the spiritual path take excessive pride in doing so, and cling to the knowledge acquired in this field almost as if it *were* a material possession. This should be avoided if "true spirituality" (Trungpa 1973, 14) is to be realized. I try to make the same paradoxical, yet meaningful, juxtaposition of the two philosophical terms. I am grateful to Jana Campbell (Ani Yeshi Llamo) for very many interesting discussions on this topic.

Bibliography

Atesoglu, H.S. and J. Smithin. 2006a. Inflation targeting in a simple macroeconomic model. *Journal of Post Keynesian Economics* 28: 673–688.

———. 2006b. Real wages, productivity, and economic growth in the G7, 1960–2002. *Review of Political Economy* 18: 1–11.

———. 2007. Un modelo macroeconomico simple. *Economia Informa* 346: 105–119.

Arnold, G. 2014. *The Financial Times Guide to Banking*. London: FT Publishing.

Bell, S. 2001. The role of the state and the hierarchy of money. *Cambridge Journal of Economics*. (As reprinted in *Concepts of Money: Interdisciplinary Perspectives from Economics, Sociology and Political Science*, ed. G. Ingham, 496–510, Cheltenham: Edward Elgar, 2005).

Bellafiore, R. 1989. A monetary labor theory of value. *Review of Radical Political Economics* 21: 1–25.

———. 2004. Marx and the macro-monetary foundation of microeconomics. In *The Constitution of Capital: Essays on Volume I of Capital*, eds. N. Taylor and R. Bellofiore, London: Palgrave.

Blaise, C. 2000. *Time Lord: Sir Stanford Fleming and the Creation of Standard Time*. London: Weidenfield and Nicholson.

Blanchard, O.J. and S. Fischer. 1989. *Lectures on Macroeconomics*. Cambridge, MA: MIT Press.

Bloom, A. 1987. *The Closing of the American Mind*. New York: Simon and Schuster.

Bodkin, R., L. Klein and K. Marwah. 1988. Keynes and the origins of macroeconometric modelling. In *Keynes and Public Policy after Fifty Years, vol. 2, Theories and Method*, eds. O.F. Hamouda and J. Smithin, 3–11, Aldershot: Edward Elgar.

Boettke, P., D. Lavoie and V.H. Storr. 2001. The subjectivist method of Austrian Economics and Dewey's theory of inquiry. Paper presented at the symposium *John Dewey, Modernism, Postmodernism and Beyond*. Simon Rock College of Bard, Great Barrington, MA, 28pp.

Boettke, P. and P. Leeson. 2002. Hayek, arrow and the problems of democratic decision-making. *Journal of Public Finance and Public Choice* 1: 19–21.

Brofenbrenner, M. (ed). 1969. *Is the Business Cycle Obsolete?* New York: Wiley.

Burstein, M.L. 1995. *Classical Macroeconomics for the Next Century*, manuscript. Toronto: York University.

Chick, V. 1983. *Macroeconomics after Keynes: A Reconsideration of the General Theory*. Cambridge, MA: MIT Press.

Cohen, A. and G.C. Harcourt. 2003. Whatever happened to the Cambridge capital controversies? *Journal of Economic Perspectives* 17: 199–214.

219

Colander, D.C. and H. Landreth. 1996. *The Coming of Keynesianism to America: Conversations with the Founders of Keynesian Economics.* Cheltenham: Elgar.

Collins, R. 1986. *Weberian Sociological Theory.* London: Routledge.

Collis, R. 2016. *An Examination of Canadian Macroeconomic Data*, manuscript. Toronto: York University.

———. 2018. *Three Essays on Monetary Macroeconomics: An Empirical Examination of the Soundness of the Alternative Monetary Model and Monetary Policy in Canada.* PhD thesis in Economics, York University, Toronto.

Cottrell, A. 1994. Comments on "Keynes's vision: Method analysis and tactics" by C.G. Harcourt and C. Sardoni. In *The State of Interpretation of Keynes*, ed. J.B. Davies, New York: Kluwer.

Davidson, P. 1974. A Keynesian view of Friedman's theoretical framework for monetary analysis. In *Milton Friedman's Monetary Framework: A Debate with his Critics*, ed. R.J. Gordon, Chicago: University of Chicago Press.

———. 1991. *Controversies in Post Keynesian Economics.* Aldershot: Edward Elgar.

———. 2009. *The Keynes Solution: The Path to Global Economic Prosperity.* London: Palgrave Macmillan.

———. 2011. *Post Keynesian Macroeconomic Theory, Second Edition.* Cheltenham: Edward Elgar.

Davig, T. and E.M. Leeper. 2007. Generalizing the Taylor principle. *American Economic Review* 97: 603–635.

De Soto, H. 2000. *The Mystery of Capital: Why Capitalism Triumphs in the West and Fails Everywhere Else.* New York: Basic Books.

Devaney, R.L. 2011. *Mastering Differential Equations: The Visual Method: Course Guidebook.* Chantilly, VA: The Great Courses.

De Vroey, M. 2016. *A History of Macroeconomics: From Keynes to Lucas and Beyond.* Cambridge: Cambridge University Press.

Dillard, D. 1988. The barter illusion in classical and neoclassical economics. *Eastern Economic Journal* 14: 299–318.

Domar, E.D. 1946. Capital expansion, rate of growth, and employment. *Econometrica* 2: 137–147.

Dow, S. 1985. *Macroeconomic Thought: A Methodological Approach.* Oxford: Basil Blackwell.

———. 2016. The political economy of monetary reform. *Cambridge Journal of Economics* 40: 1363–1376.

Dyson, B., G. Hodgson and F. van Lerven. 2016. A response to critiques of "full reserve banking." *Cambridge Journal of Economics* 5: 1351–1361.

Fisher, I. 1911. *The Purchasing Power of Money.* New York: Macmillan.

Fleming, J.M. 1963. Domestic financial policies under fixed and under floating exchange rates. *IMF Staff Papers* 9: 369–379.

Fletcher, G. 1987. *The Keynesian Revolution and its Critics: Issues of Theory and Policy for the Monetary Production Economy.* London: Macmillan.

———. 2000. *Understanding Dennis Robertson: The Man and his Work.* Cheltenham: Edward Elgar.

———. 2007. *Dennis Robertson: Essays on his Life and Work.* London: Palgrave.

Fontana, G. and M. Sawyer. 2016. Full reserve banking: More "cranks" than "brave heretics." *Cambridge Journal of Economics* 5: 1333–1350.

Friedman, B.M. 2000. The role of interest rates in Federal Reserve policymaking. NBER Working Paper 8047, December.

Friedman, M. 1960. *A Program for Monetary Stability.* New York: Fordham University Press.

———. 1968. The role of monetary policy. *American Economic Review* 58: 1–17.

———. 1983. Monetarism in rhetoric and in practice. *Bank of Japan Monetary and Economic Studies* 1: 1–14.

———. 1989. Quantity theory of money. In *The New Palgrave: Money*, eds. J. Eatwell, M. Milgate and P. Newman, 1–40, London: Macmillan.

Friedman, M. and R. Friedman. 1980. *Free to Choose*. New York: Harcourt Brace Jovanovich.

Godley, W. and M. Lavoie. 2007. *Monetary Economics: An Integrated Approach to Credit Money, Income, Production and Wealth*. London: Palgrave MacMillan.

Goodhart, C.A.E. 1989. Monetary base. In *The New Palgrave: Money*, eds. J. Eatwell, M. Milgate and P. Newman, 206–211, London: Macmillan.

———. 1998. The two concepts of money: Implications for the analysis of optimal currency areas. *European Journal of Political Economy* 3: 407–432.

Graeber, D. 2011. *Debt: The First 5000 Years*. Brooklyn, NY: Melville House Publishing.

Graziani, A. 1984. The debate on Keynes's finance motive. *Economic Notes* 1: 5–32.

———. 1990. The theory of the monetary circuit. *Economies et Societes* 24: 7–36.

———. 1997. The Marxist theory of money. *International Journal of Political Economy* 27: 26–50.

———. 2003. *The Monetary Theory of Production*. Cambridge: Cambridge University Press.

Hahn, F. 1983. *Money and Inflation*. Cambridge, MA: MIT Press.

Hamouda, O.F. and J. Smithin. 1988a. Some remarks on "uncertainty and economic analysis." *Economic Journal* 98: 59–64.

———. 1988b. Rational behaviour with deficient foresight. *Eastern Economic Journal* 14: 277–285.

Harcourt, G.C. 1969. Some Cambridge controversies in the theory of capital. *Journal of Economic Literature* 7: 369–405.

Harrod, R.F. 1939. An essay in dynamic economic theory. *Economic Journal*. (As reprinted in *Growth Economics*, ed. A. Sen, 43–64, Harmondsworth: Penguin, 1970).

Hayek, F.A. 1931. The "paradox" of saving. (As reprinted in *Contra Keynes and Cambridge: Essays, Correspondence*, ed. B. Caldwell, 74–120, Indianapolis: Liberty Press, 1995).

———. 1932. Reflections on the theory of pure money of Mr. J. M. Keynes (continued), *Economica*. (As reprinted in *Contra Keynes and Cambridge: Essays, Correspondence*, ed. B. Caldwell, 174–197, Indianapolis: Liberty Press, 1995).

———. 1935. *Prices and Production* (second edition). (As reprinted by Augustus M. Kelley: New York, 1967).

———. 1939. Introduction. (As reprinted in *An Inquiry into the Nature and Effects of the Paper Credit of Great Britain*, ed. Henry Thornton, 11–63, New York: Augustus M. Kelley, 1991).

———. 1994. *Hayek on Hayek: An Autobiographical Dialogue,* eds. S. Kresge and L. Wenar. Chicago: University of Chicago Press.

Hayes, M.G. 2017. Keynes's liquidity preference and the usury doctrine: Their connection and continuing relevance. *Review of Social Economy* 75: 400–416.

Heilbroner, R. 1992. *Twenty-First Century Capitalism: The Massey Lectures 1992*. Toronto: House of Anansi Press.

———. 1999. *The Worldly Philosophers* (seventh edition). New York: Touchstone.

Heilbroner, R. and W. Milberg. 1995. *The Crisis of Vision in Modern Economic Thought*. New York: Cambridge University Press.

Heinsohn, G. and O. Steiger. 2000. The property theory of interest and money. In *What is Money?* ed. John Smithin, 67–100, London: Routledge.

Heydoorn, O. 2014. *Social Credit Economics*. CreateSpace Independent Publishing Platform.

————. 2016. *Social Credit Philosophy*. Irving, TX: International Academy of Philosophy Press.

Hicks, J. 1935. A suggestion for simplifying the theory of money. *Economica*. (As reprinted in *Money, Interest and Wages: Collected Essays on Economic Theory: Volume II*, 61–82, Oxford: Basil Blackwell).

————. 1937. Mr. Keynes and the "classics": A suggested interpretation. *Econometrica*. (As reprinted in *Money, Interest and Wages: Collected Essays on Economic Theory: Volume II*, 121–142, Oxford: Basil Blackwell).

————. 1949. Harrod's dynamic theory. *Economica*. (As reprinted in *Money, Interest and Wages: Collected Essays on Economic Theory: Volume II*, 171–197, Oxford: Basil Blackwell).

————. 1967a. The two triads: Lecture I. In *Critical Essays in Monetary Theory*, 1–16, Oxford: Clarendon Press.

————. 1967b. The "classics" again. In *Critical Essays in Monetary Theory*, 141–154, Oxford: Clarendon Press.

————. 1967c. A note on the *Treatise*. In *Critical Essays on Monetary Theory*, 189–202, Oxford: Clarendon Press.

————. 1982. *Money, Interest and Wages: Collected Essays on Economic Theory: Volume II*. Oxford: Basil Blackwell.

————. 1985. *Methods of Dynamic Economics*. Oxford: Clarendon Press.

————. 1989. *A Market Theory of Money*. Oxford: Oxford University Press.

Hume, D. 1752. Of money. (As reprinted in *Essays, Moral Political and Literary*, ed. E.F. Miller, 281–294, Indianapolis: Liberty Classics, 1987).

Humphrey, T.M. 1982. The real bills doctrine. *FRB Richmond Economic Review*. (As reprinted in *Money, Banking and Inflation: Essays in the History of Economic Thought*, 21–31, Aldershot: Edward Elgar).

————. 1983. Can the central bank peg real interest rates? A survey of classical and neoclassical opinion. *FRB Richmond Economic Review*. (As reprinted in *Money, Banking and Inflation: Essays in the History of Economic Thought*, 35–43, Aldershot: Edward Elgar).

————. 1998. Mercantalists and classicals: Insights from doctrinal history. *Annual Report*, 1–27, *FRB Richmond Economic Review*.

Ingham, G. 1996. Money is a social relation. *Review of Social Economy* 54: 243–275.

————. 2000. "Babylonian madness": On the historical and sociological origins of money. In *What is Money?* ed. J. Smithin, 16–41, London: Routledge.

————. 2004a. *The Nature of Money*. Cambridge: Polity Press.

————. 2004b. The emergence of capitalist credit money. In *Credit and State Theories of Money*, ed. L.R. Wray, 173–122, Cheltenham: Edward Elgar.

————. 2018. A critique of Lawson's "Social positioning and the nature of money." *Cambridge Journal of Economics* 42: 837–850.

————, K. Coutts and S. Konzelmann. 2016. Introduction: "Cranks" and "brave heretics": Rethinking money and banking after the Great Financial Crisis. *Cambridge Journal of Economics* 5: 1247–1257.

Innes, A.M. 1913. What is money? (As reprinted in *Credit and State Theories of Money*, ed. L.R. Wray, 14–49, Cheltenham: Edward Elgar, 2004).

————. 1914. The credit theory of money. (As reprinted in *Concepts of Money: Interdisciplinary Perspectives from Economics, Sociology and Political Science,* ed. G. Ingham, 354–374, Cheltenham: Edward Elgar, 2005).

Jones, C.I. 1998. *Introduction to Economic Growth*. New York: W.W. Norton and Company.

Kaldor, N. 1955/56. Alternative theories of income distribution. *Review of Economic Studies* 23: 94–100.

———. 1982. *The Scourge of Monetarism* (second edition). Oxford: University Press.

———. 1983. Keynesian economics after fifty years. In *Keynes and the Modern World*, eds. David N. Worswick and James R. Trevithick, 1–27, Cambridge: Cambridge University Press.

———. 1985. *Economics without Equilibrium*. Armonk, NY: M.E. Sharpe.

Kam, E. 2000. *Three Essay on Endogenous Time Preference, Monetary Non-Superneutrality and the Mundell-Tobin Effect*. PhD thesis in Economics, York University, Toronto.

———. 2005. A note on time preference and the Tobin effect. *Economics Letters* 89: 137–142.

Kam, E. and J. Smithin. 2004. Monetary policy and demand management for the small open economy in contemporary conditions with (perfectly) mobile capital. *Journal of Post Keynesian Economics* 26: 679–694.

———. 2008. Unequal partners: The role of international financial flows and the exchange rate regime. *Journal of Economic Asymmetries* 5: 125–137.

———. 2011. ¿Capitalismo en un sólo país?: Una re-valoración de los sistemas mercantilistas desde el punto de vista financier. In *Las Instituciones Financieras y el Crecimiento Económico en el Contexto de la Dominación del Capital Financiero*, eds. N. Levy Orlik and T. López González, 37–58, Mexico City: Juan Pablo.

———. 2012. A simple theory of banking and the relationship between commercial banks and the central bank. *Journal of Post Keynesian Economics* 34: 545–549.

Kam, E. and A. Tabassum. 2016. The long-run non-neutrality of monetary policy: A general statement in a "DGE" model. Paper presented at the annual meetings of the Canadian Economics Association, Ottawa, May.

Kaldor, N. 1955/56. Alternative theories of distribution. *Review of Economic Studies* 23: 83–100.

———. 1983. Keynesian economics after fifty years. In *Keynes and the Modern World*, 1–27, eds. D. Worswick and J. Trevithick, Cambridge: Cambridge University Press.

———. 1985. *Economics without Equilibrium*. Armonk, NY: M.E. Sharpe, Inc.

Kalecki, M. 1937. A theory of the business cycle. *Review of Economic Studies* 2: 77–97.

———. 1943. Costs and prices. (As reprinted in *Selected Essays on the Dynamics of a Capitalist Economy 1933–1970*, 43–61, Cambridge: Cambridge University Press, 1971).

Keen, S. 1995. Finance and economic breakdown: Modelling Minsky's "financial instability hypothesis." *Journal of Post Keynesian Economics* 17: 607–635.

———. 2009. The dynamics of the monetary circuit. In *The Political Economy of Monetary Circuits: Tradition and Change in Post Keynesian Economics*, eds. J.-F. Ponsot and S. Rossi, 161–187, London: Palgrave Macmillan.

Keynes, J.M. 1921. *A Treatise on Probability*. (As reprinted in *Collected Writings* VIII, ed. D. Moggridge, London: Macmillan, 1973).

———. 1923. *A Tract on Monetary Reform*. London: Macmillan.

———. 1930. *A Treatise on Money*, vol. 1. (As reprinted in *Collected Writings* V, ed. D. Moggridge, London: Macmillan, 1971).

———. 1931. *Essays in Persuasion*. (As reprinted in *Collected Writings* IX, ed. D. Moggridge, London: Macmillan, 1972).

———. 1933a. A monetary theory of production. (As reprinted in *Collected Writings* XX1, ed. D. Moggridge, 408–411, London: Macmillan, 1973).

———. 1933b. The distinction between a co-operative economy and an entrepreneur economy. (As reprinted in *Collected Writings* XXIX, ed. D. Moggridge, London: Macmillan, 1979).

———. 1934/35. Keynes-Shaw correspondence of 1934–5. (As reprinted in *Collected Writings* XXVIII, ed. D. Moggridge, London: Macmillan, 1982).

———. 1936. *The General Theory of Employment Interest and Money*. (As reprinted by Harcourt Brace: London, 1964).

———. 1937. The general theory of employment. *Quarterly Journal of Economics* (As reprinted in *Collected Writings* XIV, ed. D. Moggridge, 109–123, London: Macmillan, 1973).

King, J. 2012. *The Microfoundations Delusion: Metaphor and Dogma in the History of Macroeconomics*. Cheltenham: Edward Elgar.

———. 2015. *Advanced Introduction to Post Keynesian Economics*. Cheltenham: Edward Elgar.

Knapp, G.F. 1924. *The State Theory of Money*. (As reprinted by Augustus M. Kelley: Clifton, NJ, 1973).

Kresge, S. 1995. Introduction. In *Hayek on Hayek: An Autobiographical Dialogue,* eds. S. Kresge and L. Wenar, 1–35, Chicago: University of Chicago Press.

Laidler, D.E.W. 1989. The bullionist controversy. In *The New Palgrave: Money*, eds. J. Eatwell, M. Milgate and P. Newman, 60–71, London: Macmillan.

———. 1999. *Fabricating the Keynesian Revolution: Studies on the Inter-war Literature on Money, the Cycle, and Unemployment*. Cambridge: Cambridge University Press.

Lakatos, I. 1978. *The Methodology of Scientific Research Programmes*. Cambridge: Cambridge University Press.

Landes, D.S. 1983. *Revolution in Time*. Cambridge, MA: Harvard University Press.

Lau, J.Y.F. and J. Smithin. 2002. The role of money in capitalism. *International Journal of Political Economy* 32: 5–22.

Laudan, L. 1977. *Progress and Its Problems: Towards a Theory of Scientific Growth*. London: Routledge & Kegan Paul.

Lavoie, M. 1992. *Foundations of Post-Keynesian Economic Analysis*. Aldershot: Edward Elgar.

———. 2007. *Introduction to Post Keynesian Economics*. London: Palgrave Macmillan.

———. 2010. Changes in central bank procedures during the sub-prime crisis and their repercussions on monetary policy. *International Journal of Political Economy* 39: 2–23.

———. 2014. *Post Keynesian Economics: New Foundations*. Cheltenham: Edward Elgar.

Lavoie, M. and M. Seccareccia. (eds). 2004. *Central Banking in the Modern World: Alternative Perspectives*. Cheltenham: Edward Elgar.

Lawson, T. 1997. *Economics and Reality*. London and New York: Routledge.

———. 2003. *Re-orienting Economics*. London and New York: Routledge.

———. 2016. Social positioning and the nature of money. *Cambridge Journal of Economics* 40: 961–996.

Leeson, R. (ed). 2003a. *Keynes, Chicago and Friedman*, vol. 1. London: Pickering & Chatto.

———. (ed). 2003b. *Keynes, Chicago, and Friedman*, vol. 2. London: Pickering & Chatto.

Leijonhufvud, A. 1968. *On Keynesian Economics and the Economics of Keynes*. New York: Oxford University Press.

———. 1981. The Wicksell connection: Variations on a theme. In *Information and Coordination: Essays in Macroeconomic Theory*, 131–202, New York: Oxford University Press.

Lerner, A.P. 1943. Functional finance and the federal debt. *Social Research* 10: 38–51.

———. 1947. Money as a creature of the state. *The American Economic Review* 2: 312–317.

Lucas, R. 1988. On the mechanics of economic development. *Journal of Monetary Economics* 1: 3–42.

Mankiw, N.G. 2001. US monetary policy during the 1990s. NBER Working Paper 8471, September.

———. 2003. Program report: Monetary economics. *NBER Reporter*, 1–5, Spring.

Marshall, A. 1890. *Principles of Economics*. London: Macmillan.

Marterbauer, M. and J. Smithin. 2000. Fiscal policy in the small open economy within the framework of monetary union. WIFO Working Paper 137, Vienna, November.

———. 2007. Políticas monetaria y fiscal con dinero endógeno, bajo regímenes cambiarios alternatives. In *Politicas Macroeconomicas para Paises en Desarrollo*, eds. N.O. Levy-Orlik and M.G. Mántey de Anguiano, 245–265, Mexico City: Porrua.

Marx, K. 1859. *A Contribution to the Critique of Political Economy*. (As reprinted by Progress Publishers, Moscow: 1970).

———. 1867. *Capital: Vol. I.* (As reprinted by Penguin Books: London, 1976).

———. 1885. *Capital: Vol. II.* (As reprinted by Penguin Books: London, 1976).

———. 1894. *Capital: Vol. III.* (As reprinted by Penguin Books: London, 1976).

Meltzer, A.H. 2003. *A History of the Federal Reserve, Volume I: 1913–1951*. Chicago: University of Chicago Press.

Mendoza Espana, A.D. 2012. *Three Essay on Money, Credit, and Philosophy: A Realist Approach per totam viam to Monetary Science*. PhD thesis in Economics, York University, Toronto.

Menger, C. 1892. On the origin of money. *Economic Journal* 2: 239–255.

Minsky, H.P. 1986. *Stabilizing an Unstable Economy*. New Haven: Yale University Press.

———. 1992. The financial instability hypothesis. Working Paper No.74, Levy Economics Institute.

Mints, L.W. 1945. *A History of Banking Theory in Great Britain and the United States*. Chicago: University of Chicago Press.

Mises, L. von. 1934. *The Theory of Money and Credit*. (As reprinted by Liberty Press: Indianapolis, 1980).

———. 1960. *Epistemological Problems of Economics*. New York: New York University Press.

———. 1978. *Ludwig von Mises: Notes and Recollections*. South Holland, IL: Libertarian Press.

Mishkin, F. 2015. *The Economics of Money, Banking and Financial Markets: Business School Edition*. New York: Pearson.

Moore, B.M. 1988. *Horizontalists and Verticalists: The Macroeconomics of Credit Money*. Cambridge: Cambridge University Press.

Moseley, F. 2016. *Money and Totality: A Macro-Monetary Interpretation of Marx's Logic in Capital and the End of the Transformation Problem*. Leiden: Brill.

Mosler, W. 1997–98. Full employment and price stability. *Journal of Post Keynesian Economics* 2: 167–182.

———. 2011. *The Seven Deadly Innocent Frauds of Economic Policy*. Guildford, CT: Valence Co. Inc.

Mundell, R.A. 1961. A theory of optimum currency areas. *American Economic Review* 51: 509–517.

———. 1963a. Inflation and real interest. *Journal of Political Economy* 71: 280–283.

———. 1963b. Capital mobility and stabilization policy under fixed and flexible exchange rates. *Canadian Journal of Economics and Political Science* 2: 475–485.

Nell, E.J. and M. Forstater. (eds). 2003. *Reinventing Functional Finance: Transformational Growth and Full Employment*. Cheltenham: Edward Elgar.

Okun, Arthur. 1962. Potential GNP: Its measurement and significance. *Proceedings of the American Statistical Association* 7: 98–111.

Palley, T.I. 2015. Money, fiscal policy and interest rates: A critique of modern money theory. *Review of Political Economy* 27: 1–23.

Paraskevopoulos, C.C. and J. Smithin. 1998. Economic and financial integration: Implications for nationally-based public policy. In *Global Trading Arrangements in Transition*, ed. C.C. Paraskevopoulous, 3–10, Cheltenham: Edward Elgar.

———. 2002. Integracion economica y financier: implicaciones sobre la political fiscal y social de una nacion. *Revista Economica de Castilla La Mancha* 2: 197–209.

Parguez, A. 1996. Beyond scarcity: A re-appraisal of the theory of the monetary circuit. In *Money in Motion: The Post Keynesian and Circulation Approa*ches, eds. E.J. Nell and G. Deleplace, 155–199, London: Macmillan.

Parguez, A. and M. Seccareccia. 2000. The credit theory of money: The monetary circuit approach. In *What is Money?* ed. J. Smithin, 101–123, London: Routledge.

Paschakis, J. 1993. *Real Exchange Rate Control and the Choice of an Exchange Rate System.* PhD thesis in Economics, York University, Toronto.

Paschakis, J., C.C. Paraskevopoulos, and J. Smithin. 1996. Financial integration between Canada and the USA: An empirical analysis. In *Economic Integration in the Americas*, eds. C.C. Paraskevopoulos, R. Grinspun and G. Eaton 199–120. Aldershot: Edward Elgar.

Paschakis, J. and J. Smithin. 1998. Exchange risk and the supply-side effects of real interest rate changes. *Journal of Macroeconomics* 4: 703–720.

Patinkin, D. 1948. Price flexibility and full employment. *American Economic Review* 38: 543–564.

———. 1956. *Money, Interest and Prices.* Evanston, IL: Row Peterson.

Pheby, J.D. 1988. *Methodology and Economics: A Critical Introduction.* Basingstoke: Macmillan.

Pigou, A.C. 1943. The classical stationary state. *Economic Journal* 53: 343–351.

Pollin, R. 1991. Two theories of money supply endogeneity: Some empirical evidence *Journal of Post Keynesian Economics* 13: 366–396.

Polyani Levitt, K. 2017. Kari Polyani Levitt on Karl Polyani and the economy as a social construct. *Review of Social Economy* 75: 389–399.

Popper, K. 1945. *The Open Society and Its Enemies.* London: Routledge.

Radford, R.A. 1945. The economic organization of a POW camp. *Economic Journal.* (As reprinted in *Concepts of Money: Interdisciplinary Perspectives from Economics, Sociology and Political Science*, ed. Geoffrey Ingham, 20–32, Cheltenham: Edward Elgar).

Rawls, J. 1971. *A Theory of Justice.* Cambridge, MA: Harvard University Press.

Rebelo, S. 1991. Long-run policy analysis and long-run growth. *Journal of Political Economy* 99: 500–521.

Ricardo, D. 1817. *The Principles of Political Economy and Taxation.* (As reprinted by Liberty Fund: Indianapolis, 2004).

Rima, I.H. 1988. Keynes's vision and econometric analysis. In *Keynes and Public Policy after Fifty Years*, vol. 2, eds. O.F. Hamouda and J. Smithin. New York: New York University Press.

Rima, I.H. (ed). 1995. *Measurement, Quantification and Economic Analysis: Numeracy in Economics.* London: Routledge.

———. 1996. *Development of Economic Analysis* (sixth edition). London: Routledge.

Robbins, L. 1967. Introduction. In *Collected Works of John Stuart Mill: Essays on Economy and Society 1824–1845,* ed. J.M. Robson, vii–xli. (As reprinted by Liberty Fund: Indianapolis, 2006).

———. 1998. *A History of Economic Thought*, eds. W.J. Samuels and S.G. Medema. Princeton, NJ: Princeton University Press.

Rochon, L.-P. 1999. *Credit, Money and Production.* Cheltenham: Edward Elgar.

Rochon, L.-P. and M. Setterfield. 2007. Interest rates, income distribution, and monetary policy dominance: Post Keynesians and the "fair rate" of interest. *Journal of Post Keynesian Economics* 29: 13–42.

———. 2012. Models of growth and distribution with conflict inflation and Post Keynesian nominal interest rate rules. *Journal of Post Keynesian Economics* 34: 497–520.

Robertson, D.H. 1922. *Money*. (As reprinted in a second edition by London: Nisbet and Co, 1948).

———. 1934. Industrial fluctuation and the natural rate of interest. *Economic Journal*. (As reprinted in *Essays in Monetary Theory*, ed. P.S. King, 83–91, London, 1940).

———. 1939. Mr. Keynes and the rate of interest. (As reprinted in *Essays in Monetary Theory*, ed. P.S. King, 1–38, London, 1940).

———. 1940. *Essays in Monetary Theory*. London: P.S. King and Son.

Robinson, J. 1962. *Economic Philosophy*. London: Pelican Books.

———. 1979. Introduction. *In a Guide to Post Keynesian Economics*, ed. Alfred S. Eichner, xi–xix, White Plains, NY: M.E. Sharpe.

Robinson, D.N. 2004. *The Great Ideas in Philosophy: Second Edition: Course Guidebook*. Chantilly, VA: The Great Courses.

Romer, P. 1986. Increasing returns and long-run growth. *Journal of Political Economy* 5: 1002–1037.

Romer, D. 2000. Keynesian macroeconomics without the LM curve. *Journal of Economic Perspectives* 14: 149–170.

Rothbard, M.N. 1998. *The Ethics of Liberty*. New York: New York University Press.

Rowthorn, R. 1977. Conflict inflation and money. *Cambridge Journal of Economics* 1: 215–239.

Salin, P. 2014. The neglected importance of the Austrian thought in public economics. In *A Handbook of Alternative Theories of Public Economics*, eds. F. Forte, R. Mudamby and P. Navarra, Cheltenham: Edward Elgar.

Samuelson, P. 1947. *Foundations of Economic Analysis*. (As reprinted in second edition by Harvard University Press: Cambridge MA, 1983).

Samuelson, P. 1964. *Economics: An Introductory Analysis* (sixth edition). New York: McGraw-Hill.

Sargent, T.J. 1979. *Macroeconomic Theory*. New York: Academic Press.

Scarth, W. 2014. *Macroeconomics: The Development of Modern Methods for Policy Analysis*. Cheltenham: Edward Elgar.

Schmitt, B. 1988. The international debt problem and the "clearing union." In *Keynes and Public Policy after Fifty Years*, vol. 2, *Theories and Method*, eds. O.F. Hamouda and J. Smithin, 194–201, Aldershot: Edward Elgar.

Schumpeter, J.A. 1934. *The Theory of Economic Development: An Inquiry into Profits, Capital, Credit, Interest, and the Business Cycle*. (As reprinted by Transactions Publishers: New Brunswick NJ, 1983).

———. 1954. *History of Economic Analysis*. (As reprinted by Routledge: London and New York, 1994).

Searle, J.R. 1995. *The Construction of Social Reality*. New York: The Free Press.

———. 1998. *Mind Language and Society: Philosophy in the Real World*. London: Weidenfield and Nicholson.

———. 2005. What is an institution? *Journal of Institutional Economics* 1: 1–22.

———. 2010. *Making the Social World: The Structure of Human Civilization*. New York: Oxford University Press.

Sen, A. 1970. Introduction. In *Growth Economics*, ed. Amartya Sen, 9–40, Harmondsworth: Penguin.

Sennholz, H.R. 1978. Postscript. In *Ludwig von Mises: Notes and Recollections*, 145–176, South Holland, IL: Libertarian Press.

Simmel, G. 2004. *The Philosophy of Money*, ed. David Frisby. London: Routledge.

Skidelsky, R. 2009. *Keynes: The Return of the Master*. New York: Public Affairs.

———. 2015. The failure of austerity. SPERI Paper No. 23, University of Sheffield, 11pp.

Smith, A. 1776. *An Inquiry into the Nature and Causes of the Wealth of Nations*. (As reprinted by Liberty Fund: Indianapolis, 1981).

Smithin J. 1982. *The Incidence and Economic Effects of the Financing of Unemployment Insurance*. PhD thesis in Economics, McMaster University.

———. 1986. The length of the production period and effective stabilization policy. *Journal of Macroeconomics* 8: 55–62.

———. 1990a. *Macroeconomics after Thatcher and Reagan: The Conservative Policy Revolution in Retrospect*. Aldershot: Edward Elgar.

———. 1990b. Empirical and conceptual problems in contemporary macroeconomics. *British Review of Economic Issues* 27: 73–90.

———. 1994. *Controversies in Monetary Economics, Ideas, Issues, and Policy*. Aldershot: Edward Elgar.

———. 1995a. Econometrics and the "facts of experience." In *Measurement, Quantification, and Economic Analysis: Numeracy in Economics*, ed. I.H. Rima, 363–378, London and New York: Routledge.

———. 1995b. Geldpolitik und demokratie. In *Europaische Geldpolitik zwischen Marktzwangen und Neuen Institutionellen Regelungen: Zur Politischen Okonomie der Europaische Wahrungintegration*, ed. C. Thomasberger, 73–96, Marburg: Metropolis-Verlag.

———. 1996. *Macroeconomic Policy and the Future of Capitalism: The Revenge of the Rentiers and the Threat to Prosperity*. Aldershot: Edward Elgar.

———. 1997. An alternative monetary model of inflation and growth. *Review of Political Economy* 4: 395–409.

———. 2000. What is money?: Introduction. In *What is Money?* ed. J. Smithin, 101–123, London: Routledge.

———. 2002a. Review of Fletcher *Understanding Dennis Robertson: The Man and His Work* (2000). *Eastern Economic Journal* 28: 440–442.

———. 2002b. Phillips curve. In *An Encylopedia of Macroeconomics*, eds. B. Snowdon and H.R. Vane, 581–585, Cheltenham: Edward Elgar.

———. 2003a. *Controversies in Monetary Economics: Revised Edition*. Cheltenham: Edward Elgar.

———. 2003b. Interest parity, purchasing power parity, "risk premia" and Post Keynesian economic analysis. *Journal of Post Keynesian Economics* 25: 219–235.

———. 2004a. Keynes, Friedman and Chicago: A review essay. *Journal of Economic Studies* 31: 76–88.

———. 2004b. Macroeconomic theory, (critical) realism and capitalism. In *Transforming Economics: Perspectives on the Critical Realist Project,* ed. P.A. Lewis, 53–75, London and New York: Routledge.

———. 2005. The real rate of interest, the business cycle, economic growth and inflation: An alternative theoretical perspective. *Journal of Economic Asymmetries* 2: 1–19.

———. 2007. A real interest rule for monetary policy? *Journal of Post Keynesian Economics* 30: 101–118.

———. 2009a. *Money, Enterprise and Income Distribution: Towards a Macroeconomic Theory of Capitalism.* London: Routledge.

———. 2009b. Review of Fletcher, *Dennis Robertson: Essays on his Life and Work* (2007). *Eastern Economic Journal* 35: 269–271.

———. 2010. The importance of money and debt-credit relationships in the enterprise economy. In *Introducing Macroeconomic Analysis: Issues, Questions, and Competing Views*, eds. H. Bougrine and M. Seccareccia, 49–60, Toronto: Esmond Montgomery Publications.

———. 2011. Getting back on track: Macroeconomic management after the financial crisis: Comment. Panel 3, 2nd annual INET conference, *Crisis and Renewal: International Political Economy at the Crossroads*, Bretton Woods, NH, April.

———. 2012a. Interest and profit. In Keynes's *General Theory after Seventy-Five Years*, ed. T Cate, 306–324, Cheltenham: Edward Elgar.

———. 2012b. Inflation. In *The Elgar Companion to Post Keynesian Economics* (second edition), ed. J.E. King, 288–293, Cheltenham: Edward Elgar.

———. 2013a. *Essays in the Fundamental Theory of Monetary Economics and Macroeconomics*. Singapore: World Scientific Publishing.

———. 2013b. Credit creation, the monetary circuit, and the formal validity of money. In *Monetary Economies of Production: Banking and Financial Circuits and the Role of the State: Essays in Honour of Alain Parguez*, eds. L.-P. Rochon and M. Seccareccia, 41–53, Cheltenham: Edward Elgar.

———. 2013c. Requirements of a philosophy of money and finance. In *Financial Crises and the Nature of Capitalist Money: Mutual Developments from the work of Geoffrey Ingham*, eds. G.C. Harcourt and J. Pixley, 19–29, London: Palgrave Macmillan.

———. 2013d. Three short essays on numerical methods. Prepared for the Institute for New Economic Thinking (INET), New York, August.

———. 2013e. Keynes's theories of money and banking in the *Treatise* and *General Theory*. *Review of Keynesian Economics* 1: 242–256.

———. 2014. Economic growth: Free trade, public finance, and the paradox of thrift. *Review of Keynesian Economics* 4: 456–463.

———. 2016a. Endogenous money, fiscal policy, interest rates and the exchange rate regime: A comment on Palley, Tymoigne, and Wray. *Review of Political Economy* 28: 64–78.

———. 2016b. Some puzzles about money, finance, and the monetary circuit. *Cambridge Journal of Economics* 40: 1259–1274.

———. 2016c. Endogenous money, fiscal policy, interest rates and the exchange rate regime: correction. *Review of Political Economy* 28: 609–611.

———. 2018. *Money and Totality*: A review essay. *Journal of Post Keynesian Economics*, forthcoming.

Smithin, J. and E. Kam. 2018. Hicks on Hayek, Keynes, and Wicksell. In *Economic Growth and Macroeconomic Stablization Policies in Post-Keynesian Economics: Essays in Honour of Marc Lavoie and Mario Seccareccia: Book Two*, eds. H. Bougrine and L.-P. Rochon, Cheltenham: Edward Elgar, forthcoming.

Smithin, J. and H. Smithin. 1998. Spolecna mena: nove moznosti, nebo hrozba? *Novy domov* 49, August.

Smithin, J. and B.M. Wolf. 1993. What would be a "Keynesian" approach to currency and exchange rate issues? *Review of Political Economy* 3: 365–383.

———. 1994. The macroeconomic and microeconomic consequences of alternative exchange rate regimes: Implications for European monetary union. In *Economic Integration Between Unequal Partners*, eds. T. Georgakopoulos, C.C. Paraskevopoulos and J. Smithin, 243–251. Aldershot: Edward Elgar.

———. 1999. A world central bank? In *Global Instability: The Political Economy of World Economic Governance*, eds. J. Grieve-Smith and J. Michie, 212–226, London and New York: Routledge.

Smithin, J. and F. Zhou. 2014. *Monetary Macroeconomics*. Mini-course delivered at the INET-CIGI *Young Scholars Initiative*, Fields Institute for Mathematical Research, University of Toronto, April.

Solow, R.M. 1956. A contribution to the theory of economic growth. (As reprinted in *Growth Economics,* ed. A. Sen, 161–192, Harmondsworth: Penguin, 1970).

———. 2000. Towards a macroeconomics of the medium run. *Journal of Economic Perspectives* 14: 151–158.

———. 2007. Heavy thinker. *New Republic*, May 21. 12pp. httpps://newrepublic.com/articles/61183/heavy-thinker (9/21/2016).

Soros, G. 2009. General theory of reflexivity. Lecture delivered at the Central European University, Budapest, 29/10/2009.

Sraffa, P. 1932. Dr. Hayek on money and capital. *Economic Journal*. (As reprinted in *Contra Keynes and Cambridge: Essays, Correspondence*, ed. B. Caldwell, 198–209, Indianapolis: Liberty Press, 1995).

———. 1960. *Production of Commodities by Means of Commodities*. Cambridge: Cambridge University Press.

Stalin J. 1924. *Foundations of Leninism: Lectures Delivered at the Sverdlov University.* (As reprinted by Foreign Languages Press: Peking, 1975).

Swan, T.W. 1956. Economic growth and capital accumulation. *The Economic Record* 2: 334–361.

Sweezy, P.M. 1942. *The Theory of Capitalist Development: Principles of Marxian Political Economy*. (As reprinted by Modern Reader Paperbacks: New York, 1970).

Tabassum, A. 2012. *Three Essays on the Impact of Financial Evolution on Monetary Policy*. PhD thesis in Economics, York University, Toronto.

Taylor, J.B. 1993. Discretion versus policy rules in practice. *Carnegie-Rochester Conference Series on Public Policy* 39: 195–214.

Tobin, J. 1958. Liquidity preference as behavior towards risk. *Review of Economic Studies* 25: 65–86.

———. 1965. Money and economic growth. *Econometrica* 33: 671–674.

Toporowski, J. 2008. Minksy's "induced investment and business cycles." *Cambridge Journal of Economics* 32: 725–737.

Turnovsky, S.J. 2000. *Methods of Macroeconomic Dynamics* (second edition). Cambridge, MA: MIT Press.

Tymoigne, E. and L.R. Wray. 2015. Modern money theory: A reply to Palley. *Review of Political Economy* 27: 24–44.

Walsh, C.E. 1998. *Monetary Theory and Policy*. Cambridge MA: Cambridge University Press.

Warner, A.M., M. Forstater and S.M. Rosen. (eds). 2000. *Commitment to Full Employment*: *The Economics and Social Policy of William S. Vickrey*. Armonk, New York: M.E. Sharpe.

Weber, M. 1927. *General Economic History*. (As reprinted by Dover Publications: Mineola, NY, 2003).

Weintraub, S. 1959. *A General Theory of the Price Level, Output, Income Distribution and Economic Growth*. Philadelphia: Chilton.

Wickens, M. 2008. *Macroeconomic Theory: A Dynamic General Equilibrium Approach*. Princeton, NJ: Princeton University Press.

Wicksell, K. 1898. *Interest and Prices*. (As reprinted by Augustus M. Kelley: New York, 1965).

Woodford, M. 1998. Doing without money: Controlling inflation in a post-monetary world. *Review of Economic Dynamics* 1: 173–219.

———. 2003. *Interest and Prices: Foundations of a Theory of Monetary Policy*. Princeton, NJ: Princeton University Press.

———. 2010. The simple analytics of the government expenditure multiplier. NBER Working paper 15714, January.

Wray, L.R. 1998. *Understanding Modern Money: The Key to Price Stability and Full Employment*. Cheltenham: Edward Elgar.

———. 2004. Conclusion: The credit and state money approaches. In *Credit and State Theories of Money*, ed. L.R. Wray, 223–262, Cheltenham: Edward Elgar.

———. 2012. *Modern Money Theory*. London: Palgrave Macmillan.

Wray, L.R. and S. Bell. 2004. Introduction. In *Credit and State Theories of Money*, ed. L.R. Wray, 1–13, Cheltenham: Edward Elgar.

Zelmanovitz, L. 2016. *The Ontology and Functions of Money: The Philosophical Foundations of Monetary Institutions*. Lanham, MD: Lexington Books.

Index

About the Author

John Smithin is Professor Emeritus of Economics and Senior Scholar at York University, Toronto, Canada. He was on the Faculty of York University for a period of thirty-four years. He previously held teaching appointments at the University of Calgary, and Lanchester Polytechnic at Coventry (now Coventry University) in England. In the academic year 1995–96 he was elected Bye Fellow at Robinson College, Cambridge. He holds a PhD and MA from McMaster University and a BA (Hons) from the City of London Polytechnic (now London Metropolitan University). His research interests are in the fields of monetary theory, macroeconomic policy, and the philosophy of money and finance. He is the author and/or editor of *Essays in the Fundamental Theory of Monetary Economics and Macroeconomics* (2013), *Money, Enterprise and Income Distribution* (2009), *Controversies in Monetary Economics* (2003, 1994), *What is Money?* (2000), *Macroeconomic Policy and the Future of Capitalism* (1996), and *Macroeconomics after Thatcher and Reagan* (1990).

Lightning Source UK Ltd.
Milton Keynes UK
UKHW051249180521
383930UK00003B/24

9 781498 542814